An Illustrated History of the
HOME GUARD
From the LDV of 1940 to Stand Down 1944

ARTHUR COOK

HALSGROVE

DEDICATION
To Sam, Harry and Bill

First published in Great Britain in 2011

British Library Cataloguing-in-Publication Data
A CIP record for this title is available from the British Library

ISBN 978 0 85704 105 0

HALSGROVE
Halsgrove House,
Ryelands Industrial Estate,
Bagley Road, Wellington, Somerset TA21 9PZ
Tel: 01823 653777   Fax: 01823 216796
email: sales@halsgrove.com

Part of the Halsgrove group of companies
Information on all Halsgrove titles is available at: www.halsgrove.com

Printed and bound in the UK by the MPG Books Group

Contents

BOOK
PRODUCTION
WAR ECONOMY
STANDARD

THIS BOOK IS PRODUCED IN
COMPLETE CONFORMITY
WITH THE AUTHORIZED
ECONOMY STANDARDS

Abbreviations

A.C.	All Clear	Me (109)	Messerschmitt
A.R.P.	Air Raid Precautions	N.C.O.	Non Commissioned Officer
A.U.	Auxiliary Unit	O.C.	Observer Corps
B.E.F.	British Expeditionary Force	O.P.	Observation Post
B.E.M.	British Empire Medal	O.B.	Operating Base (A.U. Underground Shelter)
B.R.A.	Brigadier Royal Artillary	O.B.E.	Order of the British Empire
C.D.	Civil Defence	R.A.	Raiders Approaching or Royal Artillery
D.A.	Delayed Action (Bomb)	R.E.	Royal Engineers.
D.D.V.	Dock Defence Volunteers	R.A.F.	Royal Air Force
F.A.P.	First Aid Party	R.M.	Royal Marines
F.W. 190	Focke Wulf 190	V.A.D.	Voluntary Aid Detachment (Red Cross)
G.H.Q.	General Headquarters	W.D.	War Department
G.T.C.	Girls Training Corps	W.H.D.	Women's Home Defence
H.E.	High Explosive	W.A.S.	Women's Auxiliary Service
H.G.	Home Guard	W.H.G.A.	Women's Home Guard Auxiliary
H.Q.	Headquarters	W.V.S.	Women's Voluntary Service
M.B.E.	Member of the British Empire		

Acknowledgements

Many thanks to my friend John Dyer. John was responsible for all of the Studio and Location Photography. I could not have made this book or my previous book *Exmouth at War* without him. For colour reference of items featured in this book visit.

www.jsdyer.co.uk

Thanks to Lee Marshall and Alan Marshall (The Lee Marshall Collection), for allowing me to photograph their extensive private collection of Home Guard equipment and documents.

Thanks to Phil Trayhorn and all at Brixham Battery. For helping me to photograph equipment from their displays and allowing me access to the Battery restoration project. For more info contact.

Brixham Battery Heritage Centre Group,
Fishcombe Road,
Brixham,
TQ5 8RU.

Website: www.brixhambattery.org
E-Mail: hiightres@tiscali.net

Thanks to Preston, Tim and Di Isaac.
Cobbaton Combat Collection
North Devon.
Website: www.cobbatoncombat.co.uk
E-Mail: info@cobbatoncombat.co.uk
For access to their collection and documentation

Lieutenant Tony Atkinson and the staff in the Armoury at Commando Training Centre Lympstone, for their help with information regarding vintage firearms.

Thanks to the following for their help with research and the lone of equipment to photograph. Clive Stewart, Steve Parsons from South West Airfields Heritage Trust (S.W.A.H.T.) and Andy Youngs.

Nina Hanniford Devon (C.A.R.T.) and Tom Sykes Coleshill Auxiliary Research Team (C.A.R.T.), for the use of photographs and information.
E-Mail: cartdevon@gmail.com

Regional Home Guard Living History Groups
Blitz and Peaces. Equipment and talks about the Home Guard.

For colour reference of items featured in this book visit. www.blitzandpeaces.co.uk

Dale Johnson. 'The Real Dads Army'.
Website: www.therealdadsarmy.co.uk

John Hellis The Fortress and Pill Box Studies Group

Without the following people and organisations help, it would have been impossible for me to undertake the research for this book. Thank you all!

Interviewees and Eyewitness Accounts
Bernard Bradford, Hazel Bradford, Laurie Butler, Pearl Cawse, Ray Challis, Barry Clarke, Dennis Davey, Jim Dyer, John Fletcher, Peter Gardner, Edwin Hawker, Bernard Greenaway, Bill Gorfin, Mike Heard, Roy Hole, Rene Ide, Ron Lavis, Ron Lee, Roy Marshall, Betty Mattholie, Peter Mattholic, Ken Parker, John Pascoe–Watson, Geoff Perriam, Ivor Pike, Joe Radgick, John 'Jack' Sage, Bill Sleeman, Ray Towill.

Additional Information and Help
Jenepher Allen, David Beasley, Peggy Burnett, John Cartwright, Dave Clarke, Rhys Davey, Daniella Deighton, Ellen Donkin. Sid Dingle, Katherine Dunhill, Andy and Julie Green, Anne Hamilton, John Hellis Dale Johnson, Chris Long, Fran McElhone, Mike Oldham, Roger Russell, Richard Tarr, Lesley Schlaefli, Sally Stocker, Steve Spencer and Andrew White, Ian Wright.

Museums
Exmouth Museum.
Honiton Museum.

Information from Books, Old Newspapers and Audio Sources
Bill Gorfin's wartime articles.
Dennis Pratt's wartime articles.
George Pridmore's post-war newspaper articles about the war.

Ted Gosling. post-war articles about the war.
Lionel Howell and Becca Gliddon, Homefront Recall.
The Exmouth Chronicle.

Media Sources and Help
Bay F.M. Radio 107.9, B.B.C. Radio Devon, *Exmouth Journal*, special thanks to David Beaseley, *Exmouth Herald, Express and Echo, Western Morning News.*

Libraries
Thanks to the staff from:
Exmouth Library, The West Country Studies Library Exeter,
Exeter Library, Honiton Library, Budleigh Salterton Library, Barnstaple Library.

Photographers
Militaria and location Photography: J.S. Dyer.
Wartime Photography: W.A. Puddicombe and Eric G.
Castle Studio. The Bill Sleeman photographic Collection. Special thanks to Julian Sleeman and the Sleeman Family. (Photography was illegal in certain circumstances during the war and also, expensive and difficult to get the materials. Thanks to all the unnamed photographers that that took the trouble to record this important period in history).

Local Organisations
Age Concern. Exmouth.

Useful Websites
www.blitzandpeaces.co.uk
For colour photographs of the equipment.
www.jsdyer.co.uk
For colour photographs of the equipment.
www.devonheritage.org A great site, useful for verifying casualties in enemy actions against Devon.

Introduction

I loved the B.B.C. TV programme 'Dad's Army' when I was growing up and still do. My own children love it. I regularly visit schools to give talks about the Home Front and always ask the children there whether they watch 'Dad's Army' and whether they think it's funny. The answer is invariably 'yes!' from boys and girls alike of all ages. What the characters were actually doing in the programme is a lot less clear to them.

There is no doubt that Croft and Perry's endearing and humorous series, which looked at the activities of the Home Guard in wartime Britain, is a comic masterpiece. It has transcended the topical humour of its day and made its own mark in history. It has retained its popularity with those already familiar with it and is now reaching a new audience with the generations growing up in the present century.

Apart from enjoying the programmes, I didn't really think about what the Home Guards role really was when I was younger, until I started talking to veterans from its ranks when I was in my late teens. It then became obvious that although the stories and the entertainment value of the programme were very much appreciated by the veterans most were irritated by the way in which they were portrayed. Many men had concerns that this was the way they would be remembered for all eternity, as bumbling, argumentative incompetents, struggling to manage the simplest of tasks. When interviewing people for my first book *Exmouth at War*, many Home Guard veterans came forward and many tried to put the record straight.

I listened with interest to tales of the 50-hour, or more, working weeks from men in reserved occupations that had joined the Home Guard. On duty some worked a further 12 hours a week mounting coastal patrols in freezing weather, then also carried out a further 12 hours a week helping with fire watching parties! I also learned about the tragic deaths of some Home Guardsmen when on duty, through no fault of their own, due to accidents with weapons or faulty equipment. No laughing matter.

For a long time Britain was under the threat of constant invasion by the Germans. Our regular army's resources and effectiveness to defend Britain had been greatly reduced by the Battle for France and the evacuation from Dunkirk, and these events must be taken into consideration when evaluating the part played by Home Guard. I could see very quickly that the responsibilities and duties of the volunteers who joined the Home Guard were, in fact, deadly serious.

When initially formed as the Local Defence Volunteers in May 1940 there was no real idea of structure or strategy, weapons were at the best scarce, and at worst non-existent, yet still tens of thousands of British men enlisted (women enlisted later on) in this part time army to help defend a nation threatened with impending invasion, in whichever way they could.

I have used Exmouth my home town and Devon (although not exclusively) to try and show what life was really like for the average man in the Home Guard. Exmouth geographically is on the south-west coast of Devon. It has two miles of golden sands and nearby cliffs to defend. Woodbury Common rises behind the coast, ideally suited to glider and parachute landings. Exmouth has a large, easily accessible estuary, with a reasonably-sized dock. During the war Exmouth also had light industry, military establishments and thousands of American troops billeted in the town (post 1943) making it an ideal target for bombing raids. It had anti-aircraft guns, coastal artillery and 'Z' rocket batteries all of which were weapons used by the Home Guard during WWII.

It proved quite easy to build a picture of what the men of the Home Guard locally had to go through by carefully interviewing people over a period of five years. Home Guardsmen from other areas also came forward with information and photographs too. Private collectors and living history groups also helped me put together a collection of equipment and uniforms to show to the veterans and photograph for the book. These items would have been used by most platoons in all areas of Britain.

In short what I have attempted is to produce a book (not without some humour) which can be used anywhere in the country to see what life was like in the Home Guard. Photographs, diagrams, ephemera and maps have also been used where suitable to help illustrate the text. The book is also designed to be used with existing Home Guard publications to help illustrate them.

The testimony and text has been carefully chosen to reflect the situations of most Home Guardsmen in any area of Britain, with information on uniforms following the chronology of distribution where possible, in order to help the research of living history groups. For people wanting to research their own photographs of family members who served in the Home Guard, help is given in understanding how to read the badges and ranking systems to help identify the role of the individual.

The Home Guard received very little recognition for what they actually achieved during WWII. They were, contrary to popular belief, tested against the enemy in certain areas of Britain and this is explored in the book.

Edwin Hawker, one of the interviewees, is still trying to claim his Defence Medal for his service in the Home Guard. When I interviewed him, Steve Parsons, a local 'living history' expert, helped him fill out his application forms, whilst checking his eligibility and documents relevant to his record of service with the Home Guard. Due to a minor technicality (misplacing his Home Guard certificate nearly 70 years later), it looks like he will never receive his medal. Edwin, who was on a reserve occupation during the war, had agreed to talk to me, in the first instance, because he did not want the role of the men in his Home Guard platoon to be forgotten forever.

During the making of this book several of the veterans who served with the Home Guard have passed away, in particular Mike Heard and Bill Sleeman, I had a very enjoyable time with these men during our interviews. I hope I have shown them and the other members in a realistic and positive light and done them a service by attempting to balance popular opinion a little.

Chapter 1
War with Germany

WWI Central Association Volunteer Training Corps

This organisation commonly known as the Volunteer Training Corps, (V.T.C.) existed between December 1914 and October 1918. They served in the same role as the Home Guard during WWI, in case of an invasion of mainland Britain. It was modelled on the same lines as the regular army and had a similar ranking system. Information on officers is still available as the officers are listed in the Volunteer Force List, but very little is known about the men as no personal service records exist.

Men who served in the V.T.C. had to remain at home to carry out vital war work and they wore a distinctive badge whilst in their civilian clothes to prevent, confrontations with people who thought they may be conscientious objectors.

No campaign medal was ever presented to the men for home service in the V.T.C., but members would have been eligible for other awards if they had previously served in army units or moved on to join another service later in the war.

Badge of the Volunteer Training Corps

The Inter-war Years and Espionage

It is now unbelievable to think that it had been made clear some years before the Second World War that Exmouth, along with other West Country towns, had some supporters of Nazi ideology and had helped Oswald Mosley's Black Shirts, develop a small local following. For instance, in Exmouth, only a few years before the outbreak of the war, rallies and openly inflammatory and aggressively orchestrated meetings were held in the town. Thankfully the majority of the population hated what these far-right wing parties stood for and would have nothing to do with them. The left wing parties also hated them.

One particular incident involving the British Union of Fascists was reported in the *Exmouth Chronicle* on Saturday 5 August 1933, where a report titled 'Street Fight on Chapel Hill' talks of a running street battle between 'Socialists wearing the hammer and sickle badge and uniformed Black Shirts' after a Black Shirt meeting. It ended with 9 casualties. By 1937-38 any real support locally for the B.U.F. had finally fizzled out.

It was known by British Military Intelligence that certain pre-war Black Shirt group members, Nazi sympathisers and German agents, were sending, or taking Ordnance Survey maps, street maps and local street directories back to Germany, from all over Britain. These street and trade directories were used to find out where Britain's potential war material manufacturing industries were located and the maps were converted by German Abwehr (the Intelligence Service) cartographers, into military maps showing military objectives in red and strategic objectives marked in purple. Examples of theses maps of the south-west of England, Torquay and Plymouth are kept in the West Country Studies Library in Exeter. These documents are written in German and mostly date from 1940-41. They were rescued from the wreckage of a German bomber.

This would indicate that the Germans were in receipt of their information for the documents some years before the German publication date. Tourist maps and brochures from beaches were also collected to give the Germans the best possible advantage of local knowledge and suitable landing grounds if an invasion was to go ahead.

Extract of a map of Exmouth taken from German Chart

The plans and the accompanying information were also studied by the Luftwaffe Intelligence Service which then passed it to the relevant Luftflotte H.Q., which then passed it to the most suitable squadron and was acted on accordingly during the bombing raids over Britain. During the later night-time bombing raids and the hit-and-run raids which caused Exmouth so many problems post-March 7 1942, it was clear that the German crews knew exactly what they were doing and that very little was left to chance.

It is interesting to note that the gasometer and hospital were amongst other targets which were identified for special attention and are marked in purple as strategic targets on the German maps dating from 1940. On 26 February 1943 at 12.15 Exmouth was badly bombed by eight Focke Wulf 190A fighter-bombers in a hit-and-run raid and the gasometer was set alight by cannon fire and the impact by a 500 kg bomb, which fortunately passed right through it, exploding on nearby house down the road.

There is no doubt in my mind that things could have been very different for the town of Exmouth if the Germans had had things all their own way and so it must be understood that the threat to the local population of Exmouth during wartime was very real.

If this is true of our small town, then we can only assume that this was true for most of the south and south-east coastal towns, as well as the larger cities and manufacturing centres elsewhere in Britain.

The British Public's Understanding of Lightning War

From 1937 the British had realised that the Germans aggressive policy of 'Blitzkrieg' (lightning war) could become a reality in Britain too. With the aid of the Luftwaffe (the German Air Force) the German armed forces could raze to the ground any city they chose. One such city was Guernica, which was virtually destroyed by the Spanish Nationalists and the Luftwaffe on 27 April 1937 during the Spanish Civil War.

More recently the world had also followed closely the progressive and aggressive expansion policies of the Third Reich, with the occupation of the Sudetenland and the invasion of Czechoslovakia, where Britain had seen how people, with differing views from the Nazis, had been brutally suppressed by the secret police units of the Gestapo.

By the time Operation Sea Lion, (the German invasion of Britain) was being planned, the Germans had enough information on Britain to fill a suitcase for each agent landed on our shores, some of which would prove extremely useful and much of which was open to debate!

Topics of the information held included aerial photographs of most towns and cities and dock installations, Ordnance Survey maps of all the areas and major towns and cities in Britain. These were overprinted in German with strategic and military targets marked. Topographical information included local street directories for most towns and cities, conversion charts from metric to imperial measurements for all aspects of life in Britain, translated summaries of the history of the British Constitution, the names and addresses of all potential political adversaries correct to the end of 1937, the locations of synagogues, lists of police officials and their responsibilities etc. etc. The Germans had certainly prepared themselves well for the invasion of Britain.

German military geographical maps and books

Information about inland waterways, density of population, tourist route maps from A.A., tourist guides, bed capacities of hospitals, suitability of terrain for armoured warfare, positions of telecommunication centres, airfields, permanent military installations, arterial roads and junctions, permanent-way key depots and junctions had all been included in the intelligence gathering sweeps of pre-war Britain.

There was even a book specially prepared for the Gestapo. The publication marked 'Geheime' (Secret) was called the Informationsheft G.B. It included information about rival political groups and their leaders, details about the locations and key figures in public schools, religious groups and leaders hostile to the Nazi cause, and information about the Upper Class hierarchy and others though to be in opposition to Nazi Policy.

Civil Defence

Civil Defence plans and Policies were starting to be adopted all over Britain by 1938 and one of the most important of these was the evacuation of children from metropolitan areas deemed at risk from German air raids. Also the issue of gas masks to every man, woman and child in Britain was a sensible precautionary measure as it was feared that the Germans would use sprayed poisonous gases.

Leaflets had already been distributed to most British households by July 1939, covering many topics of concern about war. Every attempt was made by the government to put the nation's mind at rest, whilst also educating the masses to help them react in a suitable fashion to the prospect of war.

On Friday 1 September 1939, it was Poland's turn to be invaded. Many towns, including the nation's capital city Warsaw, were now to be subjected to blitzkriegs. It was now that the British were certain in the knowledge that they would have the same tactics used against them in a 'Total War' with Germany, and so Great Britain and France declared war on Germany. On this day over 700 Evacuees from Lambeth London arrived at Exmouth Railway Station ready to be billeted with residents.

It was clearly understood by most quarters of the British population, that the possibility of German air attacks and an invasion of Great Britain was a real possibility in the near future.

11.00a.m. Sunday 3 September 1939

It was a sunny, September Sunday, when the news that Britain had declared war on Germany was broadcast. Where possible people had either stayed in to listen to the impending news on their wireless (radio) sets, or had gone to their neighbours to listen to the Prime Minister Neville Chamberlain's fateful speech to the nation. Some Exmouth people can remember exactly

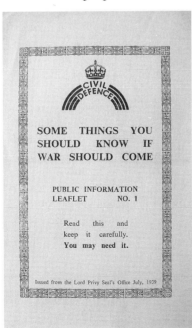

British Public Information Leaflet No. 1 July 1939

where they were and what they were doing when war was declared.

Bill Sleeman
'I was en route to Woodbury Common on a cycling trip with friends at the time. We stopped at a house which had the neighbouring families leaning in through open windows listening to the wireless.'

Ivor Pike
'I can remember Neville Chamberlain's declaration of war speech, on the Sunday morning; I was six at the time. The family were gathered round the wireless listening quietly. Amy Davis the milk lady, who used a horse and cart to deliver her milk, which she ladled out into jugs, was with us.'

Ron Lee
'I was a policeman in Exmouth, on duty in uniform at the police station in Victoria Road. We heard the news on the wireless. Sergeant Buckingham and other constables were there listening very intently to the news'

'We had sealed instructions which were delivered some weeks before the war started and other information in envelopes, which we had to open if war was declared. The first job we then had to do was put sand bags outside the door of the Victoria Road Police Station, in case of bombing raids.'

The Phoney War
Elizabeth Maycock
'There was a lull after war had been announced and nothing seemed to happen, I was expecting to find German soldiers around every corner and always thought that they were on the way!'

A few weeks after the first evacuations, Britain entered a period know as the 'Phoney War'. The country was technically at war with Germany, but they were not engaging the German's in large-scale land battles.

The war at sea had already begun and Exmouth had already lost men in an engagement at sea where H.M.S. *Courageous* was sunk, killing four local men, just two weeks after the declaration of war. From 12 October the B.E.F. were fully deployed and there were skirmishes along the Western Front.

Air engagements between enemy aircraft and planes of the R.A.F. were few, and most encounters were with German reconnaissance planes which had over flown most parts of the British Isles to take photographs of military or strategic targets, bridges, industrial areas and potential landing grounds.

Chapter 2
The Early Days

10 May 1940

Germany Invades France, Luxembourg, Belgium and Holland

Without any warning, Germany put operation Yellow, into effect. France and the Low Countries, was invaded with a total of 77 divisions, which included 10 panzer divisions and two parachute divisions. The Allied force completely outnumbered the German force in men, tanks and equipment, but was used in an outmoded 'static warfare' linear role, similar to that of the First World War.

In Britain Neville Chamberlain resigned and Winston Churchill became Prime Minister and formed a coalition government, to get the best from the country's available politicians. Discussions started immediately about the defence of Britain.

Sir Alan Brooke

'Why do we in this country, turn to all the old men when we require a new volunteer force? Old men spell delay and chaos!'

The comment above was made by Sir Alan Brooke, when attending an early lecture on the formation of the L.D.V. For quite a while there were mixed feelings about a voluntary force, to act as a second line of defence, behind the British Expeditionary Force, which at the time was fighting on the French–Belgian border.

The peace-time size of the Territorial Army had already been increased from its normal pre-war establishment to double its size, and some of these men were already fighting in France and Belgium. In certain dusty political quarters it was unthinkable that a further volunteer force would be needed!

Winston Churchill had already proposed that a second line of defence should be put in place as early as October 1939. This force was to be made up of men over the age of 40 and not already serving in the armed forces. The role of this volunteer army of a proposed five million men was to guard vulnerable points such as ports, railways and tunnels, key road junctions, possible sites for amphibious invasion and moorland areas which could be attacked by gliders and paratroops. Realising that the threat was even more likely now, Churchill was determined to have his way.

11 May 1940

The Ministry of Home Security and the War Office met to discuss the use of German parachute troops during the invasion of France and the Low Countries. It was determined at this meeting, suggested by General Sir Walter Kirke, that a regional defence force based on a town and village structure should be implemented as soon as possible whereby local men could be trained to be flexible and defend their region in the event of a parachute invasion. Kirke had been considering this idea for several months

Due to the perceived threat of invasion small groups of men in various parts of the country had already started to form groups of combatants to offer resistance to the German threat, although this was strictly illegal as it had not been sanctioned by Government.

The medical prerequisite of entrants to the L.D.V. was initially only that the applicant should be aged between 17 and 65 male, and be capable of free movement.

May 13 1940

It was decided that the plans should go ahead and H.M. Stationery Office was subsequently ordered to print the L.D.V. enrolment forms. On May 13 German paratroops had landed in Holland, broken through in the Ardennes, while the Maginot Line, once thought impassable, was seriously damaged. An announcement was broadcast by the B.B.C. which declared that 'any German parachute troops would be shot in the air or on landing if they were not wearing recognisable uniform.' The *Daily Mail* also announced (prematurely), that a new 'Home Guard' of older men who had previous military training and were crack shots was to be formed.

In return Germany broadcast this warning to the British civilians, warning them of the danger of signing up to what they considered was an illegal army of saboteurs and guerrillas:

'Civilians who take up arms against German soldiers are, under international law, no better than murderers. Whether they are priests or bank clerks. British people will do well to heed our warning.'

The Formation of the Local Defence Volunteers (L.D.V.)

On Tuesday 14 May 1940, at around 9.15 p.m., after the 9 o'clock news, the Minister for War, Anthony Eden appealed to the nation for the formation of the Local Defence Volunteers. The L.D.V. as it became known would constitute a part-time, defensive army, to be trained by the regular army, with the aim of defending Britain's shores against German airborne or seaborne invasion.

May 14 1940

Anthony Eden's speech

'I want to speak to you tonight, about the form of warfare which the Germans have been employing so successfully against Holland and Belgium, namely the dropping of troops, by parachute, behind the enemy main defence lines.'

An explanation followed about the strategy and tactics of this type of warfare. He then went on to say.

'In order to leave nothing to chance, and to supplement resources as yet untapped and the means of defence already arranged, we are going to ask you to help us in a manner which I hope will be welcome to thousands of you. Since the war began, the Government has received countless enquiries from all over the kingdom, from men of all ages who are for one reason or another not presently engaged in military service and who wish to do something for the defence of their country.'

'Now is your opportunity. We want large numbers of such men in Great Britain who are British subjects, between the ages of fifteen and sixty-five, to come forward now and offer their services in order to make assurance doubly sure. The name of the new force which is now to be raised will be the Local Defence Volunteers. This name describes its duties in three words. You will not be paid, but you will receive uniform and you will be armed. In order to volunteer, what you have to do is to give your names at your local police station and then, as and when we want you, we will let you know.'

And so, with this appeal to the nation and a following conference it was agreed that the L.D.V. would become a part of the fighting forces of the Crown. The Local Defence Volunteers was formed.

The L.D.V. Concept

The original concept and principal tasks of the L.D.V. were to guard and protect Britain from airborne invasion by parachute troops and gliders, by setting up regular patrols of potential landing sites.

In the Exmouth area, Woodbury Common was believed to be a probable site for airborne invasion, as were Dartmoor and Exmoor which, due to their immense size were equipped with horse patrols. All over Britain the wheels were put in motion to form units to defend against perceived airborne invasion.

Amongst other priorities for the newly-formed L.D.V. would be the need to defend Britain's railway, dock and inland waterway infrastructures against potential attack from paratroops. Prevention of sabotage by clandestine 'Fifth Columnists' (traitors and saboteurs) which may have been formed in Britain was high on the agenda of the L.D.V.

L.D.V. candidates were asked to enrol at their nearest local police station. No enrolment forms were available because of the rushed nature of the need for volunteers. The police were instructed by the Chief Constable to register the names and addresses only, of those who came forward and it was made clear that the local police would not be directly concerned with the organisation or control of this new part time army. The police were however obliged to ask the following questions.

Are you familiar with firearms?
What is your occupation?
What military experience, if any, have you?
Are you prepared to serve away from home?

It was decided that the minimum entry requirement in respect of physical fitness, was that a man 'need only be capable of free movement.'

It was originally agreed that men would only enlist initially for a period of 6 months and that the first 14 days of this period would be probationary. Either party could terminate the agreement if it was considered by either side that the candidate was not suitable.

There was a fear that enemy parachutists and agents who had already arrived in the

Saturday May 18th 1940 Exmouth Chronicle *article.*

The Exmouth Chronicle

L. D. V.

Great Response in Exmouth

By the time Mr. Anthony Eden had ceased giving his broadcast appeal for volunteer in the new spare time army (Local Defence Volunteers), which will guard Britain from an invasion by parachute troops, a small queue was formed outside Exmouth Police Station, ready to sign on the dotted line.

Recruiting has been going on steadily ever since and by last night nearly 400 had signed on.

Since Tuesday the type of form has been altered slightly so that the first 250 who signed are asked to go to the Police Station and re-sign unless they have already done so.

Within twenty-four hours of the appeal being broadcast, more than a quarter of a million men up and down the country applied for enrolment.

Members of the force will enlist for the duration of the war. They will not be paid and will live at home.

Training will be arranged for the convenience of volunteers, including night workers.

They must be reasonably physically fit and know something about the use of firearms.

When they have been enlisted they will be given uniforms and arms, and will be trained in the use of arms. If necessary, they may be given Bren guns.

Volunteers are needed particularly in small towns, villages and less densely-populated areas, where parachutists would probably try to land.

The force will be under the command of the G.O.C.-in-Chief of the Home Forces. Members will still be liable for military service.

It should be particularly noted that if you are already doing Civil Defence work, your officer should be consulted before registering.

In connection with the above, the Exmouth Miniature Rifle Club has offered its services to instruct volunteers in shooting. Names of all interested should be sent to Mr. G. Langdon, The Garage, or Mr. E. Burch, 85, Egremont-road.

National Identity Card.

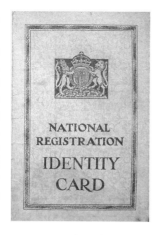

NATIONAL REGISTRATION IDENTITY CARD

British Isles would join the L.D.V. National Identity Cards had to be produced at the police station by individuals when enrolling and then carried everywhere afterwards to produce if challenged by other L.D.V. members or the police.

In Exmouth, Bill Gorfin was purported to be, in his own words, *'The first man, to register for the Exmouth Local Defence Volunteers.'*

In his position as the Editor of the *Exmouth Journal* newspaper he was aware of the government's planned Home Defence initiative in an advanced press notice, the night before the radio announcement. This notice was to be published in the local paper in the next available publication and so he registered his name at the Victoria Road Police Station before the national radio announcement was even made. The following extract is taken from his unpublished memoirs.

Bill Gorfin

'With the break-through of the Germans in May 1940, came the appeal for volunteers for the L.D.V. The force (in concept) was formed at 9.15 p.m. on Monday May 14 when Mr. Anthony Eden made his appeal for volunteers after the 9 o'clock news. My application to join was stamped by Sergeant (later Superintendent) Buckingham as the clock struck nine.

I had a message from the Ministry of Information during the day (Monday) and acted upon it without waiting for the radio appeal, so I feel I must have been the first to join 'Dad's Army'! Which, believe it or not, did a lot of valuable service during the war.'

John (Jack) Sage

'After hearing the appeal on the radio by Anthony Eden on 14 May 1940, I registered the following day. First I phoned Honiton Police Station with my details, I was then officially in the Luppitt Home Guard, from its formation on 19 May 1940, when I had to go in person to register with Honiton Police Station, taking my identity card and some other documents.'

Volunteers

The National target figure that the government had hoped for within the first few months was 175,000 volunteers. They were surprised that 250,000 men between the ages of 17 and 65 (not being in the fighting services already), had come forward in the first 24

hours to sign on the dotted line. Some lied about their age, young and old, and during the course of the war it was found that some were as young as 14 years old and others as old as 80 had volunteered to serve the colours. Most of these men were too old for the regular army, or too young, some were not quite fit enough to join the regulars, but were welcomed into the L.D.V., and some men had reserve occupations, which meant that their job was crucial to the war effort and therefore they could not join the regulars.

Although this huge number of volunteers created an administrative nightmare for the local police forces, by the time the British Expeditionary Force was being evacuated from the beaches at Dunkirk in the 'little ships', 400,000 men had volunteered. By the end of June 1940 the L.D.V. had an astonishing million and a half men under its command, the same size as Britain's pre-war regular army.

Torquay L.D.V. members guarding Greathill Reservoir May 1940.

A large proportion of these volunteers had fought in the 1914-18 war and already had military training and front-line experience. These men would were the ideal material for Senior N.C.O.'s, who would pass on their skills and train the younger volunteers. The men in the Greathill Reservoir photo (above) are typically dressed for an early L.D.V. unit. They have no uniform items, not even home-made L.D.V. armbands. The man in the centre of the photograph wears his civilian respirator slung over his left shoulder, the string is just visible.

What is astonishing about this photograph, is how well armed these man are! They have five P-17 Rifles and the man with the spectacles on the left is holding a Spanish, Trocaola .45 Service Revolver. These revolvers were purchased by their hundreds by the British Army in 1915 as a stop gap to fill the demand for 'man stopper' pistols for use in trench fighting; some were of dubious quality. Whether or not the Torquay L.D.V. had any ammunition for these weapons at the time is not known, but it would have been highly unlikely. One of the reasons why they may have been so well armed is that reservoirs were considered the perfect spot for flying boats to land spies.

Early L.D.V. members on parade in Torbay.

Some Members of Parliament and military advisors wanted the concept of the Local Defence Volunteers to be trained to become fighting 'savages' with what ever was to hand. It is clear through talking to Home Guard members over the years that they were definitely 'up for it'!

16 May 1940

The Zone Commander for Kent visited Chatham Command and obtained 1500 rifles and 15 000 rounds of ammunition for his unit. Around 500 were then transported to Ashford where they arrived at around 4 o'clock on the afternoon of 17 May. The grease was removed from the weapons and they were checked. They were later transported to the newly formed L.D.V. detachments in the area and by 10.30 p.m. they were on patrol with 1000 L.D.V. troops in the East Kent area. This was a remarkable feat and was only made possible by the generosity of the public who helped with the cleaning of the rifles and the use of their private cars and petrol to get them to their final destinations. Most units were not so lucky with the allocation of weapons.

17 May 1940

The royal assent was given to the formation of the L.D.V., on the proviso that no men with known connections to groups or organisations hostile to the crown or had serious criminal records were enrolled.

The Defence Regulations (L.D.V.) were passed in parliament on the 17th May 1940 under the Emergency Powers (Defence) act of 1939, and this ensured the legality of the Local Defence Volunteers Force. Each volunteer had to sign a legally binding enrolment contract, pledging submission to military law, with a promise to give 14 days notice to terminate this agreement to leave the service. One of the reasons for signing this contract was to prevent the L.D.V. members being shot as spies or 'terrorists' in the event of a German occupation of the British Isles.

18 May 1940

By this time the vanguard of the German advance had reached the English Channel. Within 16 days it would be all over for the British Expeditionary Force and the last British and French soldiers were boarding ships for return to Britain.

The Evacuation of the British Expeditionary Force From Dunkirk

From the first stages of the invasion of France and the Low Countries on 10 May, to June 4 the final day of evacuation of the troops from Dunkirk, the government was busy forming the Local Defence Volunteers, who in turn, were desperately organising and training themselves to be able to defend against attack. It was a complete reversal of standard military procedure, duties first, then, gradual training to improve the function of the L.D.V.

In total 338 000 British and Canadians were evacuated from Dunkirk, along with 140 000 French troops.

John Fletcher
'When Dunkirk fell it was expected that the Germans would invade very soon. A couple of 'Squaddies' from the local Battalion came to our house and set up a machine gun nest in the back garden of number 36 Camperdown Terrace, Exmouth, for a few days. The wall in the back garden dipped in the centre a little; we could look over the wall into the estuary. It made an ideal place for the machine gun as it gave a good view of the estuary with the wall for protection. It was very exciting for us boys having the gun in the back garden.'

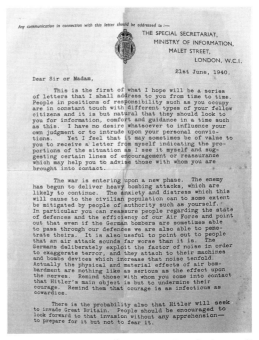

Letter to L.D.V. Commanders concerning the impending invasion

We are fortunate in the fact that the greater part of the B.E.F. is safely home in the island. All those men are confident in their ability to defeat the Germans —and they constitute the largest armed force we have ever had in Great Britain.

Our Air Force is as strong to-day as when the intensive war began six weeks ago. Fighting in France and Belgium they have never failed to bring down two, three or even four enemy 'planes to every one of their own. Fighting in their own country they will be at a far greater advantage and we may look forward to Germany's numerical superiority in 'planes being rapidly reduced to equality and then to inferiority.

Moreover it is a great advantage to have our men fighting on their own soil for their own homes. There will for the present be no more Expeditionary Forces with all the anxiety that separation entails. Our loved ones will be near us and we shall have daily news of them. So fighting side by side for the fields and villages and cities that we love we shall have greater confidence, knowing that our cause is just, that the life of our country is at stake and that we shall never surrender.

Hitler's belief is that he can frighten the British people into surrender before the autumn. If he fails to do that he will have failed to win the war and the great tide of power will begin to turn upon our side.

These are the sort of things which, in my opinion, you should be able to say to people and thereby to bring them comfort and strength. I shall be writing to you again shortly giving you further suggestions.

Yours truly,

Duff Cooper

Reverse of letter to L.D.V. Commanders

Issued by the Ministry of Information on behalf of the War Office and the Ministry of Home Security

STAY WHERE YOU ARE

IF this island is invaded by sea or air everyone who is not under orders must stay where he or she is. This is not simply advice: it is an order from the Government, and you must obey it just as soldiers obey their orders. Your order is "Stay Put", but remember that this does not apply until invasion comes.

Why must I stay put?

Because in France, Holland and Belgium, the Germans were helped by the people who took flight before them. Great crowds of refugees blocked all roads. The soldiers who could have defended them could not get at the enemy. The enemy used the refugees as a human shield. These refugees were got out on to the roads by rumour and false orders. Do not be caught out in this way. Do not take any notice of any story telling what the enemy has done or where he is. Do not take orders except from the Military, the Police, the Home Guard (L.D.V.) and the A.R.P. authorities or wardens.

What will happen to me if I don't stay put?

If you do not stay put you will stand a very good chance of being killed. The enemy may machine-gun you from the air in order to increase panic, or you may run into enemy forces which have landed behind you. An official German message was captured in Belgium which ran:

"Watch for civilian refugees on the roads. Harass them as much as possible."

Our soldiers will be hurrying to drive back the invader and will not be able to stop and help you. On the contrary, they will

Obverse of 'Stay Where You Are' leaflet

---

have to turn *you* off the roads so that they can get at the enemy. You will not have reached safety and you will have done just what the enemy wanted you to do.

How shall I prepare to stay put?

Make ready your air-raid shelter; if you have no shelter prepare one. Advice can be obtained from your local Air Raid Warden or in "Your Home as an Air-raid Shelter", the Government booklet which tells you how to prepare a shelter in your house that will be strong enough to protect you against stray shots and falling metal. If you can have a trench ready in your garden or field, so much the better, especially if you live where there is likely to be danger from shell-fire.

How can I help?

You can help by setting a good example to others. Civilians who try to join in the fight are more likely to get in the way than to help. The defeat of an enemy attack is the task of the armed forces which include the Home Guard, so if you wish to fight enrol in the Home Guard. If there is no vacancy for you at the moment register your name for enrolment and you will be called upon as soon as the Army is ready to employ you. For those who cannot join there are many ways in which the Military and Home Guard may need your help in their preparations. Find out what you can do to help in any local defence work that is going on, and be ready to turn your hand to anything if asked by the Military or Home Guard to do so.

If you are responsible for the safety of a factory or some other important building, get in touch with the nearest military authority. You will then be told how your defence should fit in with the military organisation and plans.

What shall I do if the Invader comes my way?

If fighting by organised forces is going on in your district and you have no special duties elsewhere, go to your shelter and stay there till the battle is past. Do not attempt to join in the fight. Behave as if an air-raid were going on. The enemy will seldom turn aside to attack separate houses.

But if small parties are going about threatening persons and property in an area not under enemy control and come your way, you have the right of every man and woman to do what you can to protect yourself, your family and your home.

Stay put.

It's easy to say. When the time comes it may be hard to do. But you have got to do it; and in doing it you will be fighting Britain's battle as bravely as a soldier.

(Printed in England)

Reverse of 'Stay Where You Are' leaflet

Issued by the Ministry of Information in co-operation with the War Office and the Ministry of Home Security

Beating the INVADER

A MESSAGE FROM THE PRIME MINISTER

IF invasion comes, everyone—young or old, men and women—will be eager to play their part worthily. By far the greater part of the country will not be immediately involved. Even along our coasts, the greater part will remain unaffected. But where the enemy lands, or tries to land, there will be most violent fighting. Not only will there be the battles when the enemy tries to come ashore, but afterwards there will fall upon his lodgments very heavy British counter-attacks, and all the time the lodgments will be under the heaviest attack by British bombers. The fewer civilians or non-combatants in these areas, the better—apart from essential workers who must remain. So if you are advised by the authorities to leave the place where you live, it is your duty to go elsewhere when you are told to leave. When the attack begins, it will be too late to go; and, unless you receive definite instructions to move, your duty then will be to stay where you are. You will have to get into the safest place you can find, and stay there until the battle is over. For all of you then the order and the duty will be: "STAND FIRM".

This also applies to people inland if any considerable number of parachutists or air-borne troops are landed in their neighbourhood. Above all, they must not cumber the roads. Like their fellow-countrymen on the coasts, they must "STAND FIRM". The Home Guard, supported by strong mobile columns wherever the enemy's numbers require it, will immediately come to grips with the invaders, and there is little doubt will soon destroy them.

Throughout the rest of the country where there is no fighting going on and no close cannon fire or rifle fire can be heard, everyone will govern his conduct by the second great order and duty, namely, "CARRY ON". It may easily be some weeks before the invader has been totally destroyed, that is to say, killed or captured to the last man who has landed on our shores. Meanwhile, all work must be continued to the utmost, and no time lost.

The following notes have been prepared to tell everyone in rather more detail what to do, and they should be carefully studied. Each man and woman should think out a clear plan of personal action in accordance with the general scheme.

Winston S. Churchill

STAND FIRM

1. What do I do if fighting breaks out in my neighbourhood?

Keep indoors or in your shelter until the battle is over. If you can have a trench ready in your garden or field, so much the better. You may want to use it for protection if your house is damaged. But if you are at work, or if you have special orders, carry on as long as possible and only take cover when danger approaches. If you are on your way to work, finish your journey if you can.

If you see an enemy tank, or a few enemy soldiers, do not assume that the enemy are in control of the area. What you have seen may be a party sent on in advance, or stragglers from the main body who can easily be rounded up.

'Beating the Invader' leaflet June 1940

Chapter 3
The Local Defence Volunteers (L.D.V.)

Winston Churchill on the Evacuation of the B.E.F. from Dunkirk

'If the British Commonwealth and its Empire last for a thousand years, men will say,' "This was their finest hour."'

After the evacuation of Dunkirk, the army's first duty was still to keep its divisions intact for service elsewhere, at home and overseas. Its second duty was to press on with training and re-equipping the new personnel and making good the losses sustained by the B.E.F., which was mainly artillery and vehicles as they had returned with none.

After the Minister for War, Anthony Eden's appeal to the nation for the formation of the L.D.V. as it became known, men all over Britain flooded in to join the ranks. It would constitute a part-time, defensive army, to be trained by the regular army, to defend Britain's shores against a German invasion. Candidates were asked to enrol at their local Police station, which in Exmouth was situated at Victoria Road.

Bill Sleeman

Bill described himself as *'A founder member of the Exmouth Home Guard,'* joining at the Victoria Road Police Station at 11 o'clock on the morning of Wednesday 15th May 1940 after hearing and responding to Anthony Eden's announcement on the B.B.C.

Bill was 18 years old at the time and was not alone in his desire to defend his country.

Laurie Butler

'I was around the age of 14-15 when I joined the Home Guard I put my age on when I enrolled and no one seemed to be bothered. It was in 1940 and things were very serious at the time. As I was so under age I thought I'd better ask my mother if I could join. All she really said was "As long you wrap up warm!"'

In a short while the newly designed AFW 3006 L.D.V. enlistment forms started arriving and the men were asked to fill out these documents at the early meetings.

Peter Gardner

'I volunteered for the Dunsford (Devon) area L.D.V. when the appeal went out in May 1940. We drilled with broomsticks and had very few weapons to start with. One of our jobs was to look after the Southern Railway track and tunnel that went through the Teign Valley near Dunsford. We had a hand-pumped railway cart which we would use to travel along the track in the pitch black, you couldn't show a light because of the black out.'

'The first night I went on one of these railway patrols, it was freezing cold and damp and it the only way we knew where we were going was because of the track. It took a very long time to get along the track and to the end of the long dark tunnel and when we arrived at the other end of it to meet up with the next patrol, no one turned up! We were on our own. We guessed that they couldn't be bothered to turn up because of bad weather.'

'Needless to say I wasn't in the L.D.V. for long after that and volunteered for the Royal Marines.'

Jack Sage

'When the L.D.V. was asked for by Anthony Eden, it was formed as a volunteer force. Later in the war they conscripted men into the Home Guard because they were taking the men away so fast for the armed forces. Some as young as 16 joined the Luppitt Home Guard, but most that joined, who were mainly farmers, or had some other reserve occupation, were 17.'

Early Meetings

Most L.D.V. men were in reserve occupation employment, or ran local shops and businesses. This meant that most men were occupied during the daylight hours and could only spare 6-8 hours a week volunteering. It was quickly decided that the main function of this new force would not be to engage the enemy, (for lack of weapons), but to mount patrols and watches reporting back information regarding any enemy activity so that the regular army Home Defence Battalions, could be called in to counter any threat.

Bill Sleeman

'*The first meetings of the L.D.V. were held at the Grammar School at Gypsy lane, all of our initial training was done here under the instruction of our old School Master, Mr Heath.*'

'*After the taking of registers etc. the basic training and drill instruction was using broom handles for drill, as rifles were not yet available.*'

'*No one was really sure of what was expected of them initially and everything, although very primitive at the time, was taken very seriously, not at all like the impression given by the programme 'Dads Army'. The threat of invasion was very real and a coastal town with a large estuary and two-and-a-half miles of beach and potential landing grounds to defend, meant that Exmouth could have easily been a target.*'

Jack Sage

When we first enrolled in the L.D.V. we had virtually no weapons and used to drill with broomsticks. This was useful for discipline and learning how to march but very little else. As I was on the farm I had a 12-bore shotgun and used to take that along to the meetings and when we did the early patrols.'

Nick-Names

A nick-name was not necessarily deemed derogatory in the war years, most people had them and they were created more out of affection for people or organisations rather than to deliberately defame. The world has sadly changed in this respect and nick-names, an important facet of British humour for all manner of organisations and individuals, are now becoming a thing of the past, for fear of offending due to over zealous policies of political correctness.

Ron Lavis

'*We knew the L.D.V. men and we had our own nick-names for the L.D.V. in Exmouth. They were christened the 'Last Desperate Venture', 'Long Dentured Veterans', or the most popular name was Look, Duck and Vanish. We didn't mean any real harm by these names; everyone had a nick-name in those days.*'

The L.D.V. was subjected to some gentle mockery in the early days of their existence. In Torquay they were known as the Lurking Dervish Volunteers. I personally feel a lot of this was just born out of the Englishman's ability to laugh at himself and his predicament rather than from any real malice.

The L.D.V. earned the nick-name of 'The Broomstick Army' from the regular soldiers, which was an irony in itself, as a small proportion of the regulars in the B.E.F. had thrown their own rifles into the sea at Dunkirk.

Understandably, in some cases this had to happen, either to prevent the weapons falling in to enemy hands, or just to facilitate getting on board a ship. It must be remembered though that most soldiers would have been loath to do this, for fear of court martial and a fine of £5.

This act had contributed to the lack of arms available for use by the L.D.V. and that at time of international emergency the men of the L.D.V. volunteered to fight and defend their homeland, even without the prospect of having any real weapons!

The nick-name 'Look, Duck and Vanish', was widely used, but upon the change of the name to the Home Guard, the more affectionate nick-name, 'Dads Army' came into being, refering to the number of WWI veterans which had now swelled the ranks. Older members in Exmouth in turn had then christened the 17 year olds, who were joining up in droves prior to receiving their call up papers, the 'Battle Patrol.'

The writer George Orwell, who had volunteered himself, referred to the newly formed L.D.V. affectionately as 'A Peoples' Army officered by Blimps'. Noel Coward wrote songs, like 'Won't You Please Oblige Us with a Bren Gun!' which list the difficulties of trying to defend the country with substandard, or no weapons! George Formby composed 'Guarding the Home of the Home Guard', 'Get Cracking' and 'The Home Guard Blues' all laced with his brilliant innuendo and references to the problems which beset the early units. Britain's ability to laugh at itself in times of trouble certainly helped bolster the morale of the country and I personally hope it a skill that is not lost by future generations.

Nearly every organisation in Britain had its own acronym at the time (A.R.P. Air Raid Precautions etc.) and comics everywhere could not resist the temptation of giving the L.D.V. members yet another new nick-name'.

Scrounging

It is inconceivable to think now but, the L.D.V. was started without any form of national or local government support in most areas. This was mainly due to the 'rushed' nature of implementing the idea in its simplest form and getting the men out on patrol quickly as was humanly possible, to help defend against the possibility of an immediate attack. No funds were available to buy the smallest and simplest of things needed to administer and function in the most basic way, apart from some donations from generous public spirited individuals.

Initially some L.D.V. officers paid for the whole platoon's expenses out of their own pockets, most, though not all were reimbursed. Therefore, the art of scrounging was quickly mastered by the earliest members of the L.D.V. and pencils, paper, wood and materials and furniture to build observation posts, warm clothing and old obsolete weapons were amongst the things which were needed immediately to get started.

Local women also helped to make armbands, balaclavas, scarves and gloves to keep the men warm while on cold patrols in desolate places.

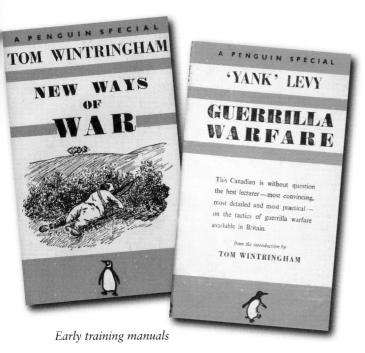

Early training manuals

Early Training Manuals

Training manuals, dating from 1940, could be privately purchased by Home Guard members. It was the sort of manual written by Tom Wintringham and others that were used until the army had produced proper training manuals. Wintringham had developed his guerrilla tactics fighting for the Communists during the Spanish Civil War and his manuals provided excellent information and tactical advice for early L.D.V. formations.

Laurie Butler

'I didn't buy any books about Home Guard training, but we could borrow books about general Home Guard issues and training when they became available.'

Colonel Mac Conaghy was an ex-Indian Army Cavalry Officer and the local man responsible for the organisation and training of the L.D.V. in Exmouth. In the early days, he did an extremely good job of training the volunteers in the skills of infantry soldiers.

Bill Sleeman

'Colonel Mac Conaghy was well organised and of really good character and was well known and respected locally'

Saluting

Because of the voluntary nature of the Home Guard no authority was ever given to the saluting of officers in the rules and regulations. Initially it was left to groups and individuals to decide whether to adopt it as a general policy for their unit. Most units did decide to adopt saluting as a mark of respect for the officers and a mark of pride in their uniform. Later on as the army rank system became operational and officers carried the Kings Commission, all Home Guardsmen saluted.

The Potential Threat of a German Invasion

The principal tasks of the L.D.V. were to guard Britain's potential airborne invasion sites by setting up regular observation patrols. As previously noted, areas such as Woodbury Common, Dartmoor and Exmoor in Devon were believed to be probable sites for airborne invasion. Dartmoor and Exmoor were quickly equipped with horse patrols due to the immense size of the areas. These patrols often included women riders, who owned their own horses.

Amongst other priority tasks for the L.D.V. was the need to defend Britain's coastline, railway, docks and inland waterway infrastructures and manufacturing industries against potential attack, either by invading regular forces or by spies and saboteurs who had already been infiltrated into Britain. Spies were thought to have landed by parachute or by submarines running in close to shore.

Bill Sleeman

'It was feared that paratroops may land on Woodbury Common or some act of sabotage may occur, from the enemy landing on the coast at night. We were instructed only to watch and report back to our H.Q. After Dunkirk however, everybody thought that was the end of it, most of us expected and invasion of some sort.'

When asked if he was prepared to kill an enemy invader, as he was so young at the time, Bill thought for a while and said:

'Yes, I suppose so, because that's what they trained us to do!'

In other areas of Britain where there were large docks some units became known as the Dock Defence Volunteers (D.D.V.) but they gradually lost this title to take the title Local Defence Volunteers.

Guarding Against Sabotage

The main concern for factories and other vulnerable points was 'Fifth Column' sabotage. Docks, bridges, viaducts, railway tunnels, important road junctions, canals, rivers and estuaries, signal boxes, rail junctions and marshalling yards and locomotive depots were all considered high-risk targets.

5 June 1940

At an informative, realistic and candid speech to the newly formed L.D.V. officials and higher ranks by General Ironside:

'What we want to know from you – and it will not be the ordinary spy rumours that you will send in to us – we want to know what is going on. Is there anything peculiar happening? Are there any peculiar people? I have made up my mind I am not going to have any more of these people, the 'Fifth Column', making trouble in this country. We do not want spy complex, but we do not want any Fifth Column trouble.'

6 June 1940

The following orders were issued by the Military Authorities. 'All troops should be warned that parachutists are expected and special vigilance is necessary. Enemy landing is regarded as imminent. All posts should be warned the probability of invasion has increased very considerably and is now definitely expected.'

The Invasion Alarm

In July 1940 after the fall of Dunkirk, the risk of invasion was very high and the British Government decided that the best way of informing the population that an invasion was underway was to have the church bells rung. Consequently the bells could not be rung for Church gatherings or weddings at the time as this may spark a false alarm; so the bells would only be rung in the event of an invasion and, around the 25 July 1940, it was decided that this job would be executed by the Home Guard. This put the local vergers and bell ringer's noses out of joint for a while as no one had informed the churches that this was the case and that the Home Guard would need access to the locked belfries and bell towers. The government had not realise there was any skill involved in ringing church bells, some of which weighed several hundredweight, and that they had to be started and stopped in a very specific way to avoid serious injury to the operators or damage to the ancient bells.

After much governmental wrangling it was decided that the bell ringers would be the obvious choice to ring the bells and as they had already offered to

Leaflet distributed to British households in July 1940

IF THERE IS AN INVASION

AIR MARSHAL'S ADVICE

Very practical advice on what to do in the event of this country being invaded was given recently by Air Marshal Sir Philip Joubert.

Keep your head, keep your mouth shut, stay where you are and ring up the police if you see anything suspicious. Above all, do not gossip and do not spread rumours. Believe only what you see yourself and not always that !

If the population takes these hints, Sir Philip said, then " it can safely leave the Home Defence forces to deal with the German invader."

Advice in the Exmouth Journal July 1940

volunteer their services they would be only too pleased to ring them, after notification by the Home Guard.

In Colyton, Devon, the Lord of the Manor Mr T. E. Newman formed his own private army from members of his staff, servants and tenants which collectively joined the L.D.V.

He exercised an ancient right which gave him permission to do this to protect his land. The last time this right had been exercised in Colyton was in 1646 during the Civil War. Newman, with his private army, was photographed addressing his men for *The War Illustrated* magazine of July 12 1940. He is equipped with denims, probably privately made and a rifle. His men all wear civilian clothing; some are armed with a selection of shotguns and rifles. Curiously they wear their L.D.V. armbands on the left sleeve.

Airborne Invasion

At this time of the war many national newspapers had christened the L.D.V. troops 'Parashots' or 'Parashootists', which referred to the fact they were to be responsible for hunting and shooting German parachutists.

L.D.V. (EXMOUTH)

Sir,—It is proposed to hold a meeting on Sunday, at the Pavilion, at 2.30. Will all members of the above please make every effort to attend. Identity cards will have to be produced.

All members will be allocated to their tasks at the meeting. It will be appreciated if members of the L.D.V. who read this will endeavour to inform other members. More recruits are wanted and should be brought to the meeting if possible.

Yours faithfully,
O.C. EXMOUTH PLATOON
L.D.V.

9 July 1940 invasion imminent, as reflected in this article in the Exmouth Chronicle

If you are researching the Home Guard using old newspapers, look out for this word as it often gives rise to early information about the L.D.V. Appeals were also made in these newspapers for shotguns, ammunition and other weapons to arm the Parashots.

In Mulbarton, Norfolk, old farm wagons were commandeered from various parts of the locality and used as road blocks and parked on the common to prevent the possibility of an airborne invasion by German glider troops; the remains of an old mill were also demolished so as not to provide a landmark to glider troops.

At a Mulbarton Parish Council meeting on 18 July 1940, when the invasion threat was at its highest point, the Town Clerk suggested that only the centre of the common should be decommissioned and asked for ideas from the council as to how to render the common unusable to the enemy. One of the suggestions which was reported by the Chairman was that:

'He had been in conversation with Colonel Beck on the question... and he advised the council to await instructions from the Military... The Clerk was instructed to write to R.D.C. to ask for permission to place a Bus on the common to be used as a Guard Room for the Local Defence Force Corps, providing that the Military would bear the expense of moving the old Bus to the required position.'

Seaborne Invasion

By the end of June 1940 the orders had changed slightly, as an amphibious assault was expected on the south-east and south coasts of Britain.

The three main purposes of the L.D.V were now.

• Observation and information regard enemy landings, invasion by sea and fifth column activities.

• Preventing initial movement by enemy forces in the event of an invasion. Denying access to motor vehicles and petrol and making road blocks.

• Patrolling and protecting vulnerable points. Especially in the country and rural areas and south coastal regions.

• Co-ordinated action between the hours of twilight and darkness, being the most susceptible to attack, 'From Dusk to Dawn'.

September 7-8 1940

The alarm of the church bells ringing coincided with the first Blitz of the City of London.

The invasion imminent code word 'Cromwell' is sent by G.H.Q. Home Forces to Southern Command and Eastern Command. Elements of the regular army and the Home Guard are put on action stations. German S-Boats were laying mines in the Straights of Dover and church bells were rung out over the south and south-east of England to sound the invasion warning.

Bill Sleeman wrote in his diary.

Bill Sleeman
'Church bells were rung in parts of Somerset, Devon and Cornwall, but no invasion was attempted.'

Rupert Cooper 'C' Coy 10 Battalion
Suffolk Home Guard
'When the invasion was thought to be imminent, I can remember coming in from work at eight o'clock at night, getting changed and then going on Home Guard duty until the next morning, and then going to work again the next day after breakfast.'

It was thought that the Germans had started their invasion on this night but luckily it turned out to be a false alarm. Unknown to the British at the time, Hitler had postponed his Operation Sea-lion until the 21st September 1940.

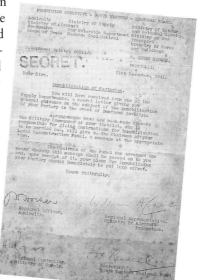

Ron Lavis's Letter ordering the demobilisation of his family business in the event of an invasion in December 1941

Chapter 4
The L.D.V. Uniforms and Equipment

This chapter looks at the equipment used by the L.D.V. in their defence of Britain. It begins with government-supplied items that they already had and weapons and personal items that they supplied themselves.

Civilian Respirators

Respirators were more commonly known as gas masks. The L.D.V. members initially used their civilian models which had been issued to them before volunteering for the L.D.V.

Civilian respirators were issued to everyone in Britain over the age of three and who were not serving in the armed forces or civil defence services. They were only used by the L.D.V. until a more suitable alternative could be found as the filter assemblies positioned on the front of the mask made firing a rifle accurately extremely difficult. These small gas masks were carried in their issue cardboard boxes, slung over the shoulder by a piece of string, or carried in privately purchased leatherette or cloth covers, which gave a little protection from the weather.

The L.D.V. used these gas masks for a few months as the shortcomings of the mask and its cardboard carrying-box soon became evident. The box was perfectly adequate for storing the mask at home or light civilian use, but was useless when used in an active military service role.

The cardboard boxes were susceptible to the wet and would frequently fall apart in the slightest amount of rain due to the poor quality of the cardboard. Around the time of the name change to the Home Guard, the volunteers in some units were issued with cylindrical metal containers (carrying-

The civilian respirator with box and metal carrying tin

tins) to replace the boxes and these could be taken on exercises, parades or patrols with the gas mask remaining dry and free from breakage from knocks and the steel parts free from rust.

Once the L.D.V. became the Home Guard, they were issued with military style Mk VI service respirators, as the threat of a German invasion became greater. Later again, Mk VII respirators were supplied to some men.

The civilian respirator in position

Armbands

Armbands, which were also known as armlets and brassards, had to be worn by men serving their country in militia units during conflicts. Identifying the men to the enemy, serving their country in a military role, was a point of international law.

It was required by the rules of the Geneva Convention, that men outside of the armed forces, serving in the militia or similar organisations in defence of their homeland, should have some kind of officially sanctioned badge or mark to distinguish them from the civilian population.

The government decided that an armband should be the identifying mark for the L.D.V., as it could be made quickly and cheaply. It was worn on the right arm by the men as a stop-gap measure, until decisions about manufacturing and supply of uniforms could be made. This would ensure that, in the event of an invasion, the

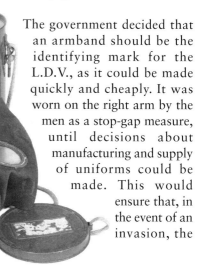

L.D.V. members would be officially recognized as a legitimate fighting force.

The government could not rule out an invasion of Britain immediately after the fall of France and the low-countries and thus contact between the L.D.V. and the enemy seemed likely. They therefore had to make sure that, internationally, the L.D.V. were easily identifiable force, sanctioned by government and with a legitimate structure, observing the rules of war and not acting as terrorists.

In the event of an invasion the potential risk to men serving in the L.D.V. was a real worry. The chance of these men being shot as terrorists or spies was a real possibility and so the government quickly sent out instructions to the newly-formed units to make improvised armbands.

This armband would afford the wearer protection under the rules of the Geneva Convention in the event that L.D.V. members fought, or were captured by, the enemy. This protection would also mean that any L.D.V. member being killed or mistreated after surrendering to the enemy, would be viewed as a serious war crime.

After the legalities of the status of the L.D.V. were eventually settled, a B.B.C. broadcast to the men of the L.D.V in mid June, by the Under Secretary of State for War, Sir Edward Grigg reported:

'Under the regulation by which you were formed, you are part of the Armed Forces of the Crown. You therefore rank as soldiers, with a soldier's rights and a soldier's obligations. The most important right is to use armed force against the enemies of your country.'

The earliest examples of L.D.V. armbands were made locally, usually by the W.V.S., Women's Institutes or similar organisations.

These home-made armbands were supposed to be made with white/off white coloured material. The Devon L.D.V. units had different colours, some blue with yellow lettering, black with white lettering, all in differing typefaces and styles.

These armbands, for practical purposes, were then thought by unit commanders to be too visible to the enemy and, in June 1940, moves were made by the War Office to standardise the colour scheme and typeface . Nationally a variety of khaki/green bands featuring different typeface styles appeared in different counties and units. In Exmouth, some greenish coloured cloth was sourced locally and a women's working party was set up to make armbands, these were then sewn together and overprinted using black paint and stencils.

The guidelines were that they should be made of khaki canvas, with L.D.V. letters stencilled in white, but they generally continued to appear in a variety of materials, styles, typefaces and colours depending on what resources were available. These armbands were sometimes stamped by the local council, to make sure the enemy knew the men were 'officially employed' by the local government if captured.

Bill Sleeman
'We wore our own clothes at first and were soon supplied with armbands with L.D.V. written on them, which were made locally.'

Home made Local Defence Volunteer armband

The L.D.V. had only been in existence a very short time before it was decided that a proper uniform was to going to be issued to the men. Unit commanders at the time gradually standardised the design of the armband, to offer at least some semblance of uniformity to the men until the national pattern armbands and supplies of uniforms arrived.

Government issue L.D.V. armband

By the end of May 250,000 of the government's standard design, mass-produced armbands became available but their use was only short-lived. All L.D.V. armbands, including the nationally-supplied ones became obsolete when the L.D.V. was renamed the Home Guard in late July 1940.

Jack Sage
'After a while we were issued with L.D.V. armbands and a bit later on we had proper uniforms and equipment.'

Uniform Clothing

The proposal to issue a uniform to the L.D.V was made on the 15 May 1940, but the logistics of sourcing and distributing them presented a difficult prospect. As uniforms could not issued rapidly it was deemed desirable to have at least some type of collective identity and many of the early L.D.V. chose work uniforms or smart, practical clothing upon which they wore their armband on the right sleeve.

It is worth remembering that the various regions of Britain formed their L.D.V. units at slightly different times and also possessed varying degrees of efficiency and administrative know-how. This, coupled with items of clothing being in short supply, or in some cases not yet even designed-for-purpose, meant that many units received their uniforms and equipment at different times, as and when supplies became available.

Bill Sleeman from the Exmouth Company 2 'Clyst' Battalion remembers they wore their own clothes initially and were soon supplied with government-issued L.D.V. armbands. Field service caps were the next thing to arrive, followed shortly by some blouses of the tobacco-brown coloured denim overalls.

A few months later serge battledress blouses arrived and, later, trousers and steel helmets were supplied along with American rifles.

Eventually, great coats arrived, nearly a year and a half after the original formation of the units.

The Field Service Cap

On the 22 May 1940 Sir Edward Grigg, speaking in the House of Commons, announced that 250 000 Field Service caps were now available for the L.D.V. with 90 000 already having been delivered. In most areas of Great Britain this was the first official piece of

The khaki field service cap

uniform clothing that the L.D.V. received. They were frequently in extra-large or extra-small sizes as most of the more common sizes had already been issued to the army.

Denims

Some of the earliest denim clothing issued to the L.D.V were the tobacco-brown denims, originally provided for work duties to soldiers late in the nineteenth century. Much of this was in extremely poor condition. Denim blouses and trousers of the newer 1938 pattern also became available at the same time. These were issued from mid 1940.

The blouses and trousers arrived separately in some cases and the colour and sizes varied enormously from green to greenish and from brown to a washed-out pinkish colour, resulting in some startling colour combinations. The men complained that the small sets were 'too small' and the large sets were 'too large'. The reason for this was that the regular army had been issued denims for work duties using most of the national stock in the most common sizes. For instance a set of denims for a man with a 40" waist would fit a 6'4" man perfectly, but there were not very many men of this height at the time. The problem was compounded by the fact that most men were either very young fit and slim, or older and slightly more portly! An order was passed to organise 'fitting under local arrangements' with Exmouth tailors, but who would foot the bill? After some debate it was decided by the Territorial Army Supply Depot that it was 'fair enough' to expect them to pay for uniforms that would actually fit! Some denims examples arrived in brand new condition but had no buttons. The buttons were manufactured to be easily removed from the denim blouse for washing and because of this they were supplied separately in some cases they took several weeks to arrive after the clothing.

1938 pattern denim blouse

The War Illustrated, a weekly publication dated 7 June 1940, shows an older and younger man of the Kent 'Parashots' (L.D.V.), armed with P-17 Enfield rifles, a full set of 1938 pattern denims (without an L.D.V. armband), Field Service Cap and a bicycle, guarding a crossroads.

Even though Kent was one of the areas that the government thought the Germans would be most likely to invade and so prioritised the men of the L.D.V. in this area, it is the exception rather than the rule to see early L.D.V. members as well equipped as this. The photograph would have been taken around a week before the publication date, around 30 May, just 16 days after Anthony Eden's rousing appeal. It could possibly have been a staged photograph to boost morale.

The L.D.V. member (left) is Alfie Parsons aged about 17. He was a Guardsman of the

Stinsford L.D.V. member dressed in 1938 pattern denims and armed with a P-17 rifle and shotgun

Higher Bockhampton Platoon. The photograph was probably taken around August 1940 as he still has his L.D.V. armband and shotgun. He has also been issued with a rifle, 1938 pattern denims, F.S. cap and county regiment badge, so it must be post-August 3 1940. The photograph was taken outside Mellstock House.

Helmets looked like an olive-green, upturned soup plate, but there were some differences in manufacture over the years. The shape of the helmet was already an icon of the British 'Tommy' in the trenches during WWI and later marks didn't change much from the original 1916 'Brodie' Pattern Mk I, named after its inventor.

The Mk I 'Brodie Pattern' Steel Helmet

This was the original rimless WWI pattern steel 'Tommy' helmet which had a very basic liner with a string for size adjustment. It also had an adjustable leather chin strap. Some Territorial Army Quartermasters stores still had limited supplies of these helmets and these were made available to early the L.D.V. units, although in most areas steel helmets were in very short supply initially. Some of these early helmets were recalled and given a rim, a new liner and a sprung strap and were re-designated Mk I* as they were re-issued.

It was a real bone of contention with the L.D.V. members that they could not be issued with helmets earlier, as the A.R.P. services and even telephonists and A.F.S. messenger boys had already received their MK II steel helmets as early as 1939. It was usually quicker for the L.D.V. members to privately purchase a Mk I* or Mk II steel helmet, as they were available in some retail shops, and many did this.

A few were issued but in relatively small numbers. Most men had to wait for one to be supplied by the government, which in some cases took several months. As the war progressed Mk II helmets became an easily obtainable item and a lot of the newly-formed Home Guard Light Anti-Aircraft Artillery and 'Z' Rocket Batteries were issued with the re-vamped Mk I* helmets.

During the first Blitz of London which started on the 7 September 1940 and lasted for 94 days, most of the London Battalions had not been issued with helmets and they were terribly exposed to enemy bombings, strafing and risk of head injuries from falling masonry, or from British anti-aircraft shrapnel returning to earth.

WWI Mk I 'Brodie' Pattern steel helmet

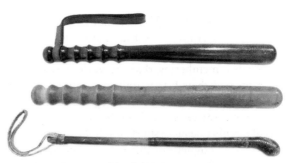

Police truncheons and lead-filled cane cudgel

Personal Weapons

The items above belonged to Sergeant Bob Parsons of the Bognor Regis Home Guard and are typical of the type of simple weapons intended to be used by the L.D.V., along with a frightening array of medieval weapons made in sheds all over Britain by the early members.

Early Devon L.D.V. units had very little weaponry as the list from the inaugural meeting of the Torquay L.D.V. (later 10 'Torbay' Battalion Devon Home Guard) shows:

Weapons List
Police truncheon x 1.
Indian clubs x 2 (usually used for exercising and keeping fit).
Lead piping and string x 1.
Revolvers x? possibly?.
Rifles/shotguns x 1.
Ammunition x10 rounds (these will not fit the shotgun).

Although this list may seem comical now, especially the lead piping and the piece of string, which more is reminiscent of the childhood game of Cluedo, it is important to realise that Britain was in extreme danger at the time.

Just imagine trying to put together an army (which would eventually become the largest regiment in the world!), where you live. Its function would be to repel the most professional and best trained army in the world. This enemy army already had three years of battle experience under its belt! What would you use?

Personal knives and daggers, axes, home-made knuckle dusters, iron bars, crowbars, pick-axe handles with a leather wrist strap, hammers, jam-tin bombs and jar bombs were all items recommended by people in 'the know' as suitable items to be experimented with.

It was recommended by the War Office that carving knives could be mounted on broomsticks by tying them on with steel wire or strong twine, this effectively was the prototype of the much-hated pike. It was also suggested that clubs and cudgels could be made out of any suitable materials.

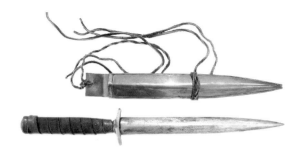

WWI trench dagger made from a half-round File

The knife above was used by an L.D.V. member in Sidmouth, Devon. It had been made from a ground down half-round file and brass shell cases, it was used by his Grandfather on the Western Front in WW I.

Hand made trench knife

Commercially made stiletto dagger

Shotguns

Firearms were in such short supply at this period of time, that even early percussion cap shotguns were considered for use by the L.D.V. The police asked for any firearm, of any style or vintage to be taken to them for inspection to see if it would have been suitable for use.

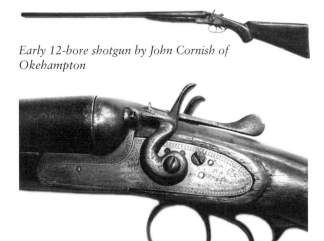

Early 12-bore shotgun by John Cornish of Okehampton

Shotgun breech detail

Shotgun owners with licences could use their own weapons once checked by the police. They were mostly .410s and 12-bore shotguns firing solid steel shot. (Effective range 50 yards).

Bill Sleeman said that they had managed to acquire some shotguns. Devon was a large farming county, a higher percentage of the population had them. Bill had his own .410 shotgun which in peace time he used to shoot rabbits on a relative's land.

Bill Sleeman
'If you had your own weapon you were considered to be elite, as rifles were in such short supply nationally.'

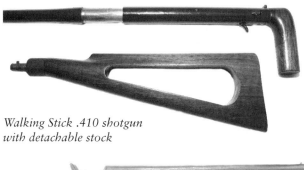

Walking Stick .410 shotgun with detachable stock

Edwin Hawker's double-barrelled Belgian Pistol

Edwin Hawker
'The Police asked for any firearms to be brought in to the Police station so they could see if they could be used by the L.D.V. They were collected in 1940. We were only able to collect them again after the war, regardless of whether they were used or not. I took a .410 double-barrelled cap and ball pistol made in Belgium by Fabrique Nationale (FDC). I collected it shortly after the war and still have it now.'

The government supplied these privately-purchased shotgun owners with free cartridges. Most were either No. 6 sized steel shot or later steel balls, which could only be fired for a short length of time as the balls would damage the inside of the guns barrel.

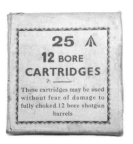

25 ⋀
12 BORE
CARTRIDGES
These cartridges may be used without fear of damage to fully choked 12 bore shotgun barrels

War Department shotgun cartridge box

(Far left) Home Guard belt bandolier. (Left) W.D. solid-shot 12-bore cartridges.

W.D. solid-shot 12- bore cartridges and box

LOCAL DEFENCE CORPS

Col. J. G. McConaghy, Exmouth organiser of the Local Defence Volunteers, wishes to make it clear that the services of every man who has volunteered will be required. Those who are anxious for immediate service are asked to communicate with Col. McConaghy, at 12, Fairfield Close, between the hours 8—10 p.m. Local owners of 12-bore shot-guns are asked to communicate with the local police.

Exmouth Chronicle's *appeal to shotgun owners*

Inert Drill Rifles

In many parts of the country the L.D.V. units borrowed inert training rifles from Officer Training Units of local schools. If inert rifles could not be borrowed then mock-ups were made, loosely fashioned on the S.M.L.E. with a similar weight and feel, in garages and workshops all over Britain.

Home-made inert drill rifles

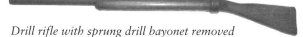

Drill rifle with sprung drill bayonet removed

The top drill rifle of the home made pair shown, was used by Bishops Nympton L.D.V and the one with the sprung bayonet was used by the men of Brixham L.D.V.

In some early training exercises for the defence of towns, the L.D.V. borrowed WW I gas rattles which had been used between the wars by the O.T.Us to represent the sound of machine gun fire on exercises. The gas rattle shown is stamped Exeter School O.T.U. and was used by the 1 'Loyal' Exeter L.D.V.

WW I gas rattle

Molotov Cocktails/Petrol Bombs

Osterley Park Training School near London was set up by guerrilla warfare expert Tom Wintringham in September 1940. His experience in WW I and with the communists in the Spanish Civil war made him the ideal candidate for the job.

One of the aspects of warfare taught at this school was the art of making Improvised Explosive Devices, mainly in respect of manufacturing simple, but effective mines, grenades and booby traps. Wilfred Vernon was the man who specialised in this area and it was his ideas that were gradually learned by Home Guardsman all over Britain from pamphlets published by the Home Office.

Home made bombs were made from any available bottle, half filled with a petrol/used oil or creosote mixture and fused with a piece of rag soaked in petrol. The idea was that the petrol would ignite easily, vaporise the oil, which in turn would ignite and burn for a longer time. Although basic they were very effective once lit and thrown at the enemy. They had a demoralising effect when used against infantry and were especially effective against soft-skinned vehicles and defensive positions.

When these home-made incendiary bombs first came into use they were intended to be used against armoured vehicles. The idea was that the burning liquid would gradually run into the engine compartment setting fire to the fuel supply or melt the wiring and thus immobilise the vehicle. These improvised bombs were effective to within a range of about 20 metres

Molotov cocktails were actually of very little use against tanks, but the Finnish Army had a lot of success

Typical home-made beer bottle Molotov cocktail

27

with these bombs against trucks and machine gun positions in their fight against the Russians at the start of WW II, shouting 'Here's one for Molotov' (the Russian leader), hence the name being used in Britain after these reports had been seen in the British press.

Mike Heard

'Firstly we made our own Molotov cocktails using petrol and used motor oil mixed together, it was a messy business making them. We found that beer bottles were best as the neck was quite narrow and it made them safer to use.'

By the end of 1941 all home made bombs and weapons were banned from use by the Government, mainly due to injuries sustained to Home Guard personnel during their manufacture and use in training.

The Molotov cocktail was still used as a weapon by the Home Guard however, as the government was now providing ready made self-igniting phosphorous bombs supplied to units in crates. These were either ignited with a commercially-produced fuse using a

W.D. Molotov cocktail with thunder-flash igniter removed

Bengal match and saltpetre impregnated cord or a thunder-flash. They were designed specifically for military use and these were deemed fit for purpose.

Molotov Cocktail Training

Mike Heard

'At the Drill Hall on the seafront, they had supplies of Molotov cocktails ready made in boxes. These were buried underground for safety reasons. In the event of an invasion they would have been ready to use. They came in wooden crates with a screw off top ready made, you just used to had to light the rag and throw them, then duck down to avoid getting hurt!'

British-made Bengal matches

Chapter 5
The Formation of the Home Guard

Winston Churchill's Speech 4 June 1940
'We shall not flag nor fail; we shall go on to the end; we shall fight... we shall defend our island whatever the cost may be. We shall fight on the beaches, the landing grounds, in the fields, in the streets and on the hills. We shall never surrender.'

It is worthwhile remembering who would be doing all the fighting. As the words left the Prime Minister's lips, the British Army had just finished being rescued from the beaches of Dunkirk by the armada of privately owned little ships under the supervision of the Royal Navy. The role of the defence of our 'island fortress' would have fallen on the combined efforts of the R.A.F., the Royal Navy, what remained of the regular and Territorial Armies, and the newly formed Local Defence Volunteers.

Bill Gorfin
'Later the force was renamed the Home Guard and there were 800 members in Exmouth when it disbanded in 1944. The Home Guard went into hard training and kept a close watch on the coast throughout the war.'

Harold Cooper 'C' Company 10 Battalion Suffolk Home Guard
'I was in the Home Guard from the start. There were 12 of us. We were not called out much, but we were keen and enthusiastic. I fired at a German plane once, but didn't bring it down! The German plane came over very low at dusk so as to avoid the ack-ack guns. They were flying very low, at about 30 feet.'

The Change of name to the Home Guard
Winston Churchill's Speech to the Commons on 14 July 1940
'Never before, in the last war or in this, have we had in this island an army comparable in quality equipment or numbers to that which stands here on guard tonight. We have a million and a half men in the British Army under arms tonight and every week in June and July has seen their organization, their

defences and their striking power advance in leaps and bounds.'

'Behind these, as a means of destruction for para-chutists, air-borne invaders and any traitors that may be found in our midst, and I do not believe there are many and they will get short shrift, we have more than a million of the Local Defence Volunteers, or, as they are much better called the Home Guard....'

'Should the invader come, there will be no placid lying down of the people in submission before him as we have seen, alas!, in other countries. We shall defend every village, every town and every city. The vast mass of London itself, fought street by street, could easily devour an entire hostile army and we would rather see London laid in ruins and ashes than that it should be tamely and abjectly enslaved. I am bound to state these facts, because it is necessary to inform our people of our intentions and thus to reassure them.'

The name of the Local Defence Volunteers was officially changed to the Home Guard, at the behest of Winston Churchill, on 23 July 1940. By this time 1.3 million men had volunteered for duty, since 14 May 1940. The Prime Minister had been using this name, the Home Guard, from around the end of June 1940 and whenever questioned by reporters or in communiqués always referred to the L.D.V. by this name, as he was determined to have his way. One of his main reasons for changing the name is that he thought that it would bolster the morale of troops fighting abroad, as they would think their wives and families would be properly protected.

The formation and leadership of the Home Guard was passed to Lieutenant-General Sir Henry Pownall, who devised the Motto of 'Kill the Boche!' for the Home Guard, amongst other more important measures. The Home Guard was now responsible for its own organisation from the Home Office down and was supplied with uniforms and equipment by the Territorial Army Stores which had been in place for many years.

Adolph Hitler's 'Last Appeal to Reason' Speech 19 July 1940

Hitler delivered this speech to the Reichstag on 19 July. It was clear that Great Britain would never have accepted his terms or dogma and, as Winston Churchill had made clear in his speech to The House of Commons on the 14 July, Great Britain was prepared for a fight. Hitler's speech had been published in full or in part, in most of the daily newspapers in Britain on 20 July 1940 and around two weeks later the Luftwaffe started a leaflet distribution campaign, dropping tons of leaflets, containing the printed text of the 'Last Appeal to Reason' speech all over Britain over the next few days.

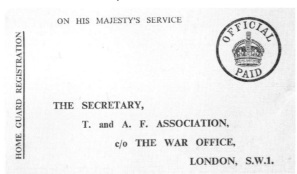

Home Guard Registration Card front

Home Guard Registration Card back

Younger Recruits

It was planned that a Home Guardsman would be on duty for one day a week. The remaining five days of the week they would be expected to carry out other duties such as training, 'fire watching', or carrying out other civil defence duties.

In 1942 the minimum age for joining the Home Guard was lowered to 16 years of age, thus younger boys could join straight from the Army cadets, so as not to break their military training. Some young boys lied about their age and were enlisted as young as 14 or 15 years of age.

Ray Towill
'I went to the labour exchange to register for something else, but was offered Auxiliary Fire Service or the Home Guard. I preferred the idea of the Home Guard because I would have a gun.'

'I joined up and the life was good. We used to go down to the Drill Hall for training went on patrol along the sea-front. Sometimes we'd stay overnight on a camp bed at the drill hall.

'Occasionally, we'd get a food allowance but I can't remember why and when. Some nights I'd come home in the early hours of the morning and then go straight off to work.'

Mike Heard
'I worked 48 hours a week at Lavis's boat yard, Saturdays as well back then! I did 12 hours a week with the Home Guard'.

Although they worked purely as volunteers, they were given one shilling and three pence for sandwiches and drinks each night they reported for duty.

By this time the Home Guard could accept younger volunteers who had been in either the army cadets or the A.T.C. Some were legally accepted as young as 16½ at the time if they possessed the right height and maturity, though 17 was a more common age to join up.

This would allow a volunteer one full year's training with drill and weapons before his 18th birthday and military service. By their 18th birthday most young Home Guards had joined the 'Battle Patrols' and were well disciplined, reasonably fit and had a good idea how to use most infantry weapons, safely and to good effect.

Some volunteers stayed on with the Home Guard even after they had been 'called up' to enlist in the forces. This was usually because they were serving as apprentices learning a trade which was classed as a reserved occupation.

Chris Long
'My Father was Harry Long, he was called up to the join the Army, but it was decided that he had a job which qualified him for a reserve occupation. He was a miller at my Grandfather, Henry Long's, mill at Withycombe and would need to return to Exmouth. He did return, against his will, as he was enjoying himself away from home and had made good friends in the Army.'

'After he had returned he resumed his job at the mill and joined the Exmouth Home Guard. His Brother Stanley Long had also joined the Home Guard, as he had a reserve occupation as a farmer. He owned Lower Halsdon Farm, a 200 acre holding, during the war and this was crucial for growing food during the war years.'

Potential regular amy men could also be refused entry to the armed forces on medical grounds. Asthma, foot problems and poor eyesight, were some of the reasons these young men were turned down for active service, which seemed a little unfair in some respects as in the Devon Home Guard units, some of the best shots wore glasses!

Dennis Davey

'I volunteered to join the Home Guard in 1941. Although I was only 16½ at the time, I was tall for my age, and was accepted into 'B' Company the Exmouth Home Guard without any problem.'

At the other end of the scale, men in their eighties lied about their age to enlist; most were rejected, but some were accepted, especially if they had previous military service or special skills.

Taking all of the statistics of age into consideration and also that a lot of the volunteers were in a reserve occupation, and therefore of 'call up age', the average age of the Home Guardsman was a lot lower than people generally think.

By 1943 the Home Guard comprised of around 1100 battalions, the average age of a serving member being 30 years of age, hardly, the ageing and decrepit defenders of the realm that the Home Guard are often portrayed as.

Stan Webber Carhampton Platoon

'My recollections of the war are of joining the Home Guard. To quite a lot of people it was quite a joke, but to us at the time it was a very serious business, albeit, we had some fun and quite a lot of laughs.'

'Our headquarters was in the gatehouse at Dunster Castle, where we drilled and were put through our paces. It was our responsibility to do guard duty on Grabbist Hill. Our turn came round once a fortnight. There were six on duty each night and each number did two hours' guard. It was quite eerie doing your stint, especially with Dunster church clock chiming every quarter of an hour, but we never had any arrests.'

'I remember the waves of German bombers going over on their way to Cardiff; it was not a pretty sight. We had a firing range in the Deer Park where we had some very interesting Sundays.'

'All night manoeuvres were another aspect of our training. I remember one particular night we were taken to Marshwood Farm, Blue Anchor, to find an 'enemy' there. It was harvest time and fields were stoked with sheaves of corn. When we were finished we were one man short and after a long search we found him under a stook of corn fast asleep. These sort of escapades made it all the more fun and took away some of the horrendous stories of the real war.'

Structure

The initial structure of the Home Guard was similar to the regular army. It comprised of seven regional commands, which were then split into areas. A further sub-division divided these areas into zones and these zones into groups. Each group was split into battalions (approx 1000 men in each battalion) of four companies. Each company then had four platoons where possible and this was then further split into three sections of approximately 12-15 men.

Devon was split into four zones, North, South, East and Plymouth. Every city, town, village, Hamlet having its own unit. Devon had 25 fully formed Battalions by stand down, which was approximately 30,000 men.

Some were highly specialist units. The 22nd 'Southern Railway' Battalion Devon Home Guard was based at Exmouth Junction, a vitally important rail hub on the Waterloo Line and were responsible for protecting the large marshalling yards near Pinhoe and the surrounding area. The Great Western Railway No. 5 Platoon of H Company 10 'Torbay' Battalion Devon Home Guard, had the responsibility for the G.W.R. railway on the other side of the river Exe at Starcross. Railway Home Guard units were given the instructions in order of priority.

1. Defeat the enemy.
2. Carry on with the operation of the railways.

The Devon General Omnibus Company No.6 Platoon of H Company 10 'Torbay' Battalion Devon Home Guard, were formed from bus drivers and conductors. They were responsible for mobilising troops to vulnerable points using the buses in the event of an invasion.

Nationally 50 000 General Post Office employees were enrolled to keep the postal and telephone systems running smoothly. They had a red broken circle with the letters G.P.O. stamped inside the circle on both sides of the letters L.D.V. or Home Guard on their armband. This additional lettering ensured that the Post Office Home Guard units were intended for a specific role and could not be sidelined by the regional commanders to do other tasks which were not under their remit.

Exeter had its own G.P.O. Telephones Home Guard Platoon. The 21 Battalion (33 General Post Office) had the sole purpose of defending and mending the telephone exchanges and telephone-connected vulnerable points. Ironically in the early days, before it was settled who would be paying for the telephone bills of the newly formed L.D.V. observation posts, some L.D.V. units had their telephones cut off by men of the G.P.O. L.D.V.

Below is a list of some of the diverse styles of Home Guard units which were formed nationally:

Welsh Coal Miners
Factories
General Service (infantry)
Coastal Artillery
Light Anti-aircraft
Heavy Anti-aircraft
Mounted Patrols (Dartmoor Exmoor)
River Patrols (Upper Thames Patrol)

The B.B.C.
The Houses of Paliament
The Stock Exchange

Hazel Rowsell

'Donald Bradford used to bring his rifle home, and used to clean his rifle and his boots, you could see your face in them. He was very proud of his uniform; he would spend hours cleaning his uniform and always looked very smart.'

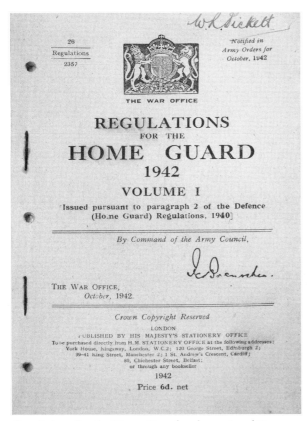
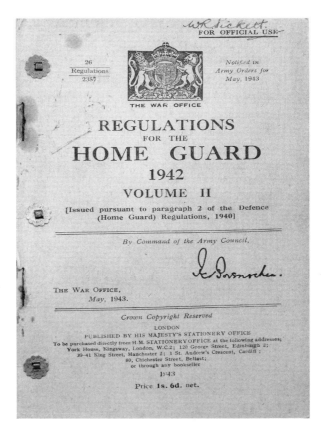

Regulations for the Home Guard, volumes I and II

Chapter 6
Home Guard Uniforms

Enamel Lapel Badges

During the change over to the name of the Home Guard these small enamel badges were produced. They had to be purchased privately and were usually worn on civilian clothing, although photographs do exist of men wearing them on their early battledress denims.

The idea was to show that you were not enlisted in the regular armed forces (who wore uniform all the time), but that you were still serving your country and gainfully occupied, whilst not wearing your L.D.V or Home Guard uniform. They were produced in a variety of shapes and sizes some later types having pin backs, with early types having a 'horseshoe' fitting for fitting into buttonholes.

Ties

In August 1940 it was decide that the Home Guard should have 'Corps' colours and these were a field of navy blue, with light blue, maroon and green stripes laid next to each other in that order. This colour scheme was adopted for ties which were commercially made and sold by tailors to Home Guard members who wanted to show their allegiance to their unit whilst off duty.

Home Guard enamel lapel badges for civilian clothing

Home Guard Arm Patches

These patches were supplied to sew over L.D.V. on the previously issued armbands and arrived, around August / September 1940. In the meantime some denims had arrived and so these were sewn directly on

Home Guard arm patch

to the right sleeve of the denims. These were khaki or khaki / green and issued from late July and August 1940 and designed to be slid onto the right arm of the denims or battledress or great coat. After the affiliation to county regiments on 3 August 1940 some armbands were over-printed with the county regiment badges either side of the words Home Guard.

Home Guard armband, armlet or brassard

Edwin Hawker

'The Quartermasters Stores were with Major Trelawney at Cotleigh House. The stores were run by Quartermaster Sergeant Frank North; during the day he was the gardener at the house.'

These photographs on the following page show Harry Simons (left) of Carhampton Home Guard with his great coat, with H.G. armband, P-17 rifle, steel helmet and respirator. In the centre Jack Robbins is seen wearing a 1938 pattern battledress with 1903 pattern belt and shotgun pouches. The photo was taken in 1943.

Harry Simons

Jack Robbins

Ernest Dorling

Ernest Dorling from Haughley Platoon is wearing Battledress and his Field Service Cap, he also has an Enfield P-17 Rifle

The Field Service Cap

A.k.a. the side cap or forage cap, it was introduced around late June 1940, it was the same pattern as the regular Army's Cap. It was made usually, though not always, from rough serge material and appeared in varying shades of khaki. From 3 August 1940 it could be worn with the County Regiment cap badge and later, as the Home Guard operated artillery and defused bombs, Army Corps cap badges.

Cap Badges

The Home Guard was granted 'County Association Status' on 3 August 1940 and County Regiment badges were allowed to be worn on the field service cap.

Once again, supplies were difficult to get hold of at first and men who had been in the local county regiments in WW I, who had retained their badges,

Examples of Home Guard field service caps, second Devonshire Regiment and third Somerset Light Infantry

wore them with a great deal of pride. Badges were scrounged, purchased and bartered from wherever they could be found. Gradually supplies of cap badges increased and a lot of men kept a 'working' badge and a permanently 'bull-shined' one for parades and special occasions.

The Home Guard were also allowed to march with the County Regiments on parades after government legislation in June 1941, but this did not meet with approval in some quarters and caused some friction between the professional soldiers and Home Guard units for a short while.

Dennis Davey
'*After D-Day our role became redundant and we were stood down later in 1944. We handed in all our weapons and equipment. I kept my cap badge as a souvenir of my wartime activities, and that was that!*'

The Devonshire Regiment cap badge

1938 Pattern Denims

Blouses and trousers in the 1938 pattern were manufactured initially in a tobacco brown colour and later on in green. Although always referred to as 'denims', both colours were manufactured in denim or cotton drill materials, depending on what was available at the time. These were issued as early as 18th May 1940 to some units.

The men of the Exmouth 477 Coastal Artillery Home Guard R.A. were never issued with denims, as it was formed after the issue of battledress. But denims could be temporarily issued for dirty jobs though and were obtainable from the Quartermasters stores at the Imperial Road Drill Hall.

The Serge Cape
Mike Heard
'*The cold weather cape was a big baggy thing! We sometimes used them to keep out the rain on really wet nights, but we were told not to!*'

Complete Early 1938 pattern denim L.D.V./Home Guard uniform

6 November 1940

In a speech in the House of Commons Sir Edward Grigg announced '*...equipping the Home Guard was otherwise going well. Battledress will before long be available for the whole force and although great coats cannot be supplied in adequate numbers, before the winter comes on... we have arranged for a large issue of trench-capes, a warm and serviceable garment made of waterproofed service-serge.*'

The great coats didn't arrive in time for the winter of 1940 for most Home Guard battalions. So the stopgap measure of the serge, shower-proof cape was distributed to the men. It was serviceable in that it gave added protection from the cold, but in wet weather it was advised not to be worn as it became soaked extremely quickly which made it heavy and cumbersome. It was generally disliked by the men.

Shower-proof serge cape

Peter Mattholie

'I was in the Home Guard for two years. I joined when I was sixteen. I had already been in the Air Training Corps. I was in Bromley in Kent. It was the Bromley 58 Battalion we had BMY 58 on our shoulders. We were issued with the battledress and gaiters, a tin hat and a side cap. Later I was issued with a rifle. I had Lee Enfield rifle, it was very accurate and I liked it a lot!'

On 6 November 1940 Sir Edward Grigg announced in the House of Commons that although *'there has been a serious shortage of steel helmets for the Home Guard'* he promised *'a much larger weekly issue in the near future.'*

The Mk II Steel Helmet

This helmet was a completely new pressing and was made from stronger chrome-manganese steel. It was of heavier construction than the earlier helmets and thus offered more protection to the wearer. The Mk II helmets had a metal sprung, canvas chin strap, which was specially produced to prevent death from strangulation and neck breaks from bomb and shell blasts and bad knocks.

Mk II helmet with Mk II liner

The Mk II helmet was simpler to produce than the earlier models and new vulcanised fibre and rubber padded liners were designed for the new helmets and proved much more suitable. These new Mk I and Mk II liners were attached to the helmet with a single central screw through the top of the helmet and not riveted, like the older ones. This allowed a uniform size shell to be fitted with the correct size of liner for the soldier's head and this also made field repairs and replacements far simpler. Most servicemen and Home Guardsman who had to wear the steel helmet lovingly referred to it as a 'tin hat'.

Mike Heard

'My helmet was quite comfortable. It looked like an up-turned soup plate! The net was green and made from string in small squares so you could push twigs, leaves and old bits of rag into it.'

Camouflage nets to cover the helmet were issued, they were made from dyed green or brown string, some had small squares and some large depending on the manufacturer. The nets were issued mid-way through

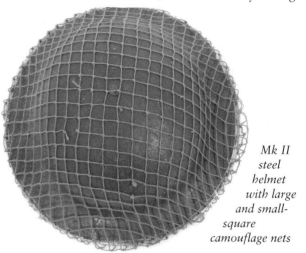

Mk II steel helmet with large and small-square camouflage nets

1941 mainly to infantry units and then later to most units. The net was intended to break up the reflective index of the helmet to make it less visible. It also allowed foliage and material scraps to be attached to the helmet to break up its distinctive outline.

Ray Towill

'We were issued with black boots and gaiters, a brown leather belt, also webbing small ammunition pouches which we were supposed to use for hand grenades too, but never did. By the time I had joined we had the 'hairy' (austerity pattern) battle dress uniforms, the shoulder titles were already sewn on when I got mine. The uniform was so itchy, it drove you mad!'

A Section of Williton Home Guard with only one man with a helmet

Ammo Boots

These were black pebbled leather with thick leather soles with 16 and later 13 metal studs. They had a smooth leather toe cap which most men polished to a bright shine. They were referred to by the army, as 'Boots Ammunition'.

Gaiters

Gaiters or anklets, were made from brown or black pebbled and grained leather. Officers and in some instances complete units, kept them brown, but most units polished them black. Some gaiters were fastened with twin leather straps and others with a leather strap passed through two inter-looped laces at the sides. Gaiters which were already coloured black also arrived from around 1942. Some H.G. units in Devon had army style khaki web gaiters issued, as can be seen from old photos from the officers and men in the 1, 10, 14, 22 Devon Battalions.

Officers, whenever possible, would try and 'win' a pair of army cotton webbing gaiters where possible as it made them look like their army counterparts. It is also safe to assume that webbing gaiters were issued to the men, as the supplies of the earlier issue leather equipment ran out.

13 stud 'Austerity' ammo boots dated 1941

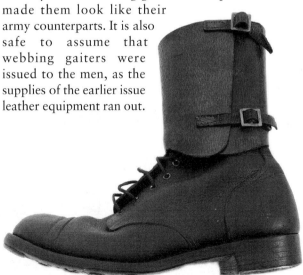

Anklet (gaiter) in position

Men of Porchfield, Isle of Wight, Home Guard wearing black and unpolished brown gaiters

The photograph above was taken on 24 August 1941 on the Isle of Wight. From Left to Right; John Cousins, Gilbert Warne and Roland Wells. It shows the differences in shades of the gaiters.

Economy boot polish

1938 Pattern Khaki Serge Battledress Blouse and Trousers

The 1938 pattern battledress was the same uniform that was issued to the regular army at the time. It was made from a warm woollen, coarse serge material, which was incredibly itchy to wear, this coupled with the fact that the uniform was impregnated with anti-gas chemicals caused some volunteers to have serious skin complaints. Most volunteers tolerated the 'prickly' nature of the material and were glad to receive at last, a proper uniform which they could wear with pride.

Standard issue of equipment to a Guardsman in 1942

The serge blouse and trousers were made available from around October-November 1940, but in most areas, it is not known whether they arrived simultaneously. Most areas of the country received the items independently and wartime photographs show a great deal of differences in different regions, some guardsmen wearing mixtures of denims and serge battledress. Once again very large and very small sizes were easier to come by but eventually this problem was addressed and solved. The denim battledress trousers can sometimes be seen being worn in conjunction with the serge blouses and sometimes vice versa. By December 1940 most Home Guard areas of Britain had received their full compliment of serge battledress.

Rubberised Cotton Rain Capes/Ground Sheets

Tobacco-brown rain capes, shown folded in the bottom left hand corner of the previous photograph were issued initially, but only to men going out on patrol as so few were available. Some of these capes had actually been issued in the Great War.

1938 and 1940 pattern serge battledress trousers

on the dressing pocket and no 'ankle cuff tabs' which puts them post 1940 and pre-June 1941.

1938 pattern serge battledress blouse from 477 Coastal Artillery

Serge Battle Dress Trousers

The design of the trousers issued to the regulars and the Home Guard changed throughout the war. The changes were made to conserve material and labour costs as part of the September 1941 austerity laws which had been introduced.

Ken Parker

'Even though I joined the Home Guard in 1943, we had our ordinary clothes and a home guard armband first off and then later on, we had our battledress issued. I wore it on patrols on Tuesday and Thursday evenings.'

The early 1938 pattern battledress trousers on the left in the following photograph have no button fastening on the open first field dressing pocket and are of pre-June 1940 issue. The pair on the right have the button

Victor Barber 'C' Coy. 10 Battalion Suffolk Home Guard 1942

1939 Pattern Great Coat

This great coat had a no gusset in the back and had a central rear vent fastened by buttons.

1940 Pattern Great Coat

The Home Guard mainly used the 1940 pattern great coat which reverted to an earlier pre-war design of having a large expanding gusset placed centrally in the back so that it could be worn over the small pack. It took a while to be issued due to wool and material shortages, but was a popular and practical, warm garment. Many of these coats were kept by the guardsmen and used for many years after the war.

Mike Heard
'My great coat was not a bad fit and very warm!'

The brass General Service buttons, with the Royal coat of arms were the last remaining remnants of heraldry left over from WWI. The button stick was needed for cleaning these buttons and cap badges, whilst protecting the cloth underneath.

General Service brass button and brass button stick

1939 pattern great coat

Corporal Bob Parsons from 'Bognor Regis' Platoon 6 Battalion Sussex Home Guard in 1941. He has his Enfield P-1917 rifle, binoculars, gasmask, haversack and newly issued 1940 pattern great coat with shoulder titles

Austerity Pattern Denim Blouse

These blouses were delivered in small numbers to some units post-June 1942. In Exmouth they were stored at the Drill Hall upstairs in the Quartermaster's Stores. They were issued for dirty jobs, then returned to the quartermaster and washed before being returned to the stores again.

'Austerity' pattern denim blouse

The new austerity design objectives which had recently been put in place, meant that attention to the new simple designs and use of raw materials had to be strictly adhered to, to minimise waste. Once again although always referred to as 'denims', some articles can be found made from cotton drill as whatever suitable material was available at the time was used.

Denims were issued for dirty jobs such as cleaning large calibre weapons, maintaining small arms and painting. They were also issued to mechanics who maintained the vehicles and dispatch riders for maintaining their motorcycles. This saved many a set of serge battledress from being ruined by grease and oil.

These 'Austerity' denims were cheaper to produce and took less time to make, also using fewer raw materials than the earlier 1938 pattern denims. They had no frontal gusset for the buttons, or chest pocket pleats. They also had fewer button holes and buttons on the trousers.

Royal Artillery Lanyard

This was a white-twisted cotton rope worn over right shoulder. It was a Royal Artillery tradition and in earlier times was intended to be attached to the gun's firing mechanism to keep the gunner safe from the recoil of the breech. It also prevented the gunners from getting burnt when the gun got too hot to touch from continuous firing.

Fully equipped, St Gerrans (Cornwall) Platoon on parade in the square

In the photograph below standing fourth row back, second from the left is Walter Preston Isaac. Preston Isaac's father is in the front row, and second from the left is James Isaac, Walter's younger brother.

4 'Cobbaton' Platoon 4 Battalion 'Barnstaple' Devon Home Guard proudly display the Devonshire Regiment colours at their stand down photograph

*Exmouth Old Comarades Association
due receipt for Jack Robbins.*

*Receipt for Home
Guardsman's equipment.
Issue as of November 1942*

Chapter 7
Home Guard Weapons

Jack Sage
'At the start our only means of obtaining any kind of self defence was to take broom handles or our own shotguns. When some American rifles arrived, our vicar kept theses at the vicarage; they were not issued to us!'

Rifles

In Exmouth most of the basic weapons and rifle drill training was done at the Wessex Drill Hall on the seafront and the Drill Hall at Imperial Road. The Home Guard platoons used to learn how to strip weapons, clean them, and then reassemble them, sometimes blind-folded and timed.

Ray Towill
'One night whilst on duty at the Drill Hall, we had an accident. 'Rummager' Gooding a local rag and bone man fired his rifle through the Drill Hall roof! They took his rifle away after that.'

US Model 1903A1 Springfield rifle .300 Calibre

These were in very limited supply initially and were not issued to many Home Guard units.

Cyril Jackson 'Land's End' Company 12 Battalion Cornwall Home Guard
'There wasn't much equipment or many uniforms in the beginning, but after some time we received our first delivery of rifles. They came packed in boxes of grease. They were American First World War rifles, .300 Remington and Springfields. They were really difficult to clean because they had so much grease on them; finally we kept pouring boiling water through the barrel and over the stock which did the trick.'

The Springfield M1903 A1 was used extensively by the American army during WW I. It had the reputation of being a cumbersome weapon to carry around, weighing in at around 4.8kg, but fired quite accurately. Its main drawback was that the Mauser bolt action, was slow and difficult to move which made 'quick firing' in succession hard to sustain. It took its name

from where it was originally produced at the Springfield Works in Massachusetts.

The original rifle was manufactured from milled parts in the typical gunsmith tradition, but later many of the parts were stamped from sheet metal. These rifles were designated M1903A3 and some rifles of both types found their way to British Home Guard units.

Some of these rifles arrived as part of the lease-lend agreement with America and were also sent over by well-meaning Americans who privately owned them as target or hunting rifles. On arriving in Britain American weapons were 'proofed' in British armouries and rifles used by the Home Guard will have full sets of British and American marks.

The rifles had red bands painted round the gun barrel and forward hand grip to make sure the men used the right cartridges as, being of .30-06 calibre, .303 rounds jammed the breech and it took a long time to get the gun serviceable again if a mistake was made. It had a five-round magazine and some of these rifles were eventually re-barrelled to accept a standard .303 cartridge.

Dennis Davey
'I was issued with my uniform, ammunition and equipment, and a Springfield .300 rifle, which we assumed were the ones used by the American Army in the First World War.'

The Canadian Ross 1910 Rifle .303 Calibre

Some WW I vintage Canadian .303 1910 pattern Ross Rifles were issued to the Exmouth Home Guard units from around September 1940. As better quality rifles became available these were withdrawn and put in to

Ross Mk II pattern 1910 rifle dated 1914

Breech, trigger and magazine of the Ross pattern 1910 rifle

storage at the drill hall. Later to be redistributed to the 477 Coastal Artillery Battery R.A. Home Guard when it was set up in September 1941.

In Exmouth it was considered that, due to the shortage of weapons, they would be issued the older Ross rifles, instead of the pikes that were just arriving. The best rifles were given to the No.3 Platoon as they arrived, as their role was that of an infantry platoon.

Ross rifles were packed into wooden crates in Canada and had a molten grease similar to Vaseline poured on top of them which then solidified as it cooled. The idea was to prevent the weapon from rusting in storage and transit. When they arrived in Devon they were allocated as they became available at a rate of around ten rifles to sixty men initially. The problem with this was that no man was in charge of his own particular rifle, and they had to be stored in a secure room at the H.Q. and signed out to guardsmen going on patrol. This meant that the man who signed for it had no idea how well the previous man had looked after it.

This coupled with uncertainty of which particular rifle you would get bothered the men immensely, as their lives would depend on them and some weapons were better cared for than others. The men would also be responsible for the maintenance, cleaning and care of their individual weapons and most of the men took a lot of pride in cleaning and maintaining their weapons, when they were eventually issued with their own.

These rifles started arriving a few weeks later than the earliest Springfields. The main benefit of this rifle was that it used standard British .303 ammunition. Once again this had the reputation as being 'a grand shooting rifle' as one Devon Home Guardsman said, but a 'an ill-balanced brute to lug about!' It also had the propensity to jam, with the least amount of dirt and therefore had to be kept spotlessly clean. This was very hard as it was extremely difficult to take the rifle

apart and put back together, often getting damaged by inexperienced hands, during the process.

This weapon had what was called a straight pull action, which caused problems for some men, giving it a poor reputation with Canadian soldiers in the trenches in WW I. It was easy to catch the bolt and load the rifle by mistake which was potentially hazardous and as a consequence of this a lot of accidents happened when these rifles were first issued. This resulted in them being badly mistrusted; some men even removed the bolt from their weapon when on duty. The bolts were then extremely hard to put back and the bolt lugs frequently became burred and this led to Home Guard units needing an armourer's facilities to repair weapons. They were eventually replaced with the American P-17 or British S.M.L.E. No.1 Mk III rifle.

Mike Heard

'Our Ross rifles came packed in grease, like Vaseline. We had to clean this off the rifle, which took a very long time. It was the Devil's own job!'

Laurie Butler

'I remember when we went on firing practice on a live range for the first time. I had a Canadian Ross rifle at the time. We had to fire 5 rounds with our rifles on a 100 metre range at the gravel pits at Woodbury Common. I fired the 5 rounds and when the instructor went with me to collect the target, I had a really good grouping and he couldn't believe it was the first time I had fired a rifle, I had previously fired shotguns, but they were very different.'

The Enfield Pattern 17 Rifle (P-17) .300 Calibre

This rifle arrived after the Ross and was a lightweight simple-to-use quality rifle, many of the Devon Home-Guardsmen who were issued with this rifle really enjoyed firing it. It fired rounds which were .300 in calibre and were given the pattern number -06, (.30-06 calibre) which referred to the year 1906.

The cartridge differed from the British .303 round, in that it had a groove running around the rim rather than the pronounced 'lip' of the British rounds. The magazine held 5 rounds of ammunition which were loaded from a stripper clip.

Barry Clarke

'My Father Bert Clarke worked for Blackmore's the undertakers. When I was very young, I used to go with him to the funeral parlour on some days, helping Dad to do odd jobs. In his spare time, Dad was in the Home Guard; he had a uniform and used to go on patrol a couple of nights a week. He had a Remington rifle for a time and kept it propped up in the hallway.'

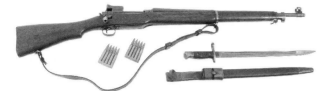

Enfield pattern 1917 (P-17) and M1917 bayonet, both made by Remington

American made bandolier for the .30-06 ammunition

The Enfield P-17 rifle breech and bolt

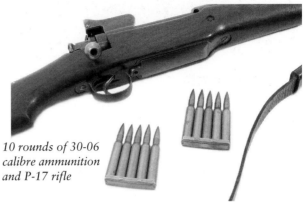

10 rounds of 30-06 calibre ammunition and P-17 rifle

Operating instructions for the P-17 and P-14 rifles

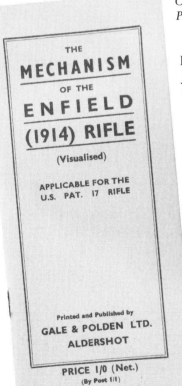

THE
MECHANISM
OF THE
ENFIELD
(1914) RIFLE

(Visualised)

APPLICABLE FOR THE U.S. PAT. 17 RIFLE

Printed and Published by
GALE & POLDEN LTD.
ALDERSHOT

PRICE 1/0 (Net.)
(By Post 1/1)

the British ones. The Remington rifles ammunition was .300 calibre and we had a cloth bandolier of 60 rounds, with two clips of 5 rounds in each section.'

Luppitt Home Guardsman, Jack Sage has a wartime stationery office note pad, in which he kept the details of the rifle register. It showed who was issued with which style of rifle. Most of the Luppitt platoon's rifles were the Enfield P-17 made by Remington; a few were made by Winchester. The register also had the dates of who was issued with ammunition and in what quantities, most men being issued two clips and a box of 50 rounds which it was decided would be best kept at home.

Rifle numbers and the transfer dates were also kept in this book as people arrived and departed from the platoon, some members stayed for the duration of the war as they were on a reserve occupation or too old or unfit to join the regular army. The younger fitter members left by the time they were 18, as and when they were called up.

Laurie Butler
'Later I had an Remington P-17 rifle. The ammunition was a different calibre to the Ross. It had a groove around the end of the cartridge, rather than a ridge like

A Corporal from Exmouth Company armed with a P-17 rifle receives his marksman's medal at Orcombe Point.

Edwin Hawker
'I carried 10 rounds of .300 ammunition in two clips, when I had the Remington Rifle. We had a red band painted on the fore-stock of the rifle, to make sure we only put the right ammunition in.'

The American Enfield P-14 Calibre .303

Some American Pattern 1917 Enfield rifles were fitted with a new .303 barrel replacing the old .300 calibre on the original. The magazine held 5 rounds of standard British .303 ammunition. This rifle then became known as the known as the P-14 to the men. It was of First World War vintage and although a little heavier and longer than the standard British S.M.L.E. it was extremely accurate and well liked. These rifles were issued from around September 1941.

The S.M.L.E. No.1 Mk III (Short Magazine Lee Enfield)

This was the rifle that the Men who had served in the front line during WW I longed for. It was the

No. 1 Mk III short magazine Lee Enfield Rifle, with 10 rounds of ammunition. 1907 pattern bayonet, scabbard and 1939 and 1914 pattern leather frogs

workhorse of the British 'Tommy' weighing in at just over half a kilogram lighter than the Ross rifle and with an accurate range of nearly 1600 metres, this was a deadly weapon in the hands of a well-trained soldier. It was comfortable to carry, relatively easy to strip and maintain and easy to load and fire. The magazine held ten rounds of .303 ammunition so it had to be reloaded less often. Photographs show that some platoons were issued with this rifle fairly early on

A sigh of relief was breathed by the veterans who knew the capabilities of this weapon. It was only issued in small numbers to Home Guard infantry platoons, or to some units thought more at risk, from the start of 1941. Ivor Pike's Father, Lesley Pike, was in the Exmouth Company 2 'Clyst' Battalion Devon Home Guard. During the day he was a painter and decorator, working for Coopers in Rolle Street.

Ivor Pike
'My Father Les (Private Leslie S. Pike 3 Platoon (Exmouth Company 2 'Clyst' Battalion) came home one night with a broom handle, which he used for drill; later on he had a uniform and later still a British .303 rifle but with no bullets! The rifle lived in the hall and later on bullets arrived.'

S.M.L.E. rifle with two clips of .303 ammunition

Ray Towill
'I had a rifle, a Lee Enfield with a bayonet, I can't remember how many rounds of ammunition, a couple of clips I think, which we kept at home with the rifle. We used to go up to Black Hill Quarry, to practice live

No. 1 Mk. III S.M.L.E. rifle breech, trigger and bolt

S.M.L.E. magazine holding 10 rounds of .303 ammunition

firing. We travelled up in Hawker's bread van. It looked like Corporal Jones's from 'Dad's Army'. Hawker was a local baker and was in our platoon.'

'There were targets erected on one side of the quarry and we used to fire across at them. Occasionally I used to win 10d or so, as we'd placed bets on who would be the best.'

Oil-bottle, 4 x 4 cleaning cloth and pull-through, stored in the S.M.L.E. rifle butt

Automatic Weapons and Machine Guns

On the 3 August 1940 when, the Home Guard was affiliated to the county regiments, an order was also given that the Home Guard would shortly be receiving automatic weapons, machine guns and hand grenades. With the responsibility of being armed with these weapons also came the responsibility to follow orders, without question and argument. Also absenteeism was to be a punishable offence, being fined or dishonourably discharged. Men were encouraged to take pride in their unit, the uniform and the county regiment's history.

Dennis Davey

'I was issued with my uniform, ammunition and equipment, and a Springfield 300 rifle, which we assumed were the ones used by the American army in WW I. Later in the war, my Springfield was exchanged for a B.A.R., Browning Automatic Rifle, an extremely heavy weapon to carry. At various times I also used a Sten gun and a Vickers Machine Gun in training. Other weapons used by some units of the Home Guard were the Thompson sub-machine guns, Lewis machine guns and Spigot Mortars, a very unreliable weapon, to be used against tanks.'

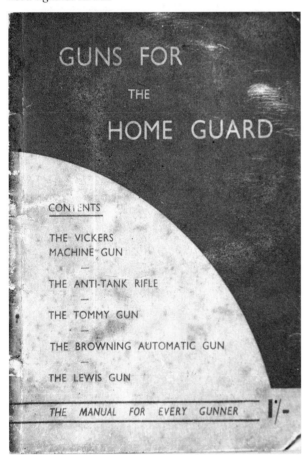

Early automatic weapon training manual

Browning Automatic Rifle (B.A.R.) .300 Calibre

This American-made gun of WW I vintage, could fire up to 40 rounds a minute in the hands of a well-trained soldier, when set to single shot fire. It was designated a 'one man' weapon and could be operated and carried by an individual soldier although it weighed around 8kg, not including the ammunition which was held in metal box magazines.

Laurie Butler

'I was issued later with a B.A.R. automatic rifle, it was a beautiful gun, but it was really heavy. The mag held 15 rounds and it could fire like a machine gun, but we used to fire it single shot, 5 rounds for target practise only, it was very accurate.'

Gas operated and air cooled, when set on automatic firing it could deliver up to 550 rounds per minute of accurate fire, with a second man to 'feed' the weapon, this made it popular with the men, except for the person who had to carry it!

It used the American .30-06 calibre rounds which were kept in 20-round box magazines. This gun eventually replaced the Vickers water-cooled heavy machine gun, which were beginning to arrive by the beginning of 1941. By the end of 1941 this gun had become the standard Light Machine Gun (L.M.G.) of the Home Guard.

Mike Heard

'Only one B.A.R. was issued to each platoon and only one man per platoon trained on this weapon. It would have been bad news if he got shot! The gun was very heavy to carry which made it unpopular, but as a weapon it was accurate with a good rate of fire and the men liked having around as it would have offered some real security in a fight.'

The Browning Automatic Rifle (B.A.R.)

Edwin Hawker

'If you used the BAR for two shots you were all right, but using it as an automatic weapon it would pull up and to the left and make you go off target. Firing single shots I could get a bull or inner ring every time but firing automatically it would be too unstable to use.'

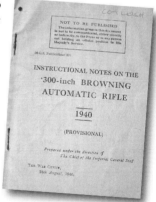

Edwin Hawker's B.A.R. manual

B.A.R. breech and magazine

Lewis Gun (Medium Machine Gun) .303 Calibre

This was a popular weapon, even though it had a tendency to jam. It was used in the infantry role in the trenches during WW I to lethal effect and was particularly suited to the light anti-aircraft role, being easy to manoeuvre on an upright pivot. It was operated by a two-man crew one carrying and firing the gun and one carrying and feeding the gun with the ready-primed circular 47-round drum magazines which clipped on the top.

The Lewis Light Machine Gun

Although considered old -fashioned by WW II the Lewis gun had a rate of fire of 120 rounds per minute and a range of 1000 yards and proved a useful tool for the Home Guard being used mainly for beach and dock defences and in the anti-aircraft role, until more modern weapons arrived.

Jack Sage

'On the 30 June 1941 our platoon had Lewis Gun instruction classes at the Vicarage. Some time later we had the chance to fire one at Harkridge where there was a firing range which we used for live firing of rifles and other small arms mainly.'

'One Sunday afternoon we were on the ranges and the instructions were to just give the targets a quick burst of live ammunition, with Lewis guns. When my friend Peter's turn came the Lewis gun jammed, still firing and the gun was jumping about all over the place it cut big chunks out of the ground all around but Peter being quite strong, managed to keep it from killing anyone until it stopped firing.'

Lewis Gun showing the inside of the magazine

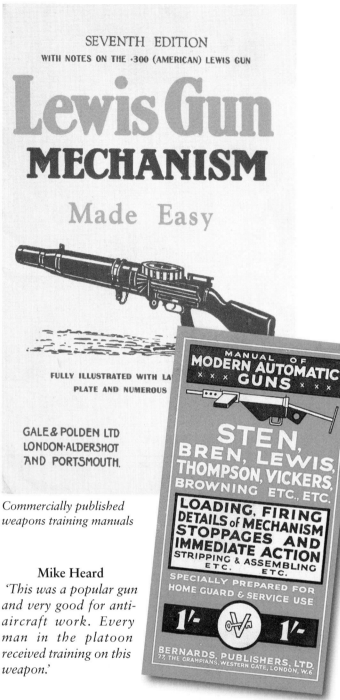

Commercially published weapons training manuals

Mike Heard

'This was a popular gun and very good for anti-aircraft work. Every man in the platoon received training on this weapon.'

Vickers Heavy Machine Gun .303 Calibre

Weighing in at 15kg this was an extremely efficient and popular weapon with old hands that had used it during WW I. Only its weight prevented its future use in the changing face of mobile warfare. Intended for use in three-man teams, one to carry the gun, one to carry the tripod and water can and one to carry the ammunition, it was gradually relegated to fixed defensive positions, as lighter machine guns became available.

The Exmouth platoons had several of these machine guns, which are mentioned in the Guardsman's memoirs as being positioned on the docks, at Orcombe Point and by the Battery Observation Post; the gun was also used in training exercises. This gun had to be

Vickers water-cooled heavy machine gun with dial sight and case, .303 ball round ammunition boxes, cleaning kit, tool kit, oil bottles, puncture repair outfit, spring balance and plotter

water cooled and when in constant use got extremely hot and would overheat if water could not be found.

Mike Heard

'It was water cooled from an old petrol can, a lovely gun, it would fire all day, but was very heavy to lug around. Every man received training on this weapon, I really liked it.'

Vickers water-Cooled M.G. dial sight and trigger

The photograph on the following page shows Company Sergeant Major Charlie Havill, with his men on manoeuvres on Woodbury Common probably in 1943. He stands in front of a Vickers .303 Heavy machine-gun, on its tripod. Hanging over the water-

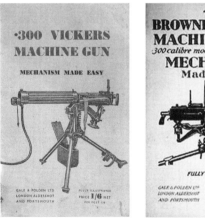

Commercially Produced Manuals for the Vickers Medium Machine Gun and the Browning Heavy Machine Gun

cooling sleeve of the barrel are two Mk II steel helmets and a set of 1939 pattern leather magazine pouches, with webbing straps. On his upper left sleeve is the 2 DVN county distinctions. All the men wear 1938 pattern battledress, and the man to the left and to the rear of C.S.M. Havill wears 1937 pattern webbing straps and 'shotgun' pouches.

Exmouth Company C.S.M. Charlie Havill and men on manoeuvres on Woodbury Common 1943

Of particular note is the American Browning Model 1917 .300 Calibre Heavy machine-gun laying on the ground to the right of the picture.

Browning Model 1917 A1 Heavy Machine Gun .300 Calibre

Browning 1917 A1 Heavy Water Cooled Machine Gun

The number of these guns issued to the Home Guard in Exmouth is unknown. They were issued to several platoons in Devon though as can be seen in a number of contemporary photographs, sometimes along with the Vickers 'K' Gun.

The Browning Heavy Machine Gun was an excellent weapon and was the forerunner of the ubiquitous Browning Model 1919 A4 which could be found on every front during World War II. The model 1917 was water cooled and therefore could fire for sustained periods of time without rounds 'cooking off' in the chamber.

Breech, tilt and traverse mechanism for the Browning 1917 A1 Machine Gun

Thompson M1928 A1 Sub-Machine Gun .45 Calibre

The 'Tommy Gun' as it was affectionately known was a familiar sight the world over due to the film industry's use of it in the popular gangster movies of the 1930s. Weighing in at around 5.5kg it made a solid

Thompson M1928 .45 calibre sub-machine gun

yet easily portable weapon. It fired heavy calibre .45 ACP rounds which could be stored in a 20-round straight box magazine or 50-round drum magazine. It was effective only over short distances due to the lack

Thompson sub-machine gun breech and magazine

of explosive charge in the cartridge case. It had a good rate of fire at 600 rounds per minute and was a portable and formidable weapon at close range. Though the Thompson only had a limited usable range of around 50 metres, they had a sinister reputation, which the soldiers loved, for being able to cut a man in half in close combat situations. Everyone wanted one!

Some units in Britain were issued with these guns as early as 1941. Their use was short lived as they were starting to be replaced in early 1943 with the Sten gun. A lot of unit's has theirs withdrawn again to supply the demand for sub-machine guns to the commandos and auxiliary units.

Sergeant Bob Parsons and son Peter clean and load his new Thompson sub-machine gun 1941

Pikes

In September 1941, because some 700 000 Home Guard volunteers had still not been issued with rifles, the Government organised the issue of 'pikes'. Some were made from 2" iron gas pipe with WW I bayonets wedged and welded in the end, and others were purpose-made one metre long tubes with a conical spike at the business end. Others had a blade which looked like a flattened out sharpened builder's trowel; these can be occasionally found with W.D. markings on the blade.

These weapons, originally dreamed up by Lord Croft (the Minister of Supply), were thought to be the perfect 'cheap' solution to engage the enemy in street fighting. They arrived at most units to exclamations of despair, as most units had already received some rifles and training with the newly arrived Thompson sub-machine guns by this time.

In early instruction manuals 'pikes' had already been suggested as a cheap and efficient way of dispatching the enemy. Diagrams on how to make them by attaching carving knives to broom handles with string or wire were distributed to the L.D.V. in some areas of Britain, and in some instances were made and used in training exercises.

Nobody really thought they had any practical use at the time, in fact many realised that they may in fact have been damaging to morale, and this is still the case. The House of Lords in 1942 complained about the *'1000 tons of valuable iron and steel being wasted on something, which is little more than an insult to the user.'* Bearing in mind the crisis that Britain was in at the time due to the threat of impending invasion this single weapon coupled with the abject stupidity of the national press mocking the Home Guard did more to damage the Home Guard's reputation, morale and public image as a serious military organisation. Thankfully most Quartermaster Sergeants had the foresight to prevent the pikes being issued.

In Exmouth, the Home Guard's rifles had started to arrive in large quantities by the time the pikes had put in an appearance and so these items deemed 'ridiculous' by the Exmouth men, were hastily stored in the toilets at the Drill Hall and remained there for the rest of the war.

The only useful function that the pike served was to provide the name for one of television's most useless and endearing characters. Pike was the obvious choice of name for the character in Croft and Perry's 'Dad's Army' programme due to his own inadequacies. It was a clever piece of writing to use him as a metaphor, for what was originally intended to be a serious military weapon.

The Sten gun (Machine Carbine) 9mm Calibre

Mike Heard

'Our nick-name for the Sten was the 'Woolworth's Gun'. They were cheap to produce, but weren't the same quality and didn't have the same hitting power as the Thompson. They were issued to us later on in the war (from early 1943) but only to Corporals.'

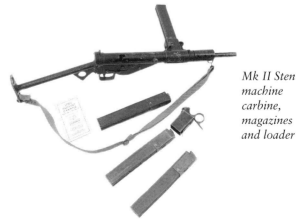

Mk II Sten machine carbine, magazines and loader

Mk II Sten gun bolt and breech

One expert described this gun as 'a spout, a handle and a tin box.' It was designed as a cheap and effective way of proving a high rate of fire power using the minimum a mount of raw materials. At a production cost of around 30/-, it had a cheap unfinished appearance and was as first ridiculed by the men of the Home Guard, incurring amongst other names 'the Plumber's Delight'.

The gun weighed in at a little over 3kg and had a rate of fire of 500 rounds per minute. It was loved by some and hated by others, probably because the tolerances from gun to gun varied dramatically.

The gun was inaccurate over a range of 50 metres and in the hands of an untrained man was potentially lethal to his own side as well as the enemy as it had a bad trait of pulling sharply upwards and away from the proposed line of fire, making it possible for ricochet shots to hit unintentional objects, lethal to friendly troops over its short range.

Upon saying all of this the toughness and reliability of the weapon was excellent provided it was kept well oiled and cleaned regularly and that the 32-round magazines were loaded carefully and correctly with only 28 rounds of ammunition.

Laurie Butler

'I was made up to Lance Corporal after I had been in for a while and it was then that I was issued with a Sten gun. I had a Mk I first then a Mk II, which wasn't so well made. It fired a 9mm round. The magazine would actually hold 32 rounds, but we would only ever load 28, as it could have jammed. The rounds were difficult to get into the magazine and we had a special loading tool which would force in the round. We carried 250 rounds loaded in magazines and carried them in a haversack; mine stayed under the stairs at home. I kept one magazine loaded all of the time and this is what I would take with me.'

Mk II Sten gun magazine and 9mm ammunition

'No bayonet was issued for the Sten gun, so I used to carry a sheath knife on my belt, it had a blade of around 6 inches long'

Ray Towill

'We had Sten gun training, we practised near Orcombe Point, on the beach under the cliffs. Targets were set up there. These guns were terrible! useless! With a very short range, good for clearing houses but nothing else. One section had a Bren gun that was a lovely gun.'

Commercially produced Sten gun manual

The Boyes Anti-Tank Rifle Calibre .55

This was a standard bolt action rifle, but made to a much higher calibre. It fired armour-piercing bullets and delivered an incredible kick to the user, which made it very unpopular. By the time it had been produced Germany had increased the armour on its tanks and the Boyes would have proved most ineffective against them.

It would however penetrate 24mm of armour at 90 degrees at 100 metres, and 9mm of armour at a 40 degree angle, which made it very effective against lightly armoured and soft-skinned vehicles.

The weapon was usually fired prone from the ground by a two man team, with a rate of fire of 9 rounds per minute. The magazine held 5 rounds. The guns were not a common item in Home Guard units.

Bayonets

Mk II 1910 pattern Canadian ross bayonet

American M1905 pattern bayonet for the Springfield rifle, with scabbard

American M1917 pattern bayonet for Enfield P-17, with scabbard and British 1939 pattern leather frog

Recognition notches on the handle of the M1917 bayonet

The American M1917 pattern bayonet had two deep cut marks in the wooden handle to distinguish it from the British 1907 pattern bayonet, by sight and feel at night. This bayonet would not fit the Lee Enfield or the Canadian Ross, 303 rifles. The bayonet was issued with a British 1939 pattern brown leather frog, which attached it to the Guardsman's leather belt.

Bill Sleeman recalled practising bayonet drill on Exmouth seafront, using bags filled with sand as the

British Wilkinson 1907 Pattern Bayonet for S.M.L.E. No.1 Rifle Marks, with Scabbard and 1937 Pattern Webbing Frog

enemy. He was keen to show me what he remembered whilst talking at his shop on Exeter Road.

Bill Sleeman
'We always had to do bayonet drill, like this!' Bill showed me how with a lunging move! *'We had to practise all the time against sacks filled with straw or sand'*

Bill Sleeman (Right) and Pals with P-17's and 'bayonets fixed'

Lustleigh Platoon 14 'Moorside' battalion Devon Home Guard displaying their weapons circa 1942

This photograph was taken outside the village hall in Lustleigh. In the front row can be seen two Thompson Sub-Machine Guns and two P-17 rifles. In the foreground is a Browing water-cooled heavy machine gun (left) and a Vickers Light Machine Gun (Right).

Officers and N.C.O's
Front Row Left to Right

Harold Olding, Mr. Stock, Mr. Farrell, Jack Gould (Officer in Charge), Mr. Laxton, Ernest Olding, Ernest Squires, Richard Bourne.

Lustleigh platoon can be seen again displaying their arsenal of weapons as they pose for the following

Lustleigh Platoon after competition shooting at Rockvale Range circa 1942

photograph. There are P-17's , a few S.M.L.E. rifles, Mk II Sten guns held by the N.C.O's and even an E.Y. Cup Discharger mounted on the Guardsman's S.M.L.E. seated on the far right in the front row. This and the earlier photograph of Lustleigh Platoon with their Lewis and Vickers machine guns, shows how well armed the Home Guard were becoming at this period of time.

Carl, Betty and Jack Robbins, Exmouth Home Guard

Chapter 8
Additional and Personal Equipment

The following information was taken from a leaflet issued to the men. This equipment listed was also taken on weekend exercises by the regular army. Variations of the equipment taken would depend on the purpose of the exercise and the role being carried out by the men.

What You Must do when the Home Guard is Mustered

Put on your uniform and take the whole of your arms and equipment to the place where you have been instructed to report.

Bring the under-mentioned articles with you, but no superfluous ones.

a. Enough food to last 24 hours, drinking mug and plate or mess tins, with knife fork or spoon.
b. Razor, lather brush, hairbrush and comb, towel, soap and toilet paper.
c. Change of underclothing, spare pair of socks,
d. Handkerchief.
e. Have a rucksack or a sandbag ready to hold the above.
f. One blanket rolled bandolier fashion.
g. Spade or pick if you have them.
i. Identity card bearing your battalion stamp.
j. All of your own ration books.
k. Envelopes, notepaper and pen or pencil.
l. Tobacco and / or cigarettes.
m. Matches and / or torch.
n. Spare pair of bootlaces.

Leather Webbing Equipment

This equipment was either from supplies left over from obsolete patterns from WWI, or the 1939 pattern equipment manufactured as a stop gap until enough cotton webbing equipment could be made for the army. The 1939 pattern webbing was made entirely from leather and supplied mainly to colonial troops fighting with the regulars in dry climates.

The Territorial Army Stores still had some WW I leather webbing equipment of the 1903 and 1906 pattern available. The 1906 pattern belt had brace buckles attached at the back to take either leather or webbing braces. It was occasionally issued with two, brown leather 1939 (emergency pattern) Bren pouches. Some of this equipment was issued as an interim, stop-gap measure to Home Guard units. The pouches were later recalled as the Sten gun became available and the fasteners were adjusted and re-riveted to allow the Sten magazines (which were longer) to be stored in the pouches and re-issued initially to Corporals armed with Sten guns.

When Sten guns were first issued to the N.C.O.s it was quite usual to see them wearing the leather 1939 pattern pouch on the left hand side of the body only. The right hand side had either a Home Guard pattern 'shotgun' pouch or just the strap supporting brace.

Later the standard 1937 pattern webbing Bren or utility pouches were supplied to the N.C.O.s who carried the Sten guns, as they were less rigid, which made crawling and certain manoeuvres easier. They could also carry either the Sten or Bren magazines.

1903 pattern leather belt with 1939 pattern pouches adjusted for the 32-round Sten magazines, Sten bayonet frog and sling

Laurie Butler
'When I had the Sten gun I had one pouch attached to my belt, with only one mag of ammunition in it. It was worn on the left hand side and had nothing on the other side just a webbing strap. The pouch was made of brown leather and was really solid. It was damned uncomfortable to lie on. We had to do things called a leopard crawl and it made life very difficult.'

Honiton Company 19 'Seaton' Battalion 16 May 1943

guns, which are slung on their left shoulders. They are also carrying the rubberised cotton Home Guard pattern haversack on their left hip and the Mk VI service respirator in the alert position on their chests.

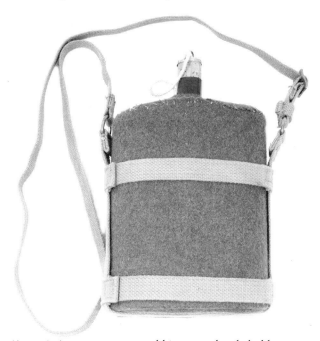

'Austerity' pattern cotton webbing waterbottle holder

The photograph of the Honiton Company parading at All Hallows Playing Fields, shows the men on parade being inspected by the Mayor of the town Mr. A.F. Studley.

The men are wearing single 1939 pattern leather pouches extended to hold the magazines for their Sten

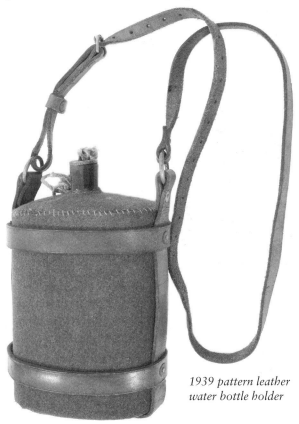

1939 pattern leather water bottle holder

Water Bottles

Initially water bottles were only issued to Corporals in the Exmouth Company. They could be drawn from the stores for use when leading patrols or on exercises. Later on, water bottles were issued to all of the infantry trained 'Clyst' Battalion members.

Most of these items were still in storage from the Great War.

They were made from pressed and welded steel and stove enamelled either blue or olive green to keep them free from rust and easy to keep sterile. The bottles were covered in serge to keep them from getting knocked and chipped and this cover could also be soaked with water to provide a way of keeping the water inside cool by evaporation.

In the photograph of a platoon 'B' Company 60 'Woodside' Battalion on their route march to Godstone, the water bottle with leather holder can be seen slung on their right hip.

'B' Company 60th 'Woodside' Battalion Surrey Home Guard, route marching smartly to Godstone

Cotton Webbing Equipment

Webbing started to be issued locally to infantry Platoons from mid 1940. The cotton webbing set comprised of the brown leather 1903 pattern belt, two 'shotgun pouches' as they were commonly known, as a box of 50 War Department 12-bore, solid ball round shotgun cartridges would fit exactly inside them. They were in fact designed to take the B.A.R. magazines also, as well as .300 and .303 rifle clips. Invariably they were used to carry grenades and other small pieces of equipment. Two webbing strap braces, supported the pouches which were also attached to the belt with a webbing sleeve, which slipped over the belt and was used to connect the braces at the back of the belt.

Donald Bradford, Doug Smaldon, Reg Dixon, Ted Bradford and Basil Mears of the Exmouth Company 2 'Clyst' Battalion Devon Home Guard on the cliffs

Standard Home Guard webbing, shotgun pouches, sleeve and 1903 pattern leather belt and bayonet frog

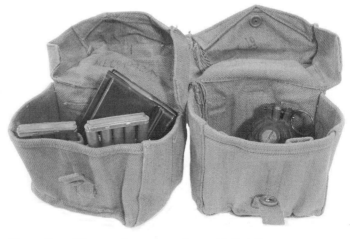

Home Guard Pattern shotgun pouches, with B.A.R. Magazines, 30-06 P.17 stripper clips and a No.36 mills bomb

Carhampton Platoon armed with Sten Guns and P-17 Rifles 37 pattern webbing with B.A.R. and bren pouches

Pouches were worn in all sorts of combinations. Devon Smith-Gun crews wore one shotgun pouch and one 1937 army webbing pouch to carry ammunition for Bren gun teams, who worked in close proximity to protect the Smith Gun position.

1937 pattern webbing with 1939 pattern supplementary pouch for Sten gun magazines

Lewis gun pouches

Lewis gun teams carried additional WW I pouches for the 47-round magazines which could be linked together in twos or in fours.

Rubberised Cotton Haversack

This was a khaki, waterproofed haversack with a rear mounted shoulder strap and single fastening strap. It was issued from around October 1940 and was made to a much cheaper standard than the 37 pattern Army webbing pattern small pack. It was issued to Exmouth infantry trained Home Guard units but not to the 477 R.A. Coastal Artillery Battery, as although they had received infantry training they were not expected to be used in the infantry role during an invasion (i.e. all their supplies etc. would be stored at the gun battery and command post).

Edwin Hawker
'We had a haversack that we carried but we didn't use it very much, sometimes we carried sandwiches or a flask in it. It was made of an oil cloth. We usually kept any ammunition in our pockets.'

After talking to many Home Guard Veterans over the years about what was kept in their haversacks, the contents seem to vary from unit to unit and

Home Guard pattern rubberised cotton haversack

Typical contents of a Guardsman's haversack when on exercise

county to county. The most common items carried in this bag were a torch, sandwiches and a vacuum flask when on patrol or on watch on cold nights. Some also carried simple stoves like the 'Tommy Cooker' to brew up a cup of tea on or warm up soup or a tin of beans. Cigarettes, penknives, pipes and tobacco and later in the war, hand grenades (mainly the No. 36. Mills bomb), were all carried in these simple bags.

'B' Company 60th 'Woodside' Battalion Surrey Home Guard route marching in full marching order

The 'Tommy Cooker' and half-pint army issue enamel mug

Mike Heard

'Every three hours, when on call out, the army would come round with a bucket full of soup and a ladle, it wasn't bad, lovely veg, but the meat was suspicious! They would also bring round buckets of tea which you dipped a mug in! But, it was always cold.'

Ken Parker

'My nick-name was 'beans', I always took a tin of baked beans to the drill hall to heat up for a meal whilst I was on duty.'

Edwin Hawker

'We always took sandwiches which we would eat when on duty. We took them with us, usually chicken but the odd lamb and pig would die mysteriously from some disease or other now and again and the meat was shared out between all of us.'

'We made our own tea in the tent, we also took bottles of cold tea, plain water, or anything else we could get our hands on.'

Mess Tins

Mess tins were issued by the Army to Home Guard units, when on combined exercises and had the responsibility for the catering. The mess tins were only issued to the men on duty during the exercises and had to be returned after the exercise had finished.

Brown or white enamel or, white pottery mugs supplied by the army, were also used when on exercises, these too had to be returned to the army caterers after use.

White or brown enamel or white utility pottery mugs were provided at the Drill Halls.

A Guardsman's eating essentials when on exercise

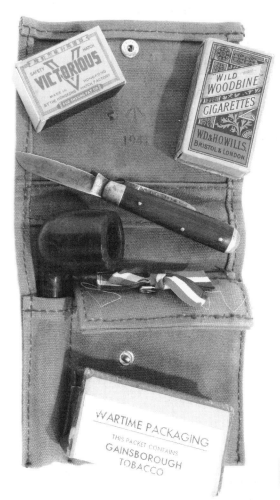

Smoking pouch, wartime tobacco, pipe and penknife, and wallet with wartime currency

Torches

Torches in the early days were issued to patrol leaders only from a pool of equipment held at the Quartermaster's stores and were 'signed out' when required due to the shortages of dry batteries.

First Field Dressing

This small dressing was carried by all Home Guard members in the small pocket on the right hand thigh of the battledress and denim trousers.

It is a cotton pouch in a waterproof cellulose cover, housing two packets, each containing a compressed cotton-lint bandage. In the event of any injury bandages were always at the scene, with instructions on how best they were to be applied to open wounds.

The dressings were intended to be used by anyone in emergencies and all Home Guardsmen had received basic first aid training. This simple pouch saved many lives of injured servicemen during WWII.

Mike Heard
'We did only the basics in first aid training, just enough to help save someone's life if they were bleeding badly'

Men of the R.A. 477 kept their dressings packet in the left hand blouse chest pockets. For some reason they did not kept them in the special field dressing pocket on the battledress trousers.

Traffic control torch, hooded torch and a signalling torch

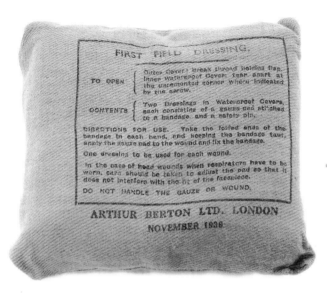

First field dressing

Army pattern fingerless gloves and trigger mittens

Personally Supplied Items

Home Guard members were expected to supply the following items themselves: pocket knife, underwear, socks, trouser braces, and gloves. Scarves and thermos flask were to be provided when on patrol).

Underwear

Home Guard personal equipment, had to be purchased privately and had also to conform to utility standards. This was included as part of the Guardsman's yearly general clothing, ration allowance.

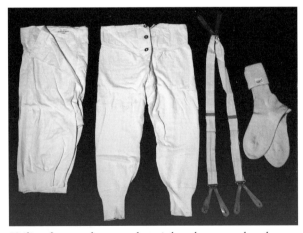

Utility short underpants, long johns, braces and socks

Gloves

These were either purchased from shops, or more usually knitted by wives, girlfriends or sisters. Early in the war gloves were knitted on four needles and they didn't have to conform to utility standards. Later specialist knitting books were produced for the Home Guard and Comfort Services (knitting for servicemen overseas), these books of patterns showed women how to make warm garments with the minimum of wool. Items such as jumpers were also unpicked and made into the new items.

Scarves

Most wore a warm scarf of a suitable colour, khaki, green, brown or grey, usually knitted by wives or girlfriends to austerity patterns.

Mk VI Service Respirator

The Service Respirator was usually referred to as a 'gas mask', they were issued to every rank who served in the Home Guard. This sturdy mask with flexible hose was far more suitable for firing weapons as the filter section was permanently housed in the haversack.

Mk VI service respirator, haversack and contents with cape anti-gas Mk I (Left)

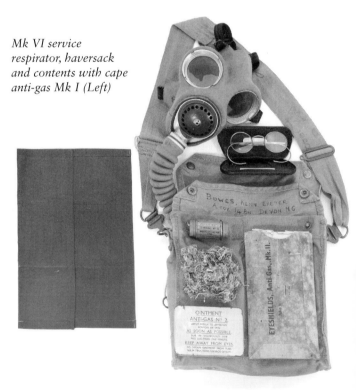

The Anti-Gas Cape Mk I

The cape was made from a cotton-oilskin material and was intended to cover the user and protect them from sprayed chemical gas attacks. It was impregnated with chemicals which would help to counter the effects of vesicant (skin burning) gases, reducing the risk of contamination to the user and increasing the speed and efficiency with which the decontamination squads could deal with the clean up operations after an attack.

It was usually carried tied to top of gas mask bag when worn in the alert position on the chest. This made it quickly accessible in the event of a gas attack.

Mike Heard

'The gas cape came in a little packet, which we kept inside our gas mask bag, or on the top of it, tied on with string when we were on alert. It was made from oilskin. Sometimes we wore it on really rainy nights, but we were told not to because the chemicals would wash out'

The reason for this was the anti-gas properties of the cape would be diminished by the action of the rain on it. The order was largely ignored as the war progressed. The crumpled gas cape can often be seen in old photographs of the Home Guard stored under the flap of the haversack.

The following list describes the items shown in the photograph above.

The Contents of a Mk. VI Service Respirator Bag

Fire Guard duty protective goggles, cotton waste to wipe off sprayed vesicant gases (mustard gas), anti-gas ointment for mustard gas burns, tinted anti-gas spray eye-shields, clear anti-gas spray eye-shields, gas mask drill instructions, demister cloths and tins first and second type.

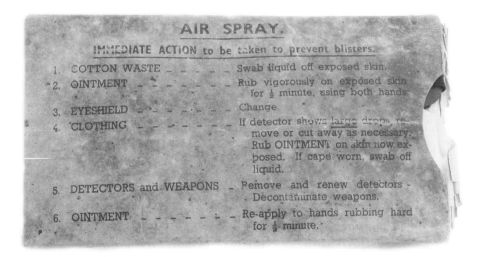

Anti-mustard gas goggles, anti-gas ointment, de-mister cylinder and cotton waste

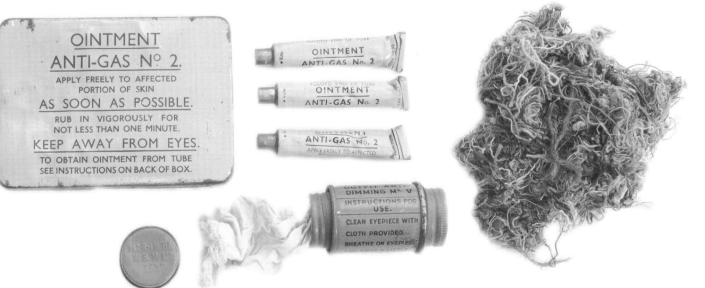

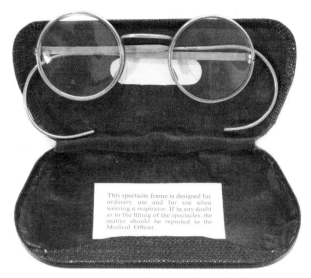

Specially designed gas mask spectacles by Hadley

Other essentials were stored in various small compartments in this haversack including specialist items like the 'flat armed' Hadley gas mask spectacles which were designed not to interfere with the air-tight seal formed by the rubber against the face. These specialist prescription spectacles were issued free of charge to Guardsmen who presented their prescription and membership details to the optician.

Dennis Davey

'A year or two after I joined the Home Guard I had my 18th birthday. I was declared to be Grade 4 when I had my army medical, because of my short-sightedness. Although I considered my sight to be normal when wearing glasses, and I was able to fare at least as good as anyone else with target practice on the firing ranges. I wore the usual type of horn rimmed glasses of the period, but I was sent to an optician to have special steel framed glasses made that would fit inside my army respirator when required.'

Gas Detection Brassard

This was a chemically impregnated, early warning device for sprayed 'vesicant' gases such as mustard gas. It was worn over the battledress on the left shoulder and in some circumstances both shoulders, with a small cord fastening round the epaulette to hold it in place. The impregnated waxed paper would change colour from the khaki/brown colour to a bright yellow if it came into contact with any gas in vapour or liquid form thus alerting the men to the presence of poisonous gas. It could also be removed and placed in pools of liquid thought to be sprayed gas, or gas deployed by bomb, to check whether the substance was dangerous or not. Thankfully gas was never used.

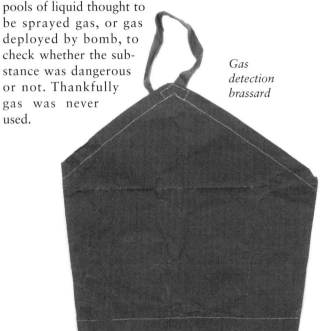

Gas detection brassard

Addiscombe Platoon Guardsmen with respirators in alert position

Chapter 9
Home Guard Officers

Bill Sleeman

'Originally it took us a while to get organised, but times were very difficult. During the course of the war the officers changed and gathered experience, I felt that we ended up with a really good set of officers.'

It was the officers who gave the character to the L.D.V. and Home Guard. They were mainly men who had served in the armed forces in WW I. They brought a lot of experience and know-how, in military matters and the more mundane, but nevertheless necessary, administration and organisational aspects of running the new force. They came from all areas of the armed forces, some having commanded battalion-strength infantry units, to officers who were in desk jobs and supply. A much smaller percentage of men came forward as ex-serving members of the Royal Navy and Royal Air Force.

There was a great deal of responsibility that fell on the shoulders of these men, they worked tirelessly to make the Home Guard a success. Some even paid for essential equipment in the early days, without any guarantee of seeing anything back. Generally speaking the Exmouth Company were happy with their officers and were proud to serve under them. They were responsible for the general administration of the units, the safe storage of weapons and explosive equipment in civilian buildings and built up areas, and also had to ensure that adequate attention was paid to the safe handling of these weapons in training programmes.

In 1941, the Home Guard mounted the guard on Buckingham Palace, for which, King George VI expressed his gratitude in a speech to the men. In 1942, a year later he took up the honorary position of Colonel-in-Chief of the Home Guard.

Later in the war the officers commanding the Home Guard were granted the King's Commission in recognition of their work, which gave them a parity of status with the regular army.

Officers Uniforms
Denims

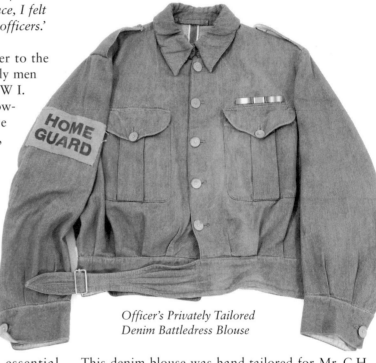

Officer's Privately Tailored Denim Battledress Blouse

This denim blouse was hand tailored for Mr. C.H. Sanders, by Bruce and Alderton of London on the 24 June 1940, little more than 5 weeks after the appeal for men to join the L.D.V. had gone out. It is made in the style of the 1938 pattern men's denim blouse and not in the pattern of the officer's battledress with an open collar. It is worth remembering that for all the rules and regulations surrounding military uniforms there are always exceptions to the rule to be found.

Officers in the Home Guard were issued with other-ranks' (O.R.s') battledress when it started to become available. Later they could have their own uniforms privately tailored at their own expense if they so desired. Some of these garments were made of extremely fine serge cloth and had satin or silk linings.

These officers' battledress blouses were privately tailored like their army equivalents. They differed from the O.R.s' 1937 and '40 pattern battledress blouses, in that they were designed to be worn open at the neck with a shirt and tie, as in the regular army. Not all officers decided to opt for a tailor-made battledress and can often be seen still wearing their O.R.s' issue battledress in their unit's stand-down photographs.

When the 1940 pattern battledress was introduced it had a cotton lining to the collar, which was intended to prevent chaffing, some officers chose to bleach this white as a personalised 'fashion statement', to be seen when worn open with a collar and tie.

As the Home Guard became more organised, officers had an allowance towards providing themselves with their clothing and equipment. The main difference between officers and O.R.s' clothing was the quality of materials used. The badges were usually of better quality too, being machine embroidered rather than screen printed. Although the men could also purchase these if they had enough money and supplies were available.

Medal Ribbons

Medal ribbons can sometimes be seen displayed on officers and O.R.s' battledress blouses. They were displayed on the upper chest next to the left arm. The most common being the campaign stars and medals for the 1914-18 war. The 1914-15 Star (Mons Star), the 1914 -18 star, the 1914-18 War Medal, and 1914-18 Victory Medal. These medals were nick-named, Pip, Squeak and Wilfred after a popular newspaper's cartoon characters.

Major Archdale O.C. 2 'Clyst' Battalion wearing a barrathea field service cap

Officers' quality embroidered shoulder titles

Headgear

Officers usually wore the standard field service cap. They also had specially tailored caps made locally from fine serge material, or barathea material if they could afford it and it became available. Some officers opted for the more traditional service dress cap with a stiff peak. The officers wore the same county regiment or corps badges like the men, but made of bronze rather than brass.

Devonshire Regiment officers' bronze cap badge

Officers' F.S. cap

Service dress cap

Lieutenant Frederick David Thomas of 'Bampton' Home Guard in 1944 wearing a F.S. cap

Webley No. 1 Mk. VI Service Revolver Calibre .455

The .455 was the standard service revolver for officers serving in the British Armed Forces during WW I. It had a six-round revolving cylinder and possessed awesome stopping power, creating horrific wounds at close quarters. It was nick named 'Big Ugly' by those who used it. This weapon served the officers very well in the trench warfare of WW I, but was cumbersome and heavy to handle and possessed a mighty kick. By

1923 soft lead bullets of high calibre, as fired by the .455 Webley, were considered to be outmoded for modern 'civilised warfare' and thus the concept for a .38 war service revolver was born. Some .45s were issued to Home Guard officers during WW II but were soon replaced by the newer .38 revolver.

Webley .455 No.1 Mark VI 'war finish' service revolver

The Webley No. 2 Mk. IV Service Revolver Calibre .38

This was the standard service revolver for officers serving in the British Armed Forces and was developed from the earlier Webley and Scott No. 1 Mk VI revolver. Home Guard officers were issued with this revolver from 1942.

Once again the gun had a six-round revolving magazine drum which stored the .38" S.A.A. ball rounds and were simple and quick to re-load. These revolvers, were extremely well made, but lacked the finish of the earlier interwar revolvers due to wartime restrictions of labour and finance. They were produced in their thousands and were popular with the men who used them. They were to be used mainly in defence at close quarters as they had good stopping power. With a maximum effective range of 50 metres, the gun was best used at 20 metre and less, where a hit anywhere from this weapon would provide deadly.

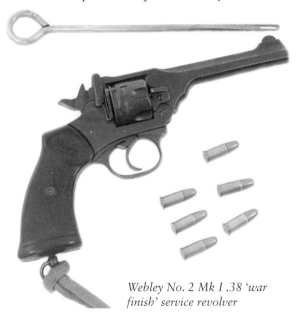

Webley No. 2 Mk I .38 'war finish' service revolver

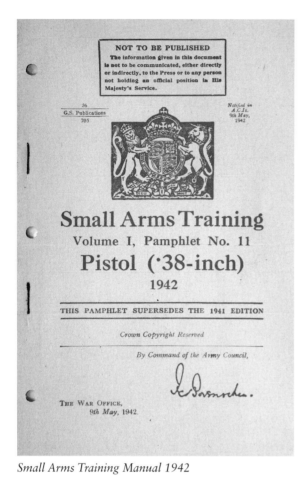

Small Arms Training Manual 1942

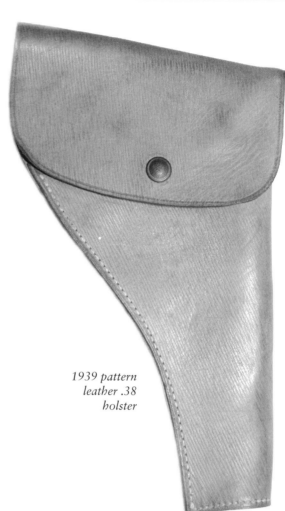

*1939 pattern
leather .38
holster*

*Drum magazine of the No 2 Mk I service
revolver*

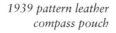

*1939 pattern leather
compass pouch*

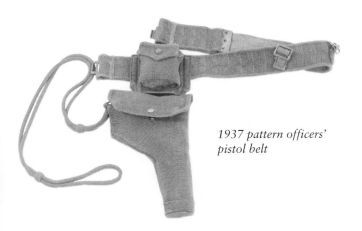

1937 pattern officers' pistol belt

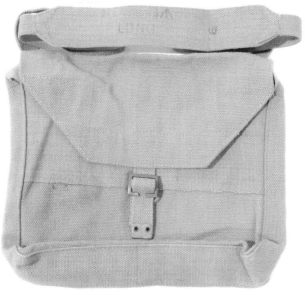

1937 pattern officer's document valise

Officers' 1937 Pattern Webbing

Some officers who had served in WW I had kept their original Sam Browne belts and fittings and, if they still fitted, wore these for a while. This practise was tolerated for a short while but was soon stopped as, in some areas, the officers started to wear their old uniforms too which was frowned upon as most were showing rank which they were no longer entitled too. When things got a little more organised they wore the 1903 pattern leather belt with WWI pattern holsters, or whatever was available.

Soon 1939 pattern holsters, pistol ammunition pouches and compass pouches were worn. 1937 pattern standard army webbing was issued when the Webley .38 pistol was introduced into Home Guard service. A full set of pouches and attachments were shortly made available to the officers as the need for live exercises with the regular army became necessary.

The complete set consisted of the following 1937 pattern items.

1x Adjustable belt.
2x Brace attachments.
2x Braces.
1x Holster.
1x .38 Pistol ammunition pouch.
1x Compass pouch.
1x Binocular pouch.
1x Officers document valise.
1x Map case.
1x Water bottle sleeve

1937 pattern map case

Field glasses or binoculars

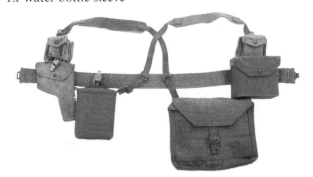

1937 pattern officers' webbing equipment

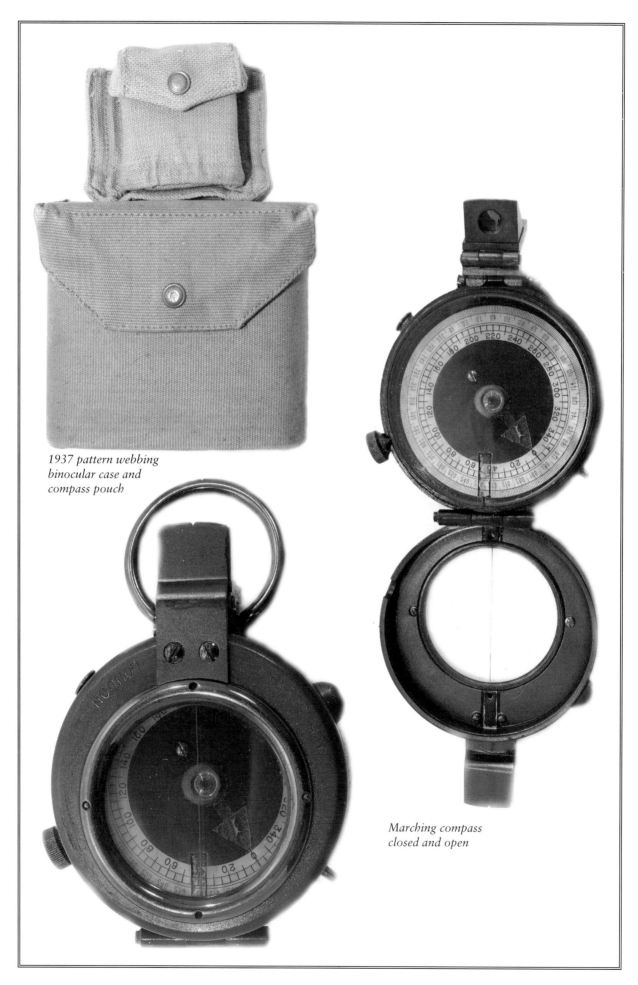

1937 pattern webbing binocular case and compass pouch

Marching compass closed and open

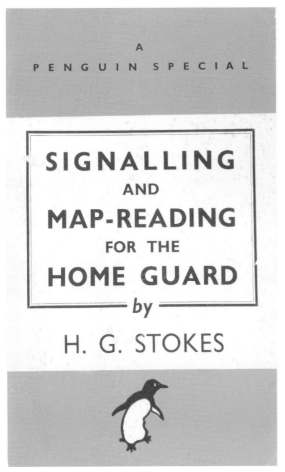

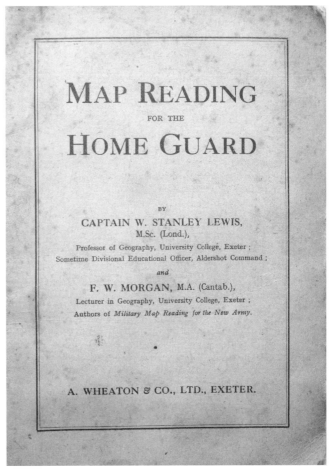

Commercially produced map-reading books

Astbury Officer's wristwatch dated 1916

Map Reading

Officers provided their own prismatic marching compass and most still had their own from WW I. Many were already used to reading military maps and if they were not, attended the same training sessions in orienteering and map reading as the men. An appeal went out for current local Ordnance Survey maps to be taken to the Home Guard headquarters buildings and these were then used by section leaders and patrols in the early days to find their way around.

Chapter 10
Training and Exercises

John Jack Sage

'We were organised into units with an army-style rank system, we then organised patrols and training sessions on Sunday afternoons.'

The first L.D.V. training school was established at the sand pits at Draycot near Cleverly by Lieutenant-Colonel Otter-Barry.

A rudimentary school of musketry (rifle skills) was started as the risk of invasion was so high. The use of rifles was taught by volunteers who had recently received tuition on how to instruct novices and had already gained previous experience of using rifles. It was intended to be a guerrilla training school, where all aspects of unorthodox methods of warfare would be taught. But it was decide instead to concentrate purely on the use of the rifle as this was deemed to be the most useful role for the L.D.V.

Osterley Park Training School

The need for a specialist training school was recognised immediately by some forward-thinking individuals. Mr. Edward Hulton, owner of the *Picture Post*, which had been running articles regularly about how to deal with the menace of the Panzer. Tom Wintringham provided the military know-how and the Earl of Jersey, who provided part of his estate for the project, were quick to set up a guerrilla training school at Osterley Park, Hounslow.

Tom Wintringham had gained a lot of experience with the International Brigade in Spain during the civil war and had gained practical first-hand experience in dealing with ambush fighting tactics with the minimum amount of training and weapons. He had also strong links and contacts with the communists and some former Spanish miners who had devised tactics for destroying tanks at close range during the Spanish Civil War. These contacts, coupled with the skills of a young artist called Hugh Slater who had also served in the International Brigade and had subsequently become an expert with machine guns, proved a very potent combination.

At the training school L.D.V. members were taught to attack and harass the enemy using simple tactics with guile and boldness and this, coupled with confidence in the weapons and training, provided an education which would be lethal to the enemy.

Lectures included camouflage and field craft, stalking and ambush tactics, observation and reporting procedures. Improvisational use of use hand grenades, anti-tank weapons and land mines, small arms and machine gun training were also part of the course.

Irregular military tactics and skills were also a high priority; pupils learnt guerrilla fighting in occupied territories, street and house-to-house fighting, defensive measures and tactics including road-blocks, anti-tank ditches and traps. A lot of emphasis was also placed on the study of modern military tactics and German military tactics of the time.

There is no doubt that Osterley Park and its instructors did a great job of training the L.D.V and Home Guard members, with 4 940 officers and men passing through its doors, until Tom

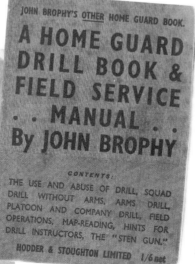

Early commercially available training manuals

Wintringham's personal politics and petty jealousy from certain members of the armed forces forced it's closure, with the War Office finally taking over the facility and moving piecemeal to a new location, still using the same principle as the men who had set the school up, but without their involvement.

One of the main legacies left by the teachings of Tom Wintringham and his band of tank-destroying miners was the myth that the tank, which was considered invincible and impervious to attempts by infantry to destroy them or hold them up, could in fact be destroyed, damaged or its ability be hindered, by simple, inexpensive improvised bombs and explosives such as the Molotov cocktail. This improved greatly the L.D.V. members' confidence in attempting to ambush and confront enemy armour. So much so that a second school specifically to deal with the German panzer menace was set up by Sir Hubert Gough at Hurlingham, and the combined successes of these initial training establishments greatly influenced the War Office in setting up the Home Guard Training Schools in most areas of Britain, where army instructors were employed to teach these methods.

Basic General Training

Responsibility for training the men in the various skills expected of a Home Guardsman fell to the following regular service units.

Musketry.	The Infantry.
Driving.	The Royal Army Service Corps.
Signals.	The Royal Signals, (Semaphore. Heliograph, Pigeons and Radio).
Gunnery.	The Royal Artillery.
Aircraft Recognition.	The Royal Air Force
Basic First Aid.	Local Red Cross and St. John Ambulance Voluntary Aid Detachments.
Unarmed Combat	Army Physical Training Instructors.

Main Training Topics Delivered at a Local Level

Physical Training. (Army P.T.I.'s)
Marching Drill.
Rifle and Small Arms Drill.
Live Firing Exercises.
Gas Drill.
Map Reading.
Unarmed Combat.
Camouflage and Concealment.
Aircraft / Vehicle Recognition.
Battle Craft. Defence and Mobile Patrols.
Hand Grenade Training.
Enemy Uniform Recognition.

Mine Laying.
Signals and Communication.
Sub Artillery Training. (Spigot Mortar, Northover Projector, Smith Gun, Vickers Heavy M.G., Browning Heavy M.G.)
Intelligence and Reconnaissance training.

In Exmouth the Home Guard drilled in the Manor Gardens when weather and other conditions were right. Every one was keen to learn new skills and mucked in, it was generally considered by the men interviewed, that the Exmouth Company were well trained and had an excellent esprit de corps.

The following list gives a good indication of how busy the Exmouth Home Guard were, bearing in mind the long hours worked by the men in their normal day jobs. The list is fairly representative for a syllabus of training for one month anywhere in Britain during the years 1941-1942.

Typical Monthly Company Training

Wednesday 1.	Recruits.
Thursday 2.	Fire Control Orders and Fire Discipline.
Friday 3.	Recruits.
Saturday 4.	Practice for Company Hand grenade Competition.
Sunday 5.	Company Exercise.
Monday 6.	P.C. Conference – Recruits.
Tuesday 7.	Use of Cover. Camouflage and Concealment.
Wednesday 8.	Recruits.
Thursday 9.	Fire Positions – Lecture.
Friday 10.	Recruits.
Saturday 11.	Company Hand grenade Competition.
Sunday 12.	Company Route March with Gas Exercises. Battle drill by Platoon or Battalion Parade for Cinema.
Monday 13.	P.C. Conference – Recruits.
Tuesday 14.	Covering Fire - Light Artillery and Anti-Tank Guns.
Wednesday 15.	Recruits.
Thursday 16.	Gas Detection, Recognition and Protection.
Friday 17.	Recruits.
Saturday 18.	Battalion Exercises.
Sunday 19.	Battalion Exercises.
Monday 20.	P.C. Conference – Recruits.
Tuesday 21.	Section Schemes.
Wednesday 22.	Recruits.
Thursday 23.	Lessons learnt on Tuesday. Section Schemes – Faults.
Friday 24.	Recruits.
Saturday 25.	————
Sunday 26.	Company Parade. Manor Gardens. Battle Drill by Platoons.

Monday 27.   P.C. Conference – Recruits.
Tuesday 28.   Reconnaissance – Reports –
                    Ambushes.
Wednesday 29. Recruits.
Thursday 30.   Lecture on Mondays work.

The regular competitions that were held were:

Bombing (Hand Grenades).
Bayonet Fighting.
Unarmed Combat.
Squad and Arms Drill.
Musketry (Rifle Shooting).

Bill Sleeman

'Inter-section rivalry between the members of the different sections was encouraged, things like shooting and aircraft spotting. We would also play competitive sports in section teams. Generally though, everyone worked as a team and were keen not to let the side down.'

Drill Halls and Headquarters

Exmouth Drill Hall at Imperial Road was in use every day of the week by the Home Guard. It was used for drill, practise and training downstairs. Upstairs was the Quartermaster's store. The armoury and rifle range, was at the back of the building. Between the main building and the Manor Gardens was a small arms firing range. The Home Guard used this and also trained members of the A.T.C., Army Cadets, Sea

Cadets, Girls Training Corps and other youth organisations to handle and fire weapons such as .22 rifles, .303 rifles and hand guns.

Ken Parker

'We were based at the drill hall behind the old Regal Dance Hall for our meetings and training. Charlie Miller was my Corporal and my Company Sergeant Major was a Charlie Havill.'

'On Saturday nights we went on training classes, or on runs with equipment to get us fit for joining the army. It was very hard work, especially in hot weather.'

Whilst on duty one winter's night around twenty men of the. 477 Coastal Battery were sleeping at the Exmouth Drill Hall. It was a bitterly cold night and the fire in the grate had been well stoked to keep the room as warm as possible.

Mike Heard

'The Drill Hall was on the corner of Imperial Road and St. Andrews Road. We used to sleep there some nights under blankets on the floor when on duty. One night when we were all asleep and the chimney caught fire. The alarm was raised and we were woken up. You couldn't see your hand in front of your face! The room was full of smoke, we managed to get some stirrup pumps and buckets of water arranged and after a while managed to douse the flames by sticking the jets of water from the stirrup pumps up the chimney. It wasn't funny at the time as we could have all suffocated, but now it seems amusing!'

Hazel Rowsell

'My Brother joined the Home Guard when he was 17 years old. One of Donald's best friends was Mike Heard, they used to be seen around together a lot and would meet at the drill hall on the Home Guard nights. The Home Guard's meetings were held at the Imperial Road Drill Hall. The entrance was just before you get to the Manor Gardens.'

Drill

After the L.D.V. changed its name to the Home Guard, it became more organised and the Exmouth sections started training in infantry tactics.

Jack Sage

'We used to drill at Calhayes Farm on Sunday afternoon's we had a barn there for wet weather drilling. We also did basic small arms drill and training here, but no live firing.'

Edwin Hawker

'Rifle drill was held Sunday at the drill hall. It was at King Street in Honiton, we also used Cotleigh Village hall for some training and lectures.'

NOT TO BE PUBLISHED
The information given in this document is not to be communicated, either directly or indirectly, to the Press or to any person not holding an official position in His Majesty's Service.

26/G.S. Publications/338

HOME GUARD

INSTRUCTION No. 13

DRILL

——
1940
——

Prepared under the direction of
The Chief of the Imperial General Staff.

THE WAR OFFICE,
25th September, 1940.

Home Guard Drill Instructions

Lustleigh Company on parade winter 1941/42

Honiton Company 19th 'Seaton' Battalion 16 May 1943

Carhampton Company Route Marching in Full Kit and great coats

Carhampton (Somerset) Guardsman included in the photograph above are Lionel Besley, George Paskey, Arthur Laramy, Clifford Yeandle, Bill Thrush, Harry Lewis, Harry Simons, Jim Downer and Joe Stephenson.

The Bitterne Platoon (near Southampton in Hampshire can be seen marching smartly up Mousehole Lane, to a Sunday morning church parade. Major Percy Stannard leads the parade, followed by Major Collins, and Captain Jack Wheatle. The platoon members in the photograph include John Hampton, Doug Prudden, Lionel Topp, Percy Sutton, Jack Hasler, Lieutenant W.M. Newman and Sergeant Ron Hawkesworth.

Bitterne Company marching on church parade

Unarmed Combat

Exmouth Home Guard were also given instruction in hand-to-hand fighting from Army Physical Training Corps instructors. The basics were learnt at the Drill Hall and in Manor Gardens. But some exercises even involved training on the sites of bombed houses and in the streets.

Dennis Davey

'The Home Guard trained enthusiastically in the Drill Hall or in the nearby Manor Gardens. We were instructed in the art of hand-to-hand street fighting in some bombed house ruins in the town. We sometimes joined regular troops on the firing ranges and in weekend manoeuvres on Woodbury Common, in fields or on the cliffs. On one occasion, another young private and myself were chosen to guide an Army unit across the cliffs to Budleigh Salterton. It was a nightmare journey in complete darkness staggering through mud and barbed wire, we got there ok, but it was never repeated.'

Close-quarter fighting manuals

Home Guard drill and instruction manuals

Gas Mask Training

Mike Heard

'First you had to apply the de-mister, it was goose-grease or something, in a small tin. With a little spit you rubbed it on to the inside and outside of the lenses with a small cloth, then, you put them on. We used to put it on neat but it didn't work. We tested the gas masks by going into a gas chamber, there was one at the back of the Imperial Road Drill Hall.'

Mk VI service respirator for use with a telephone, with a special vent on the left side of the face

Mike Heard

'They would release tear gas from a cylinder into the room and then after a couple of minutes you'd take your gas mask off and have a couple of sniffs, it made your eyes and nose sting and water and made you cough a bit.'

'The Training Instructors also handed round small phials of mustard and phosgene gas to smell. They would only let you have these for the briefest of time, one sniff and they took your breath away, I'll never forget it!'

'My Father Alfred Heard, was in the 4th Battalion of the Devons in the Great War and then later transferred to the Warwick's. He went over the bags (over the top) on more than one occasion, he was gassed and wounded by shrapnel at Ypres and he had problems with his breathing for years afterwards.'

Dennis Davey

'A year or two after I joined the Home Guard I had my 18 birthday. I was declared to be Grade 4 when I had my army medical, because of my short-sightedness, although I considered my sight to be *normal when wearing glasses, and I was able to fare at least as good as anyone else with target practice on the firing ranges. I wore the usual type of horn rimmed glasses of the period, but I was sent to an optician to have special steel framed glasses made that would fit inside my army respirator when required.'*

The trigger could not be depressed until the gun was held firmly into the shoulder to prevent breakages and dislocation of the shoulder when firing the real weapons.

Small Arms Training

Bill Sleeman

'Although the Home Guard was casual in certain aspects, due to the volunteer status of the men serving in it, it was also disciplined and strict, especially where weapons training and reporting were concerned.'

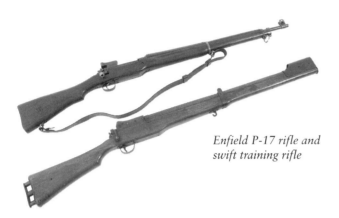

Enfield P-17 rifle and swift training rifle

Live Rifle Firing Practice

All the Exmouth Home Guard units practised live firing of small arms only very occasionally to conserve ammunition. As the war progressed ammunition became more readily available. There were firing ranges set up behind the Southern Railway Station at Littleham, open air ranges at Black Hill Quarry and temporary ranges set up under the cliffs at Orcombe Point on the beach.

Swift training rifle breech, manufactured in 1941

Laurie Butler

'I remember when we went on firing practice on a live range for the first time. I had a Canadian Ross rifle at the time. We had to fire 5 rounds with our rifles on a 100 metre range at the gravel pits at Woodbury Common. I fired the 5 rounds and when the instructor went with me to collect the target, I had a really good grouping and he couldn't believe it was the first time I had fired a rifle, I had previously fired shotguns, but they were very different.'

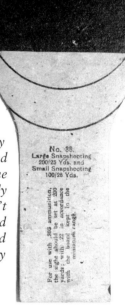

Rifle range .303 or .22 snap-shooting target

Swift rifle sprung butt

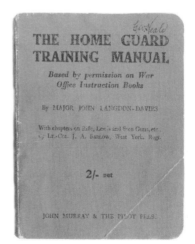

The Home Guard Training Manual

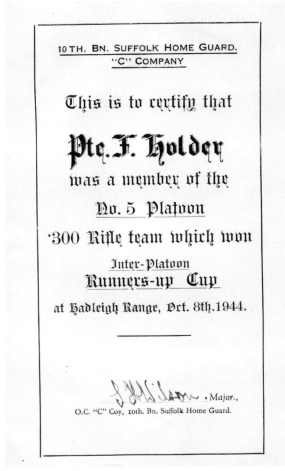

Camouflage and Concealment

Helmet nets were intended to be woven with scraps of hessian sacking, green or brown cloth straps, cotton waste, scrim and anything that could be found with an organic look. Actual foliage was used as well although the training classes suggested that for long term in the field this would needed to be changed daily as it soon died and look different from surrounding foliage.

Camouflage was specialist subject and fundamentals and practice for the Home Guard were developed at Osterley Park Training School near London. There is wartime film footage of men of a Home Guard unit wearing helmet camouflage and face veils ambushing a Valentine tank from extremely close quarters.

A surrealist painter called Roland Penrose was employed by the Government to conceal important factories and establishments from air attack and also teach camouflage and concealment techniques to the newly-formed Home Guard.

William Brett Calbourne Platoon
Isle of White Home Guard

'I was never any good at spit and polish and they used to get me out the front and give me a lacing down. We could lose the regulars when they came to train us, country-wise, we could move through the country and no bugger could see us, but you'd think it was horses going through when they tried it!'

Home made camouflage covers were also made from three yards of string, as shown in the camouflage book. They then had hessian and scrim rags attached to look like woodland plants, or hessian and household junk to look like a bomb-damaged area. For this the

Private E.H. Burley's Certificate of Proficiency for weapons

Woodland

Private F. Holders P-17 rifle shooting competition certificate

Army and Home Guard camouflage training manuals

For concealment in damaged buildings

Guardsmen were instructed to always look for and attach things to the helmet which reflected the material in their surrounding area. Generally speaking this was woodland camouflage, but urban camouflage, including the use of fake brickwork, was also used for hiding in bomb-damaged areas, for protecting against prying eyes and the close scrutiny of binoculars.

Hand Grenade Training

The Home Guard had an official armoury of fourteen different types of grenades and bombs, designed for specific jobs, by the time they stood

STEEL HELMET CONCEALMENT.

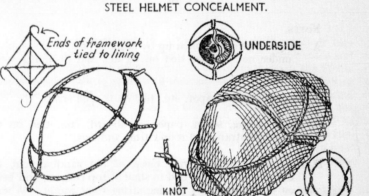

Ends of framework tied to lining

UNDERSIDE

KNOT

OVERHEAD

TWO TYPES OF STRING FRAMEWORK USING 3 YARDS OF STRING, *for use with or without netting.*

For use in BUILT UP AREAS

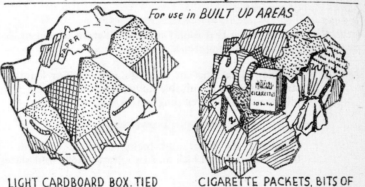

LIGHT CARDBOARD BOX. TIED TO HELMET WITH STRING AND TEXTURED & PAINTED TO SUIT SURROUNDINGS

CIGARETTE PACKETS, BITS OF CARDBOARD, BUNCHED PAPER, SHAVINGS ETC. TIED WITH STRING

THE EYE THROUGH CONSTANT REPETITION RECOGNISES CERTAIN SHAPES AVOID THIS THE SIMPLEST WAY BY BREAKING THE SHAPE & THE OUTLINE

BREAK ALL OUTLINES

HELMET OUTLINE IRREGULAR. BREAK LINE OF FACE BY TYING PIECES OF SCRIM RAG, CARDBOARD OR PAPER TO THE CHIN STRAP AND DARKEN ALL FLESH

FIG. 25.

No. 69 percussion and No. 36 H.E. grenades

(Left) Steel helmet camouflage and concealment techniques

down in 1944. I have only included the types that I know that the interviewees received training on. The metal-cased grenades like the No.36 Mills bomb arrived in cases packed in grease and every one of them had to be de-greased, cleaned and primed prior to use. This was a filthy and unpopular job with the men.

The No. 36. Grenade (H.E.) (The Mills Bomb)

Ray Towill
'We had hand grenade practise with live grenades, this was either at Blackhill Quarry or down on the beach near Orcombe Point. You would pull out the pin and throw it as far as you could and then duck down to, make sure you weren't hit by the fragments.'

Peter Mattholie
'We had a brick walled shelter, we stood behind it threw the grenade over the wall and ducked down behind it until you heard it go off. The sergeant said if you drop it, in the shelter get out quick, or you'll be killed.'

No. 36 Mills bomb

Barry Clarke
'My Dad told me that one day the Home Guard went to Woodbury for hand grenade training. Monty Richards a local newsagent and friend of Dad's were responsible for loading the live Mills bombs on the bus. The detonators were stored separately and so he wouldn't forget them and to keep them safe and save time later, he pushed the detonators into the holes on the base of the Mills Bombs. During the rickety-ride they could hear them rolling about in the luggage compartment of the bus luckily none of them detonated. The Sergeant had a fit when he opened the boot and saw the grenades primed and ready for use.'

Fuse priming cap

Ken Parker
'We went for hand grenade training on Woodbury Common occasionally, first learning how to throw dud training grenades, then we had a chance to throw a live one. It felt great to hear it explode. We also did training with an E.Y. cup discharger. It clamped to the end of the rifle and was used for launching grenades, using powerful blanks called ballastite charges.'

The E.Y. Cup Discharger (Rifle Grenade Projector)

This device was designed by Edward Yule; it could be fastened on to the end of the barrel on a rifle. It was just the right size to take a No. 36 Mills bomb with its pin removed and the handle still in position. A 'Ballastite', extra powerful blank round was put into the chamber of the rifle and then fired, which launched the grenade and allowed the handle to flick off and arm the grenade as it left the cup and was effective from 80-200 Metres.

Because of the extra blast caused by the ballastite charge and to also facilitate gripping the rifle whilst holding against the ground, coarse string was wrapped tightly around the fore-stock and the butt of the rifle and this can sometimes be seen on training photographs.

Edwin Hawker
'We had No. 36 Mills bomb training at a place near the Round Hill rifle ranges. We also used the E.Y. cup discharger to launch the hand grenades. We had to tie string round the stock and barrel of the rifle really tightly, this helped to strengthen it and also provided more grip especially in the wet. It fired the bomb about 100–150yds. We laid down and pushed the butt of the gun into the ground and then fired it.'

'We used powerful blank cartridges to fire the bombs and we had to prime the bombs with 8 second fuses instead of the ordinary 3 second fuses.'

Army hand grenade training pamphlet

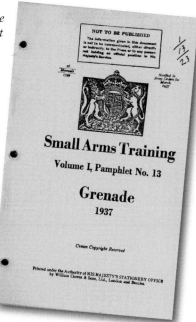

The No. 74 S.T. Grenade (Sticky Bomb)

The basic design for this bomb was thought up by Millis Jeffris the Head of M.I.R.(c). (Military Intelligence Research. Section C.) It consisted of a glass flask (later plastic), about the size of a grapefruit, which was filled with nitro glycerine based, high explosive mixture. This was attached to a bakelite handle which contained a safety pin, a spring loaded handle which operated a firing pin and a time delayed detonator. The whole device was then coated in a material 'sock' impregnated with a strong adhesive mixture. The

The No. 74 Mk II S.T. grenade or 'Sticky Bomb' with Cover and Adhesive Removed

whole device was encased in an outer aluminium sphere. In use the outer casing would be removed and shaken off, the safety pin removed and thrown, which in turn set off the firing pin. The bomb could also be stuck to a slow moving vehicle. After teething troubles these items became a reasonably good and reliable weapon.

Warning Label attached to the S.T. Grenade

Plane Spotting

Mike Heard spent a lot of time at the Battery Observation Post and had to be able to recognise German and Allied aircraft quickly and correctly, in case of attack. At the age of 83 years old, I showed Mike 20 images of German, British and American aircraft all in black and white. Initially I chose aircraft that I thought he would have been seen over the skies of Exmouth in the raids, Focke Wulf 190-A4, Messerschmitt BF109 F2, Dornier 217, Junkers JU88, Supermarine Spitfire, and Boulton Paul Defiant. Needless to say he got them all right.

Sergeant Bob Parsons of the 6 Battalion Sussex Home Guard prepares a lecture on aircraft recognition

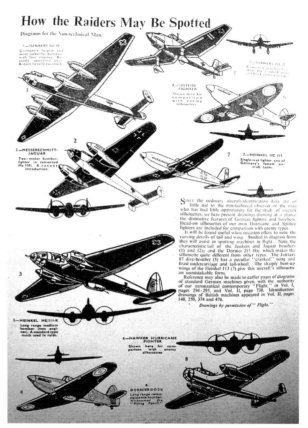

Plane-spotting chart for the L.D.V. published in The War Illustrated *in June 1940*

Commercially available aircraft recognition book

The Observation Post 'Fox Four' on Orcombe Point, was manned originally by the Home Guard; it was later taken over by the Observer Corps.

On Thursday June 17 silhouettes of German troop transports and gliders were published in Local Newspapers all over Britain to help the L.D.V. and General Public, to identify enemy planes.

Roy Marshall

'One day we at Orcombe point watching the Home Guard training. They had an aircraft flying along the seafront towing a drogue, or target behind it. The Home Guard were firing at it using machine guns. They let us stand around and watch them for quite a while, which surprised us.'

Men of Higher Bockhampton (Dorset) Home Guard with stretcher

First Aid Training

Most men only received basic training and instruction as stretcher bearers which included forging a river with a stretcher using four men.

The men in the photograph above may possibly be a first aid squad as they have a stretcher leaning against the hedge behind them.

Left to Right Back Row Alfie Parsons, Charlie Miller.
Left to Right Front Row Walt Hyde, Archie Watts, ?

Signals and Communication

People with a working knowledge of radio equipment were encouraged to join the Home Guard, operating at first the field telephones and Morse-keys of these systems and later military radio sets as and when they became available.

White and Blue signals armbands were worn by all signallers and dispatch riders.

Early Signalling

Electronic equipment and field telephones were in incredibly short supply, but did gradually appear later in the war. Semaphore lessons, Signalling with lamps, heliograph and pigeons were also included in the training of the Signals Section.

The National Pigeon Service and the Home Guard

Due to the shortage of radio sets which had the capacity to receive and transmit, also compounded by the unreliability of some of these sets, pigeons were also used. It was also known that if the Germans did invade they would cut the telecommunications systems to larger towns and cities, to prevent reinforcements arriving. The National Pigeon Service was formed to ensure there was a simple alternative to long-distance communication. Initially it desperately needed people to give up their racing birds for the service of the country and adverts for birds and help went out to local newspapers all over the country. It was also decided to set up regional homing pigeon lofts run by the National Pigeon Service members who had become members of the Home Guard. Most Home Guard units in Britain had access to the National Pigeon Service.

Exercises With the Regulars

Winston Churchill had declared himself, that 'The Armed Forces should be, up to concert pitch' by 1st September 1941, this included the Home Guard.

Peter Mattholie

'We went on exercise regularly, with our platoon. We went to Keston fish ponds, where we used to pretend we trained as though we were being invaded by the enemy. Another Home Guard unit would attack us and we would defend our positions. The officers would referee the exercises. All the exercises that I went on were at night time in the black out. We had to fit two headlamp covers on the van which had small slits to let on a little of the light out. It was very difficult driving when it was a really dark night.'

Jack Sage

'One day we had an exercise which was an attack on Sharcombe Farm. We had bad remarks from an adjudicating army officer who said it was like 'holiday makers on Brighton beach!' Later in the day this officers vehicle was found not immobilised, which was the rule for the time as it could then not be used by the enemy. On the way home the Luppitt Home Guard immobilised it for him, by removing the rotor arm and throwing it into the hedge.'

In 1942 war games between Regular Army Units, the Home Guard (some dressed in German uniforms), Civil Defence units and the Red Cross, were held at Wembley Stadium. The games were watched by Herbert Morrison and other members of the British Cabinet, who were also treated to mock air raids and casualty evacuation scenarios.

Edwin Hawker

'We acted as the enemy in training exercises with the army. They army officers were very concerned about Seaton because Seaton beach had deep water. They had 3 sets of concrete tank traps and many pill boxes situated on the river Axe some were camouflaged to look like houses.'

Mike Heard

'The funniest thing that happened to us was when we were at the Drill Hall (Imperial Road) We lined up for parade in front of the drill hall (not funny at the time of inspection) John Street, a friend of mine who was a Lance Corporal, had a thunder flash in his hand as we were about to go out on exercise. The man behind him lit the fuse and it went off in his hand most of us thought a bomb had dropped! We jumped out of our

skins. The man who lit it was demoted, there really wasn't a lot more they could do about it as we were all volunteers. When we got together over the years it always made us laugh thinking about it.'

A series of training exercises with regular troops was set up in and around the Exmouth area intended to 'evaluate' the state of readiness of the Home Guard.

They joined in combined exercises and night manoeuvres in fields or on the cliffs at Orcombe point, inter-unit firing exercises, on the live firing ranges at Blackhill Quarry and weekend manoeuvres with the regular Army and The Royal Marines, on Woodbury Common. The exercises included men hiding in bushes on arterial roads into the town to surprise the regulars with mock ambushes and delaying tactics, blocking roads, dealing with casualties and fighting tanks. Military umpires and technicians observed the exercises at every stage, making notes on the success of the operations and how they could be improved.

Bernard Greenaway

'The Home Guard participated in military exercises against the Royal Marines. The Home Guard would defend and the Marines would be the attackers. The Home Guard would form defensive road blocks across the road using oil drums filled with concrete to prevent tanks and other vehicles from coming up the road.'

Ken Parker

'Occasionally we would have to pretend to be the enemy and defend the top of the cliffs at Orcombe point. The American Rangers would then climb the cliffs using ropes and ladders. They were training for the D-Day landings but we didn't know this at the time.'

On Thursday July 30 1941 the Exmouth Company were involved in a training exercise with regular troops. The regular army troops were the attackers and the Home Guard took up defensive positions. Amongst other vehicles the army were equipped with Valentine tanks and broke through some of the Exmouth road blocks at speed. The Devon tall hedgerows rows made excellent defensive positions and camouflaged and concealed Home Guard units ambushed the attacking troops, using bags of French chalk to mark the vehicles as if they had been hit by hand grenades or petrol bombs. The Exmouth Company gave a very good account of itself during these war games and a long report congratulating them was published in the *Exmouth Chronicle* newspaper of Saturday 2 August 1942. Tensions were running very high at the time as an invasion was expected at any moment. On the day of the exercises Winston Churchill had given his famous 'Concert Pitch' speech.

A comment from the well known commander of the opposing forces of the regular Army said:

'*What we have seen today gives us confidence that the Home Guard is capable of dealing with any invading force that may be brought against them.*'

They were trained to initiate engagements with the enemy at a range of less than one hundred yards, using camouflage and concealment until the last minute. This was intended to give them the edge over their aggressors. It must be remembered that a lot of their sub-artillery weapons only had a very limited range and so they were always trained for defensive close combat engagements. Of particular note was their knowledge of defence-in-depth practises for which they were highly commended.

This report was published in the *Exmouth Journal* in1943.

'*An enemy tank unit crashed through a road block at one location at around 40 miles and hour catching the Home Guard by surprise but it was eventually overcome, when it ran into another surprise anti-tank measure a little way up the road.*'

A lot of the men involved in this Home Guard exercise were veterans of the 1914-18 war and were obviously well in tune by the time of the exercises.

Harts buses from Budleigh Salterton were hired to take the Home Guard to Woodbury Common for the manoeuvres with the regular troops.

On the nights of the Exeter Blitz Sunday 3 and Monday 4 May 1942 the Royal Marines based at Dalditch Common, held a mock invasion exercise, where they attacked Exmouth. The 2 Clyst battalion platoons acted as the defenders in this extremely life like exercise, complete with the constant drone of German aircraft flying overhead and the sky above Exeter burning a bright red.

Ray Towill
'*I went on an exercise to Woodbury Castle with the Home Guard; we had to hold a position which was being attacked by the Royal Marines and another platoon of Home Guard. Someone brought big tins of hot food up to feed the troops and the smells came wafting across to us. We were cold, hungry and fed up, so me and my friend just said that we had been captured and were sent back to the field kitchen at Woodbury Castle. The food was lovely we didn't see one of the enemy.*'

Men of the regular army and Looe Home Guard in Cornwall muster for an exercise on the Looe to Polperro Road

Jack Sage
'*The Government originally wanted to build the Home Defence units only, which were set up to defend the villages but later introduced secondary 'battle patrols' which were manned mainly by the younger men who would later go on to join the armed forces These men trained in the attacking role rather than the defensive role and thus provided a good grounding for the army.*'

'*Sometimes we had full-blown exercises, such as attacks on Windsor Copse which was supposed to be against enemy parachutists.*'

'*The town was divided into two sections later in the war. The Luppitt platoon grew too fast so that's why it was split in two and why there were six sergeants. In all when at its full strength, we had a total of 64 men.*'

'*My section was based in the village and this was referred to as the 'Home' base, we used the church tower as a look out post, as it gave a good all round view of the area.*'

'*The other section known as the 'Battle Platoon' was based at the Beacon an area just outside Luppitt village. It was under the command of C.S.M. Hooper.*'

Jack Sage
'*There was a big exercise all over Devon called Exercise Raleigh. It was a 24 hour exercise and also involved Somerset too. The exercise was very carefully planned; as far as I was concerned nothing much happened but I heard afterwards the General in charge of the exercise was overlooking (adjudicating) and was coming from Honiton to Langford Bridge when he saw a lot of vehicles parked by the roadside. He went to the Beacon to inform the Battle Patrol. The Sergeant sent out a recce party and checked out the vehicles that night. They crept along and got to the other side of the hedge, where they made up mud balls and threw them over the hedge at the vehicles. The soldiers with the vehicles didn't realise they were hiding in the bushes. If they had been using grenades they would have all been killed.*'

Reg Warr

'A never-to-be-forgotten experience was when the regular army from Salisbury plain had a 24-Hour manoeuvre one weekend, beginning from the Somerset /Dorset borders and on into Wiltshire, to test the Home Guard defences. For several days prior to the starting time of 12 noon on Saturday, hundreds of army vehicles and equipment travelled down the A30 before the attack began, causing some trepidation to the villagers! Could the valiant platoon fight off such odds?'

'We heard army vehicles moving in Crewkerne and the Chinnocks, but nothing came up Coker Hill Road. It was a long night. We had men in slit trenches along the top of the high banks by the bridge; there was no undergrowth on the banks then. Suddenly at 8.a.m. an army Bren gun carrier came roaring up over the hill towards us, obviously speeding up to get between the defile between the two banks. No live ammunition was allowed, but we had been given paper bags full of white flour to be thrown at the vehicles and if a hit was recorded by the referees, he we disqualify that vehicle before it could move on again. With venom, bags of flour rained down on the carrier, but corporal Freddie Strong, the village butcher had wrapped half a brick in a paper bag and his lucky shot hit the driver of the three man crew square on the head! Bren gun carriers had open tops. Fortunately, the driver was wearing a steel helmet but he lost control and steered into the bank, almost turning the carrier over.'

'The irate referee told Captain Booth, our commander in no uncertain terms that we were not allowed to throw bricks at the army! But it cheered us all up! We learned that the carrier crew had sent a wireless message to the oncoming troops to detour round West Coker and not face the local savages.'

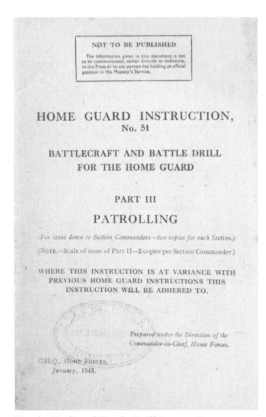

Battle Craft and Battle Drill Instructions

The Home Guard Victory Book

Chapter 11
The Volunteers

This chapter records the names (in **bold**) of those who served during the war and who were either directly interviewed by the author, or whose friends and relatives provided information (or where information and photographs were otherwise sourced), along with extracts from the interviews themselves. I hope I have represented these people in a way in which their services to Great Britain will be remembered in a realistic and positive light, which reflects well on the Home Guard, the Women's Home Guard Auxiliary and Auxiliary Unit members everywhere.

Laurie Butler

'The programme "Dad's Army" was not representative of life in the Home Guard at all; it was good entertainment, but they didn't really represent the Home Guard responsibilities very fairly. They didn't have the right equipment in the T.V. programmes, using any old pouches and equipment, which was a shame. Some of the weapons were fair enough. To a certain extent, the characters were doing similar jobs to the people I was in the Home Guard with. Some elements of the character 'Pike' was similar to my own situation, as I was so young, but the responsibilities and training that we had was by no means a joke.'

The following people were interviewed, or information was passed on to me by relatives and friends.

Private Donald Bradford. Exmouth Company 2 Clyst Battalion Devonshire Home Guard. From interviews with his sister Hazel Rowsell.

Hazel Rowsell

'My brother Donald Bradford joined the Home Guard when he was 17 years old. One of Donald's best friends was Mike Heard, they used to be seen around together a lot. The Home Guard's meetings were held at the Imperial Road Drill Hall.

'Donald's platoon went on patrols which were mostly at night. They used to patrol along the sea front and over the cliffs; the beach itself was cut off by barbed wire.'

Private William Brett. Calbourne Platoon Isle of White Home Guard. From the Halsgrove publication *The Book of Calbourne*.

Corporal Laurie Butler. Exmouth Company 2 Clyst Battalion Devonshire Home Guard. From Interview.

Donald Bradford

Laurie Butler

Laurie Butler and the Barbary Ape

'The ape was smuggled in to the U.K. by a sailor or Royal Marine, it came back from Gibraltar when it was a baby. It was kept for many years as a pet, but that's all I know about where it came from. For some time It was kept in the back garden of a house in Camperdown Terrace, it was number 12 I think, opposite our shop Butler & Son, a general stores, which was number 13. The ape was about the size of an Alsatian dog and lived in a hut with bars on the windows in the long back garden.'

'It got away once and ended up in the ladies toilet of the Beach Hotel and it was pretty bad tempered at the best of times and quite big, someone eventually managed to get it back to its hut.'

'I was about 15-16 at the time and having my lunch at home. My father was tending the shop when, Mrs. Panell the mother of the son who owned the ape ran into the shop, she had a badly wounded arm and was screaming, that she had been attacked by the ape, everyone was panicking.'

'I was called out and took her back to her kitchen, attended her badly torn arm, it was really badly injured. I wrapped it with a roller towel. By this time someone else had arrived, and had said 'This is a very bad wound, she needs to go to the hospital right away, to get it dressed.' All she was worried about was the ape attacking someone else and was anxious that it may attack schoolchildren going back to school after lunch.'

'I said to her, "Shall I put it down?" And she said, "Yes please, please do!" So I asked her again, "Are you sure?, shall I put it down?" She said, "Yes." Mrs Panell was then taken to Exmouth Hospital by ambulance.'

'I went back home and I went to the cupboard under the stairs, to fetch my Sten gun. I took the gun and a charged magazine and went to look for the ape in the back garden. I couldn't see the animal at this point and no one knew where it had gone.'

'When I did spot it, it saw me and jumped up on the wall and started coming towards me. It was bareing its teeth and looked very vicious. I immediately loaded the mag into the Sten gun, set it on single shot, took aim and fired one shot. This brought it down off the wall. I then went up the garden to check if it was dead and then shot it through the head to make sure it was.'

'I was concerned about the ape hurting people, but afterwards I was most concerned about firing the two rounds of ammunition as I was accountable for the ammunition used. I told one of the Sergeants in charge what I had done, but nobody said any more about it.'

'Mrs. Panell, who had gone to the hospital for treatment, passed away soon after from blood poisoning and shock.'

'Over the years the story has been told around Exmouth and as you would imagine gets distorted as time goes on, but that is what happened.'

Eric Burley. 'B' Company 60 'Woodside' Battalion Surrey Home Guard. From Halsgrove publication *The book of Addiscombe*.

Dennis Davey. Exmouth Company 2 'Clyst' Battalion Devonshire Home Guard. From relatives friends, more information is published on the B.B.C. People's War website

Private Bert Clarke. Exmouth Company 2 'Clyst' Battalion Devonshire Home Guard. Interview with his son Barry.

Ninkey Coe. Women's Home Guard Auxiliary, Derby. The quotes are published on the B.B.C. People's War website.

Sergeant Ron Coleman. 10 'Torbay' Battalion Devon Home Guard. Information from his friends at Brixham Battery.

Ron Coleman

Private Harold Cooper. 'C' Company 10 Battalion Suffolk Home Guard From Halsgrove publications.

Private Rupert Cooper. 'C' Coy 10 Battalion Suffolk Home Guard. From Halsgrove publications.

Peter Gardner. Dunsford and Christow L.D.V. Later part of 14 'Moorland' Battalion Devon Home Guard. From Interview.

Company Sergeant Major Charlie Havill. Exmouth Company 2 'Clyst' Battalion Devon Home Guard From ex members of the Home Guard and friends.

C.S.M. Charlie Havill

Mike Heard
'Charlie Havill Company Sergeant Major he was well loved, he used to tell us his memories of the Great War and was very nostalgic about it. He and Dad (Alfred Heard) were in the 1st Battalion of Devon's they went over the bags at Ypres where Dad was gassed and wounded.'

Hazel Rowsell
'Charlie Havill was a cobbler, he had a little shop down one of the small lanes off Chapel Street. He was a very pleasant man, he lived on Exeter Road, with his wife and had a son called Barry. He was a popular man and every one used his shoe repair business, he was also in the Exmouth Home Guard and had quite an important role.'

Private Edwin Hawker. C 'Cottleigh' Company 19 Seaton Battalion Devonshire Home Guard. From Interview.

Edwin Hawker druing the war

Edwin Hawker at the time of writing

Authors note about Edwin Hawker
'Steve Parson's introduced me to Edwin. The three of us spent about 4 hours at Edwin's Home talking about his time in the Home Guard. Although Edwin had a stroke several years ago which affected his speech,

through practise he has improved his powers of communication a great deal.'

'Edwin's main reason for wanting to talk to me was to make sure that his Home Guard friends lives weren't forgotten forever. He had made notes of their names over the years and also had some of his original equipment. He has a great sense of humour. Steve Parsons helped Edwin fill out his forms to apply for the Defence Medal whilst we were there as he had never claimed it.'

Gunner Mike Heard. 477 Coastal Artillery Battery Home Guard R.A. From Interview.

Mike Heard

Rene Lewis
'The Home Guard were all ages, but I only knew the younger ones Mike Heard was one of my favourites; a lovely fellow he was about 18 at the time and a boat builder down at Exmouth Docks. He was always seen in the company of Johnno Street, they were always together laughing and joking, they also knew my cousin Florence Tucker and were great friends of hers.'

Arthur Cook
'I interviewed Mike at several interviews and he had a fantastic sense of humour and an incredible power of recall.'

'Unfortunately Mike passed away whilst I was writing this book. I really enjoyed his company for the short time I knew him and to me he summarises the "spirit" of the Home Guard during WW II.'

'Because of his carpentry skills and his indentures, this afforded him "Reserve Occupation" status, which meant that even though he had volunteered and had signed up for the Royal Navy, they refused his application'.

'He volunteered for the Home Guard and joined in 1941 when he was 17 years old. He chose the 477 Coastal Artillery Battery, as it was newly formed and directed by the Royal Artillery.'

'Mike was on duty with the Home Guard three times a week, working 4 hour shifts on Tuesday nights, Thursday nights and Sunday mornings, each shift was 3 hours. His training specialised in gunnery and searchlight operating as well as all his basic training and small arms drill etc. In addition to this he was also called out for special duties, when invasion alerts, cordons for U.X.B's, Manoeuvres or other emergencies were on. Mike had also volunteered for the lifeboat as a "Launcher" to get the boat from the Lifeboat Station across the road and into the sea in emergencies and said that he was "always busy" and that there was "always something to do."'

Private Les Ives. Addiscombe Platoon Home Guard. From Halsgrove publication *The Book of Addiscombe.*

Les Ives
'The Home Guard did have a serious role to play in the defence of this country. It was not at all like "Dad's Army". We had all-night guard duties to perform. Remember we all had to go to work the next day. There was also night and weekend training. The Home Guard also gave help and assistance to the Civil Defence and Police. The Home Guard took their duties very seriously and believed in what they were doing and what they could achieve if asked. For myself I still keep my cap badge with pride.'

Cyril Jackson. Land's End Company 12 Battalion Cornwall Home Guard. From Halsgrove Publication the Book of Looe.

Sergeant Harry Lawes. Exmouth Company 2 'Clyst' Battalion Devonshire Home Guard. (From relatives and friends.

Bombadier Harry Long. 477 Coastal Artillery Battery Home Guard R.A. From Son Chris Long, Relatives and friends.

Harry Long with Sisters Nancy and Dorothy

Private Harry Marshall. 3 Platoon 'Exmouth' Company 2 Clyst Battalion Devon Home Guard. From Interview with son Roy Marshall.

Harry Marshall

Private **Peter Mattholie.** 58 Battalion 'Bromley' Kent Home Guard. From Interview.

Peter Mattholie

'When I was in the Home Guard my job was a van driver's boy, picking up stuff in the blitzed areas of Bromley. Sometimes it was very hard to get around as there was so much destruction.'

C.Q.M.S Tony Mc Larin

Lieutenant J.H. May. 5 'Bideford' Battalion Devon Home Guard. From his personal documents held in Barnstaple Records Library.

Company Quartermaster Master Sergeant Tony Mc. Larin. 'Exmouth' Company 2 Clyst Battalion Devon Home Guard. Information from ex members of the Home Guard and friends.

Mike Heard

'When local tradesmen were short of money and knowing times were hard, he would just say "Take the stuff and pay me when you can" and usually people did pay up. The shop was known quietly as, the most untidy shop in Exmouth. When you walked in there, there was no sense to anything, there was stuff everywhere! But you could nearly always be guaranteed that whatever it, Was, you could get it there.'

'Tony Mc Larin did a very good job as the C.Q.M.S. and we always had what we wanted, as soon as he could get it, the War allowing!'

Peter Mattholie

Private Ken Parker. Exmouth Company 2 "Clyst" Battalion Devonshire Home Guard. From Interviews.

Sergeant Bob Parsons. 6 'Bognor Regis' Battalion Sussex Home Guard. From his grandson Dave Parsons.

Sergeant John 'Jack' Sage during the war

Sergeant Bob Parsons

Private Les Pike. Exmouth Company 2 'Clyst' Battalion Devonshire Home Guard. From Interviews with son Ivor Pike.

Sergeant John 'Jack' Sage. D 'Luppitt' Company 19 'Seaton' Battalion Devonshire Home Guard. From Interview.

Jack Sage

'Life in the Home Guard was very instructive and we were good friends, it was very community spirited. I missed being at home sometimes especially when it was cold and miserable weather and

John Sage

Sergeant John 'Jack' Sage at the time of writing

it had the disadvantage of leaving your wife and families out of it, We were scared of talking to anyone for a time about what we did and where we went, as we didn't know who the enemy was, due to the invasion scare.'

Bill Sleeman

Private Bill Sleeman. Exmouth Company 2 'Clyst' Battalion Devonshire Home Guard. From Interviews.

Authors Note

'Bill Sleeman was a well known Exmothian and brilliant historian. His family have owned popular quality tailoring business in Exmouth for over 100 years. The business was started by his father in 1907 and still continues under family ownership to this day.'

'Unfortunately Bill passed away when this book was being written, so although he had a chance to see what his own entries and inclusions would entail, in our meetings at his shop, he didn't get the chance to see it in context with the whole body of work which is a great shame, because he clearly had very fond memories of his time in the Home Guard.'

'Bill was typical of the sort of man the volunteered for the Home Guard. He was 17 years old and described himself as 'A founder member of the Exmouth Home Guard' of which he was deservedly proud.'

Private Ray Towill. 4 Platoon 'Exmouth' Company 2 'Clyst' Battalion Devonshire Home Guard. From Interviews.

Ray Towill

Reg Warr. West Coker Platoon Somerset Home Guard. From Halsgrove publication *The Book of West Coker.*

The photograph below shows newly married Guardsman Dick Weaver of Leigh Platoon and his wife

A Home Guard wedding

Willand Company at Stand Down December 1944

Bampton Platoon march down Luke Street to Church Parade 1944

Louise Anne Burrows Walking through an Arch of Enfield P-17 rifles held aloft by a Home Guard guard of honour. The church is St Edburga's, and the photo was taken in Leigh in 1941.

Information from Private Stan Webber Carhampton Platoon, rom Halsgrove publication *The Book of Carhampton*.

The Junior Home Guard (non-offical Units)

Boys evacuated to Hemyock during WWII formed their own junior Home Guard Unit. This was not unusual as in most parts of Britain the youngsters

The Hemyock Boys Junior Home Guard

Influenced by their adult role models, the Royal St Omer Close Corps ready to defend Mulbarton circa 1941

worshipped the Home Guard, partly because their fathers, uncles and older brothers were in the local units, and partly because the men of the Home Guard encouraged the boys by showing them equipment and tactics they used themselves.

In Hemyock's case the boys were evacuees and the local unit commanded by Captain Cubitt and Lieutenant Lowry encouraged the boys to take an interest in the Home Guard, as their fathers were elsewhere. Hemyock Home Guard's H.Q. was at the milk factory and a lot of the men from the unit came from the depot. It was expected that most boys would go on to join the Army Cadet Force before the Home Guard and so the idea was to catch their interest early.

Some Guardsmen even held aircraft spotting classes and marching drill for the young recruits and also the locally formed Army Cadets, who fell under the responsibility of the Home Guard Units.

This photograph from the Bill Alborough Collection, shows boys living in St Omers Close, Mulbarton during WWII who formed their own Junior Home Guard unit. Some of the boys borrowed items from their fathers and other boys made their own from whatever was available.

From Left to Right Back Row Bill Alborough, Donny Abendroth, Peter Haverson, Rex Mickle Burgh.

Middle Row Left to Right John Tuddenham, Chris Mickleburgh, Barry Dent, Dennis Mickleburgh.

Front Row Left to Right Bernard Rayner, Colin Spoor, Bryant Mickleburgh, Lionell Robinson.

These boys played at being soldiers during WWII, emulating the roles, previously adopted in real life, of their fathers and in some cases grandfathers. They spent many long hours aircraft spotting, creeping about in the undergrowth and along ditches to attack the 'Rosery', and once even daring to attack nearby Flordon. The 'tin hats' were really made of tin and because the edges weren't crimped over they were sharp. Mothers dutifully taped the edges of the helmets to make sure their little soldiers would not be injured.

When Italian prisoners of war started to arrive in England after their defeat in the Western Desert the

Happy times! Exmouth N.C.O.s relax at Orcombe Point

boys would spend many happy times talking to them as they worked on the land.

Mascots

Mascots were also adopted by some Home Guard units and these boys would march with the Home Guard on parade. Hamleys, the London toy shop, even stocked miniature Home Guard uniforms, until the bite of rationing made it impossible to keep up the supply. Many youngsters had small uniforms made for them out of scraps of cloth by their mothers, aunties and sisters, Ironically in the early war period toy steel helmets were readily available as the photograph shows and some of the young L.D.V. and Home Guard mascots obtained their helmets and uniforms before the men.

Chapter 12
Duties

In the event of a full-scale invasion Home Guard battalions would come under the regional commands of the regular army. In November 1941 conscription was introduced for the Home Guard and it was also decided that, by adopting the regular army structure and ranking system, it would be simpler to implement the joining of the forces together as a cohesive fighting force if an instantaneous response to the threat of enemy invasion was needed.

Jack Sage

'At Luppitt the 4a.m. early-morning patrols were organised by our vicar, Rev. B.A. Finn. Two men were detailed to patrol the Luppitt Common area and to be on the lookout for possible enemy parachute landings. There were similar patrols at Hartridge Common.'

On 16 February 1942, although the threat of a full-scale German invasion was generally considered to be lessened, compulsory enlistment became law for specific categories of men. This applied mainly to the younger men at the age of 17. It was considered that the Home Guard would prove an excellent introduction to the regular armed forces and ensured a year's basic experience prior to their 18th birthday.

The new Home Guard conscripts would have to attend at least 24 hours of training every four weeks, plus watches and patrols. Around this time it was also decided nationally to adopt the army-style of rank system and chain of command, intended to make, liaisons and training exercises easier to administer.

Expenses claims of 2 shillings a night were also introduced to cover basic essentials and food.

Mike Heard

'My Home Guard duties were three times a week, Tuesday night, Thursday night and Sunday mornings. We went on patrol along the seafront in four hour stints usually We trained in gunnery on Sundays and I was allocated searchlight no 1.'

Orders

The Home Guard orders were published weekly in the *Exmouth Chronicle* and the *Exmouth Journal* newspapers.

Here is a typical example of a week's training orders for the, Exmouth Home Guard taken from the *Exmouth Chronicle* Saturday 22 July 1944. This would have been typical for most Home Guard companies in Britain at the time.

Home Guard Orders Exmouth Company
Week Commencing 24 July 1944.

Monday, 24.— Detail No.4 Platoon, Blackhill ranges, 19.30 hours.

Tuesday, 25.— Detail No.3 Platoon, Blackhill ranges, 19.30 hours.

Wednesday, 26.— Detail No.1 Platoon, Blackhill ranges, 19.30 hours.

Sunday, 30. — Proficiency test, Drill Hall, 10.00 hours.

No.1 Platoon, Blackhill ranges, leave Drill Hall 10.00 hours.

No.2 Platoon, field training, Lympstone, 10.30 hours.

No.3 Platoon, E.Y. rifle practise, Maer Farm, 10.30 hours.

Remainder under platoon arrangements.

No. 4 Platoon, field training, R.O.C. Post, 10.30 hours.

Here is a typical duty roster for the Exmouth Company Sergeants, each covering one day a week.

Orderly Sergeants Duty Roster for the week
beginning 9 August 1943

Sunday 9 August	Sergeant. A.W. N. Gorfin.
Monday 10 August	Sergeant. F. A. Troulan.
Tuesday 11 August	Sergeant. R. Challis.
Wednesday 12 August	Sergeant. A. E. D. Pollard.
Thursday. 13 August	Sergeant. W. J. H. Clements.
Friday 14 August	Sergeant. C. Tindall.
Saturday 15 August	Sergeant. T. E. Mathews.

'On Guard!' Exmouth Beacon 1941

Guard Duty and Patrols

Hazel Rowsell

'The Home Guard had a tent erected on the Beacon, outside the Royal Beacon Hotel; they used it as a lookout to keep watch over the mouth of the river.'

Patrols were carried out in the pitch black, over cliff tops and mostly over rough ground, defended by rolls of barbed wire. It was only permissible to use a torch in an emergency, because of the blackout and also because torch batteries were very hard to come by.

Mike Heard

'Gunners were constantly tripping and stumbling due to the black out, and on cloudy nights it was as black as the inside of a cow! When we arrived at the turning point the Budleigh patrol took over, covering the area from Budleigh Salterton to Sidmouth. The winter patrols were so cold, it was unbearable. On the very coldest nights we put on our gas masks, it kept our faces warm, but you couldn't see bugger-all when you had them on.'

He laughed and said.

'...and the de-mister grease for the glass only made it worse!'

Mike has similar recollections of the patrols as Bill Sleeman. Bill's patrol route was slightly different to the other two Home Guard platoons in the area. His route covered from the pier opposite the end of Victoria Road where it meets the Esplanade to the outskirts of Budleigh Salterton.

Fighting Patrol training manuals

The Elmsett (Suffolk) Home Guard platoon met outside the Rose and Crown pub on Sunday mornings and on weekday evenings. During the winter months they met at the Reading Room. The first leader of the unit was Alf Pearl, and later Stan Roxborough took over. They used the rifle range at Chelsworth where they held competitions. For gas mask training they were sent to Raydon.

Rupert Cooper

'We were based at the rectory (Elmsett) and I used to go round with a chap called Jack Malster, nick-named "Bodger". We worked in pairs. We had our rifles

HOME GUARD ORDERS

Exmouth Company

Week com. Monday, Sept. 28th

Monday, 28th September— No. 4 Platoon, drill and weapon training, Imperial-road Drill Hall 19.30 hours.

Tuesday, 29th September.— (a) No. 2 Platoon, patrols, Lympstone, 19.45 hours. (b) No. 3 Platoon, Spigot Mortar training, Imperial-rd. Drill Hall, 19.30 hours. Remainder, patrols, No. 1 Section R.V., Bradham Lane, Withycombe 19.45 hours. Dress, Steel Helmets and Rifles. No. 2 and 3 Sections R.V., Holly Tree Inn, Withycombe 20.00 hours. Patrol Dress and Rifles. (c) Littleham Section patrols, Littleham, 19.30 hours.

Thursday, 1st October.— Stretcher Bearers, No. 1 and Platoons, Bastin Hall, 19.30 hours. No. 1 Platoon, Conference Exercise of 20th Sept., Imperial road Drill Hall, 19.30 hours.

Friday, 2nd October.—(a) No. 4 Platoon as for 28th September. (b) Littleham Section, patrols, Littleham, 19.30 hours.

Sunday, October 4th.—(a) No. 1 Platoon, Field Training, Maer Farm, 10.30 hours. (b) No. 2 Platoon, Field Training, Lympstone, 10.30 hours. (c) No. 4 Platoon, Blackhill Ranges, 10.00 hours.

HOME GUARD ORDER

Exmouth Oompany

Week Oommencing April 26t

Tuesday, April 27th.—No. 2 Platoon, weapon training, Lympstone, 1945 hours. No. 3 Platoon, weapon training, Imperial-road Drill Hall, 1930 hours. Littleham Section, field training, Littleham, 1900 hours.

Thursday, April 29th.—No. 1 Platoon, No. 1 Section, Cricket Field. Remainder Imperial-road Drill Hall, 1930 hours.

Friday, April 30th.—No. 6 Platoon, drill and weapon training, Imperial-road Drill Hall, 1930 hours.

Sunday, May 2nd.—No. 1 Platoon, field training, Maer Farm. M.G.s, Imperial-road Drill Hall, 1930 hours. No. 2 Platoon, field training, Lympstone, 1030 hours. No. 3 Platoon, Vickers M.G.s, Harbour View. Remainder manning, 1030 hours. No. 4 Platoon, Blackhill Ranges, less Vickers M.G.s, at Harbour View, 10.30 hours. No. 6 Platoon, drill and weapon training, Cricket Field, 10.30 hours.

HOME GUARD FINED

ABSENT FROM PARADES

Before Mr. W. E. Dean (in the chair), at Exmouth Sessions, on Monday, Pte. E. L. Bridle, of 38, New-street, Exmouth, pleaded guilty to absenting himself from duty as a member of the Home Guard on June 7th, 14th, 21st and 28th, and on July 12th, 19th, and 26th.

Inspector Abrahams said this young man was a member of the Home Guard and joined as a local defence volunteer in 1940. Regulations were passed this year whereby a member of the Home Guard could be called upon to do not more than 48 hours' training in parade every four weeks. Defendant was engaged at a local cinema and it was difficult for him to do parades on week-days. The officers took this in consideration and defendant was instructed to go on Sundays, but since June he had not attended, a single parade. He had been written to on several occasions asking reasons why he had not attended, but he had ignored all the letters. He was again asked why he had not answered the letters or attended parades by Co.-Sergt.-Major Havill and replied that he did not bother to answer the letters. He had treated the matter with contempt.

Exmouth Company Orders October 1942 and April 1943

Absenteeism was taken very seriously

strapped to our bicycles and to start with we had 5 rounds of ammunition. We rode round the village and into Aldham and on to Whatfield so we were riding around all night. We had one or two nights on duty a week.'

Home Guard orders, training nights and patrols were published in the local newspapers and the men were expected to attend. There was no excuse to forget that there was a meeting, lecture or duty to be performed.

Nationally the absenteeism rates had been increasing and so fines were also brought in for not turning up for patrols or training.

In the Exmouth Home Guard Private E.L. Bridle was fined £2 for not attending regularly enough. He was only 17 years old at the time but had been with the company for two years.

In Exmouth the main worry was amphibious invasion, so regular night-time patrols were set up. Each section would report for duty on three specific allocated nights a week.

The section would assemble for patrol at around 8 o'clock in the evening for 'Coast Watching' which was achieved in three 4-hour shifts, each shift starting at a sub-station at the bottom of Gore Lane. The sub-station was a large beach hut donated by Mr and Mrs McLarin. Mr. McLarin was the Home Guard's Quartermaster Sergeant and this was a very generous gesture as it was an extremely expensive and luxurious hut.

The patrols had to walk the full length of the beach, 2 hours to Sandy Bay, then back along the front to the swing bridge at the docks, a further 2 hours, before being relieved.

During the beach patrol they would be looking for Paratroops, landing on the fields behind the cliff tops, German troops landing by sea, for a probing attack, or the enemy coming ashore to retrieve soil samples in preparation for a later invasion.

Ken Parker

'I went on patrol for the Home Guard on Tuesday and Thursday evenings. As I was aged 17, I was issued a rifle for beach patrols only. On Saturday nights I would have training exercises or go on runs.'

Laurie Butler

'We went mainly on night patrols. We met at the Pavilion, all the beach was barbed wired off. We used to meet a returning patrol there. Another patrol would take over at the top of Orcombe Point this would be the Budleigh Patrol. In the early days, sometimes they didn't turn up and sometimes we didn't, but we did our best with what we had.'

'After patrols we made our way back to the drill hall and would have a cup of tea. I was out all night when on patrol and then worked in the stores during the day. It was only once or possibly twice a fortnight though.'

'I took sandwiches with me sometimes on patrol, other men took a thermos of tea, some carried their flask or sandwiches in the gas mask haversack, occasionally we would leave the gas mask behind, but it was strictly against the regulations. I took 10 rounds of ammunition on patrol when I had the rifle and one mag when I had the Sten gun.'

'It used to be terribly cold some nights and climbing over Orcombe Point in the dark with no lights or moonlight, left us wondering where the edge was!'

By mid July 1940 Exmouth beach was covered in scaffolding obstacles and barbed wire by the Royal Engineers. All was very quiet in the evening after sun down and a curfew was in place as civilians may have been shot by the patrols.

In the summer during daylight hours certain areas of the beach were opened to sunbathers and picnickers, but only very small areas. Later in the war the entrances to these areas were guarded during the daytime by two Home Guardsmen.

There was also another patrol specifically allocated to the dock area in Exmouth. The men had to check the parts of the dock that were vulnerable to enemy attack from the estuary and sabotage from Fifth Columnists.

Dock Patrols

The dock Home Guard patrols covered from the dock to the Pier and this section was made up from people who worked at the dock and from the local Fisherman. They were also in charge of the swing bridge at the entrance to the dock, which had to be disabled every night and the positioning of concrete tank blocks in front of the approaches to this bridge. There were loop holes for firing rifles through cut in the seaward side of the swing-bridge, much later when the bridge was replaced by a new bridge these holes were cut in once again as the council thought they were decorative!

The Mamhead slipway, and the steps to the Starcross ferry were also protected by tank blocks and had Lewis guns mounted on pillars nearby which could be turned on any would-be attacker.

At the top of the Mamhead slipway on the right hand side as you would look down was a rectangular pill box, which was disguised as a hut using wooden planks. It had rectangular firing slots in it and could house Lewis guns and eventually the obsolete Vickers heavy machine guns.

Ray Towill

'We mostly went along the seafront, between the clock tower and Orcombe Point. Another platoon patrolled the dock area. Bernard Bradford was in the docks platoon, they were nick named the "Dixon's" Home Guard.'

'Ted, "Neddo" Bradford and Doug Smaldon were in this unit, they were my friends and both boat builders at Dixon's Boatyard. After the war they joined the Royal Navy.'

Joe Radgick

'I was not old enough for the Home Guard. From the boatyard we had mainly Sergeants in charge of Platoons. The boss of Dixon's, Reg Dixon, was the boss of the dock-side Home Guard. His Brother "Turps" Dixon, was in the Home Guard too and also George Dixon, making 3 brothers in all from the Dixon family.'

The Exmouth Home Guard was also responsible for occasional patrols on Woodbury Common, when the Woodbury platoon could not patrol it, due to other commitments. Woodbury Common was considered to be an ideal place for a German airborne assault.

Bomb Disposal Squads

From 1940 most men had undergone training in dealing with incendiary bombs which were dropped in their thousands. Most Home Guard units in cities that had experienced incendiary raids had already had experience of dealing with them in live situations. Many men in rural areas had also shared this experience too as the Germans bombed wheat fields to try and 'starve' Britain into submission. Bill Sleeman's diary recorded a few incidents with live bombs.

Bill Sleeman's Diary

3 September 1940
'Between 300 and 400 incendiary bombs were dropped around Kemps Farm and district, no damage was done due to the promptness of the Home Guard.'

4 September 1940
'Went out on Patrol at Bonds Lane until 6.00 next morning.

ack-ack shells bursting in the sky most of the night until 4.00.'

Most volunteers were also carrying out Fire Watching or Fire Guard duties for 12 hours a week in addition to being in the Home Guard and, by the end of 1940, the bombing situation in Britain had become critical due to manpower shortages. A supplementary service was desperately needed and civilian personnel including Home Guard members, under the name of; the Voluntary Auxiliary Bomb Disposal Service, was formed.

U.X.B. cordon sign

Royal Engineers cap badge on a bomb disposal team F.S. Cap

The units were formed from the pool of men employed on reserve occupations. They were mainly factory employees, who operated in the areas close to the proximity of their place of work.

The decision to form specialist Home Guard bomb disposal squads was taken and a total of 7000 men in 132 squads were trained and supervised by the Royal Engineers throughout the war. These volunteer bomb disposal units wore the denim uniforms for work and had serge battledress uniforms issued for best wear. Royal Engineers service strips in red and navy blue were worn on the upper middle arm and a special sleeve badge of a yellow, white and blue 'bomb' was worn on the right forearm.

They remained independent units under the command of regular Bomb Disposal Units of the Royal Engineers and their Warrant Officers and N.C.O.s were regular army Bomb Disposal Engineers.

Some of these units became so proficient at bomb disposal that they were allowed to complete procedures from extraction to disposal of U.B.X.s and did not just act as sappers.

Cordons

The Home Guard were regularly summoned to the alert to arrange cordons around bomb-damaged areas; or areas where a U.X.B. had fallen. To protect the public and also to prevent looting.

H.G. bomb disposal badge

Mike Heard
'We were also called up regularly for emergencies, U.X.B.s, clearing bomb debris, and also for invasion alerts. On top of this I was one of the Exmouth lifeboat launchers and we would turn out to drag the boat across the road and down the beach to the water's edge.'

On the night of the Exmouth Parade bombing, at 8am on 1 March 1941, Home Guard cordons were set up from Clarence Road, George Street, Albion Hill and New Street, because of the U.X.B. which had landed in the doorway of the Exmouth Inn, Exeter Road. Also another cordon was set up from Rolle Street to Creedy's Corner and The Strand. The Bomb Disposal Squad from Exeter came and defused two bombs in the Strand Gardens, the Exmouth Inn bomb and later, when it was eventually found, the Savoy Cinema bomb. Mike Heard (The Strand area) and Bill Sleeman (the Albion Street area) were both on duty this night, until 7 o'clock the following morning.

Mike Heard
'The Home Guard members then had to go home, put on our uniforms on and reassemble in The Strand, to cordon off the area to keep the area safe, due to the possibility of the bombs detonating later on'.

The Home Guard remained on duty overnight in The Strand after the Royal Engineers Bomb Disposal Squad from Exeter arrived. They removed the fuses from the bomb in the Cinema and the one stuck in the soil of The Strand Gardens. After they had been made safe, Mike and his mates in the Home Guard had to roll these bombs on to the back of a waiting lorry, by pushing them up two planks.

Mike Heard
'No one had told us!, but the U.X.B. Squad had decided to detonate the fuses of these bombs in a controlled explosion in the nearest Strand air raid shelter in order to make them safe. As we were pushing one of these big bombs up the planks there was a sharp bang and we jumped out of our skins! Thinking we were going to be killed by the explosion'.

He said it, with an amused look on his face now, but added:

'...we were absolutely terrified at the time!'

Dennis Davey
'Units of the Home Guard were called out to watch over the shattered shops and houses when the centre of the town was partially destroyed during an air raid in 1942.'

Fire Watching

Peter Mattholie
'We used to go fire watching when on guard duty. We were on top of Bromley Gaumont cinema when things were really bad in the area. We were watching for the incendiary bombs which had scattered everywhere, people didn't realise they were burning in the lofts of their houses, so we had to go and tell them and also tell the Fire Guards who would go round with a stirrup pump and a bucket and put out the fire.'

'We could see planes going over at night, they had searchlights up on the Bromley recreation ground which would light up the bombers for the ack-ack batteries, some of which were manned by Home Guard units.'

Luppitt Home Guard's Duties

Jack Sage
'The town was divided into two sections later in the war. The Luppitt platoon grew too fast, so that's why it was split in two and why there were six sergeants. In all when at its full strength, we had a total of 64 men.'

'My section was based in the village and this was referred to as the "Home" base. We used the church tower as a look out post as it gave a good all round view of the area.'

'The other section known as the "Battle Platoon" was based at the Beacon an area just outside Luppitt village. It was under the command of C.S.M. Hooper.'

Guarding Railway Tunnels

Jack Sage
'The Luppitt Home Guard Platoon had to guard the Honiton/Kilmington railway tunnel, during the months of May and June 1944. It was one mile long and guards were set up at either end. Three army bell tents were erected near the entrances to the tunnel and were used by the off-duty sleeping patrols. A railway gangers hut became the temporary HQ for the officers and N.C.O.s. The tunnel had to be guarded on Saturdays, all through the night. There were three duty points for the squad on duty, and the N.C.O.s had to keep in constant contact with all the duty points. A telephone line had been installed and could be used to call in reinforcements from Honiton Camp in the event of an emergency.'

During March 1944 as the preparations for Operation Overlord, the Liberation of Europe, were being made. The Home Guard's responsibilities would be to defend the British Isles in case of an attack or counterattack by the German Forces. The guard started on the 24 April 1944 to 10 July 1944, a total of 77 days comprising over 11 000 guard duties being attended by Home Guard members.

Operational Orders for the 19 'Seaton' Battalion April - July 1944

Home Guard units were positioned in areas along the South Coast. 19 'Seaton' Battalion were given special instructions to:-

• Provide guards on approaches to beaches to prevent landing of enemy agents.
• Guard the Honiton tunnel on the Southern Region railway line.

A battle platoon, telephone communications, runners and a first aid party were posted at each end of the tunnel to post guard every night, in the event of a serious attack by a force landed by enemy parachutists.

Battle positions in the form of trenches were made at either end of the tunnel along with double lines of field telephone wire for communications with platoon H.Q.

In the event of an attack, reserves were arranged from American troops billeted at Heathfield Camp and from the Home Guard units from Honiton.

Jack Sage
'I used to guard the railway tunnel on Saturday nights. Three bell tents were erected for shelter at the Honiton end of the tunnel. Three sections of 12 men (approx 36 guardsmen) were on duty covering 3 positions at the entrance to the tunnel. The tunnel was about a mile long and emerged the other end in the Kilmington and Yarcombe area.'

'One night we were sat on the rails near the tunnel entrance and an engine approached, free-wheeling down the slope, it was pitch black and we didn't hear it until the last moment, when we jumped aside; it nearly killed us.'

'Our H.Q. was in Honiton there were control rooms there from which we received our orders, after a while there was a direct telephone link to the H.Q. and to the other end of the tunnel.'

'Our job was to watch over the tunnel to make sure that it was not captured by enemy parachutists, which were our main threat at the time. At certain times the threat of invasion became more serious than others.'

Edwin Hawker

'We used to have three men posted at the entrance to the Kilmington end of the railway tunnel. We always had our rifles loaded when we were on guard and were prepared to fire if we needed to. There was a tent erected further up the track away from the tunnel with more guards in it.'

'The sergeant would shout down the tunnel if any noise was heard or any friendly Home Guardsmen were coming down the tunnel and ask them to identify themselves. We knew there were guards at the other end of the tunnel, so anyone who did not identify themselves would have been asking for trouble. We would have shot anyone coming down the tunnel if we had heard them, without hesitation.'

'There were no hard defences at the tunnel, none at all really! There is a hole in the tunnel wall and we used to get in there to get out of the path of the trains when they came through, it was a double track and at the time with very little space inside the tunnel.'

'We were deadly serious about guarding the tunnel and we were instructed to beware and lookout for enemy paratroopers mainly, which was our prime objective. We were also there to stop any attacks or acts of sabotage.'

'We never had any trouble, we never fired off any rounds but it was still very serious.'

Invasion Alert in Exmouth

On Good Friday 1942 the Exmouth Home Guard had received an invasion warning. When on patrol at times of special alerts, Mike Heard remembered that the Army Catering Services looked after their food rations during these long vigils.

St Hilarian was a large house situated at the bottom of Portland Avenue, opposite the old Maer Bay Hotel. During the war it was a Communications Centre used by all services and the Home Guard. The Home Guard had to defend the centre during alerts and could also be billeted there, sleeping at the centre, which was less than luxurious.

Mike Heard

'When there was an alert on, we had to sleep on the floor at St Hilarian with our great coats and blankets covering us. We could be there for up to two days at a time, but it was better than being out on the cliffs in the freezing cold.'

A Serious Business

During the Good Friday alert, two newly appointed N.C.O.s of the Queen's Regiment, whilst checking the cliff defences, found an unattended Vickers heavy machine gun by the cliff path.

They removed and hid the weapon, then roused their guard of regular soldiers who were responsible for leaving it.

Knowing they were on 'alert' status and an enemy invasion was a possibility, the soldiers looked on in disbelief as they could not find their gun! It was eventually returned to them, with a reprimand from the commanding officer who then in turn reprimanded the N.C.O.s with a severe warning to not fool around, especially in times of such serious circumstances.

One of the regular N.C.O.s, was told this on his next visit to the 477 Coastal Battery Home Guard was told.

'Not to worry, as his soldiers would have been perfectly safe in the event of an invasion, due to the fact that they were surrounded and protected by the Home Guard.'

Dispatch Riding

Reg Warr

'I liked cycling so I was given the important job of dispatch rider on my bicycle, taking messages between the two sections. It was quite scary all night long cycling up and down the A30 in the blackout, when all I wanted to do was go to sleep. "You wouldn't want to sleep if you knew the Germans were coming!" they said'.

Chapter 13
Coastal Artillery

On 13 August 1940 Sir Alan Brooke acting in the role of Commander in Chief Home Defence Forces, landed at Exeter Aerodrome and was taken on a tour of inspection of Britain's southern coastline from Exmouth to Weymouth, to evaluate the strength of the coastal defences and the potential German invasion landing sites.

The 477 Coastal Artillery Battery Home Guard (R.A.)

The Royal Artillery arrived in Exmouth complete with two 4.7" ex Naval Guns in March of 1942. The battery was positioned at the bottom of Foxholes Hill on the sea front. Initially only a skeleton Royal Artillery staff could be mustered to man the guns. The Home Guard were amalgamated with the R.A. Gun crews to supplement the numbers to become the 477 Coastal Artillery Battery. An invasion warning was received on Good Friday 1942 in the batteries earliest days and the crews had to 'stand to', luckily it turned out to be a false alarm.

Bernard Greenway

'The Home Guard was formed in Exmouth early in May 1940; it was first known as the L.D.V. and eventually ended up as a fairly substantial organisation with six different Companies. On the car park at the sea front, two ex naval guns were brought up from Plymouth they were 4.7" Naval guns manned by a Royal Artillery Home Guard trained company. Every Tuesday night they would bring out a Royal Naval boat towing a target some distance behind. They would leave from Pole Sands and tow the target right the way along the sea front, we loved to watch, one night when they were getting used to the guns they hit the rocks with a shot which ricocheted off. After a few weeks training they were good quality gunners and were very well organised.'

The Exmouth Casemates

The Royal Engineers were responsible for making and positioning of the gun emplacements and casemates. They were of brick and concrete construction with underground magazines and tunnels, used to store shells and brass cartridges ready for use to supply the guns. An Observation Post, searchlight housings, beach defences and obstacles to prevent or hinder invasion, were also placed on the beaches and the approaches to the guns.

Ray Challis

'Two 4.7" ex Naval Guns were on the seafront pointing out to sea. One was up near the new life boat station, in the car park behind the café, and the other one was about 100 yards before it, closer to the Harbour View café. They were allowed to fire on Fridays to practice, when they fired out to sea with live ammunition.'

Defences

The batteries were also equipped with anti-aircraft weaponry, initially with machine guns and later with 40mm Bofors L.A.A. guns, one on Foxholes Hill and two on the Maer, close by 'Z' rocket batteries were positioned on the seafront.

There were many occasions when the anti-aircraft defences at the battery were in action against the hit-and-run raiders attacking Exmouth These included Messerschmitt ME109s carrying a single 250 kg bomb, and later the Focke Wolfe 190s which carried a formidable 500kg bomb.

The battery was protected by a double line of barbed-wire with trenches behind, to provide cover for a compliment of 30 Home Guardsmen acting in an infantry role for localised defence. A 'Vickers' machine gun defended the track up to the battery Observation Post and covered the coast to the west of the Foxholes Hill and Orcombe Point.

The beach defences ensured that the gun positions were protected from seaward invasion and could cover all the land between the sea and the estuary and give a good field of fire over the local beaches in the event of an invasion.

The role of the Coastal Artillery Battery would then be to engage enemy forces, such as landing craft and assault ships carrying landing craft, attempting landings on Exmouth or Dawlish Warren beaches or attacks by S-boats on coastal shipping. If landings were made and a beach head established, the gun battery would be responsible for engaging the invaders and destroying any beach head which had been established.

The Exmouth Battery came under the command of the Brigadier Royal Artillery Southern Command, via the Commander of Coast Artillery South West District.

The Exmouth Battery's commander was Major A.E. Jones, who had commanded a Battery of 6in Howitzers in WWI.

He organised the Royal Artillery gunners manning the 4.7" guns, which comprised of two shifts of thirty Royal Artillery Gunners manning the guns, supplying the ammunition and staffing the Command/ Observation Post.

The Home Guard was responsible only for the local defence of the area initially, which included the battery, but later on was trained by the Royal Artillery to fire and maintain the guns. The H.G. manned the guns at Foxholes from mid 1942. From 1943-1944 there was a planned reduction and reorganisation of coastal artillery, as the threat of invasion decreased but Exmouth's guns were unaffected by this and remained in position until the end of the war.

A nissen hut was placed on the corner of Maer Road and Maer Lane for use as an office and stores.

Catering facilities had also been established in the form of a canteen, with N.A.A.F.I facilities here. A café was also placed in the gardens of a private house nearby, which Servicemen of all nations used including the Home Guard.

Life at the Battery Observation Post

Half way up the cliff path on Foxholes Hill was the Home Guard Battery Observation Post. This was a brick and concrete construction manned 24 hours a day in 4 hour shifts. When called to man the 'watches' at the Observation Post Mike Heard often found it difficult to stay alert and keep warm in the damp concrete structure.

Mike Heard

'It was usually quite boring and un-eventful, we often found ourselves hallucinating or nearly falling asleep. We got "jumpy" too, imagining we saw things which weren't there when we were tired. It was very hard to stay awake and look out into the pitch black, with binoculars, at the horizon and stay interested for very long!'

Searchlights
Mike Heard

'For a time I was allocated to searchlight No. 1 at Exmouth Battery, it was for spotting enemy targets at sea. These searchlights were never used for anti-aircraft spotting; their purpose was only for illuminating anything that we thought looked suspicious at sea.'

Watching the coast

Seaton's 90cm coastal searchlight housing

Coastal Artillery Searchlight Detail

2 Searchlights staffed at night only. Used for illuminating shipping only.
Searchlight Commander x 1
N. C. O. 1/c D.S. x 1
Switchman x 2
Lamp Attendants x 2
Engine (generator) Attendants x 2

The searchlight operator was responsible for adjusting the light beam and the vertical and horizontal positioning of the light. His duties would also include maintaining all aspects of the light; he ensures that the carbons that create the arc are burn correctly and that the beam can be focused quickly and efficiently.

The operator threw the switch to start the arc lamp burning when commanded to do so by the Command Post Operator.

Two more crew members would be responsible for the operating, care and maintenance of the Lister generator, making sure it was always primed with plenty of fuel and would start reliably first time every time.

Two ex-army anti-aircraft 90 cm searchlights were installed near the 4.7" guns on Exmouth sea front and Brixham Battery. They were positioned pointing towards the sea and were only intended to be used for observing the movement of shipping and illuminating, surface targets on the sea at night. These Searchlights were linked from the Observation Post to the gun/

searchlight positions by telephone in order to direct fire. The search lights had a beam equivalent to one million candle power and were powered by a petrol generator. The operator was responsible for adjusting the light beam and the vertical and horizontal positioning of the light. His duties would also include maintaining all aspects of the light; he ensures that the carbons that create the arc are burn correctly and that the beam can be focused quickly and efficiently.

During an invasion the operator could only throw the switch to start the arc burning when commanded to do so by the Command Post operator, so as not to give the light and guns position away too early. The Lister generator that supplied the power to the searchlight was staffed by two crew members, who would be responsible for the operating, care and maintenance of the generator, making sure it was always primed with plenty of fuel and would start reliably first time every time.

Exmouth Coastal Artillery Staffing Detail

Officer of the watch x 1
B. C. A. x 1
Telephonist x 1
Range Finding personnel x 3
2 x Gun Detachments x 36

The Guns

The two 4.7" QF (Quick Firing) guns were made by the Japanese Kura Company. The Calibre is odd by today's standards, as the calibre of the guns was governed by the weight of the projectile.

The guns could throw a 45lb (20.4 kg) shell a distance of 5900 metres armed with a time fuse, or 9100 metres with a percussion fuse fired on a flatter trajectory. The firing mechanism was designed by Vickers and these guns had a good reputation for ease of operation and reliability by gun crews that used them. Although many practice rounds were fired out to sea in training sessions the guns were never fired against enemy

Empty 4.7" gun emplacement and observation post on Exmouth sea front

shipping. This may seem remarkable, as German S-boats were known to operate in Lyme Bay, Torbay and the Exmouth area. One of the reasons for this, was that although the Home Guard were willing to 'have a go', it was decided it would have been foolhardy to have given the position of the guns away to the enemy, with no guarantee of hitting a fast moving small vessel, and so the Home Guard were instructed to observe without even illuminating, small targets such as these when they were spotted.

Ken Parker

'One 4.7" gun was positioned on a mound, where the Foxholes car park is now and the other one was near the sea-front Drill Hall by the Lifeboat Station.'

The last time these guns were fired was on October 29 1944 at the commencement of stand-down, when 'D' Company (Artillery) of the 5 'Bideford' Battalion Devon Home Guard sent their gunnery detachments to Exmouth for a training shoot. The Gunnery instructors from 477 carried out this last training shoot and were watched by the Exmouth Army Cadets.

Gordon Lawes

'During the war I joined the Army Cadets. One day we were invited by the Home Guard to visit the 4.7" guns on the seafront. They were placed in large concrete and brick casemates by this time.'

'A few of us at a time were allowed in to watch their gunnery procedures as they practised firing at towed target barges out to sea. I stood at the back of the room behind the gun to watch. As the gun fired, the blast knocked me unconscious. They had not told us to tense our stomach-muscles and open our mouths when the gun fired and the air pressure of the detonation knocked me out. I was taken to the hospital to be checked over and made a full recovery. After this they would not allow children to watch their practises.'

Field service cap with the badge of the Royal Artillery issued to coastal batteries

Brixham Battery

Brixham Battery started life as a Royal Artillery Battery. Its designation was 362 Battery Royal Artillery 'Heavy Coastal Battery', which in turn was part of 556 Heavy Coastal Battery Southern Command. The battery, which was the 'Control Battery' for Torbay, became operational in September 1940 as an 'Emergency Examination Battery' and the battalion's number can still be seen cast into the concrete flag pole base at the site.

In February 1942, the Home Guard came under the jurisdiction of the National Service Act, and each man

Guardsmen of 477 Coastal Artillery Battery pose with Royal Artillery Attached A.T.S. attached to the Anti-Aircraft Batteries on Exmouth Seafront

Brixham battery observation post

Inside the lowerlevel of the observationpost

Volunteers and 'Living History' members at Brixham No. 1 gun casemate

Brixham battery volunteers standing inside No.2 gun casemate

Firing a 4.7" gun

Brixham Home Guard on parade in Fore Street 1944

Kessingland coastal artillery battery gunners with their 4.7" gun

Kessingland coastal artillery battery at Stand Down

had to be available for a minimum of 48 hours of training and active duty a month. It was at this point; the name of the Battery was changed to 378 'Coastal Artillery' battery Home Guard R.A. and was manned by the Home Guard along with staff from the Royal Artillery.

New coastal artillery sites were set up all over the coasts of Britain during this period.

Brixham Home Guard holding their 'sports day' trophy at 'Brixham Rugby Club' grounds 1943

Included in the photograph are: Back Row Centre. Arthur Stringer. Front Row. Percy Mobbs, Poatman Read (Hank).

Living Historian Steve Parsons in the renovated underground magazine tunnels at Brixham battery

Corbyn Head Home Guard gunners

In total around 7000 Home Guardsmen were trained by the Royal Artillery and served in the coastal artillery batteries.

Kessingland Officers and N.C.O.s at Stand Down

109

Chapter 14
Badges and Insignia

Printed Shoulder Titles

Home Guard Shoulder titles were printed in off-white, on khaki cloth (officers had a woven type on wool serge backing). These shoulder titles were issued to most Home Guard units from January 1941.

Printed shoulder titles

Ken Parker

'To start with, I used my ordinary clothes and was issued with a Home Guard armband and later when a uniform became available that would fit, I had my battledress issued. It wasn't a bad fit; I had to sew on Home Guard badges on the shoulders of the uniforms.'

Late War 'Blind' Printed Shoulder Titles

Red and Blue Arm of Service Strips

These were Royal Artillery distinctions placed mid-arm for men and N.C.O.s, and just below the shoulder titles

for officers. They were made from coloured felt, two inches long by a quarter-inch wide. The strip was worn with the colour dark blue to the front of the arm and red to the rear on both arms of the Battledress blouse but not on the great coat.

The Home Guard Bomb Disposal Units also wore arm of service strips and these had the colours reversed.

Royal Artillery arm of service strip (red/blue)

Anti-Aircraft Command sleeve patch

Shoulder Distinctions

Edwin Hawker

'I was at school in Honiton until I was 14. I Finished School in 1939 and I joined the Cotleigh Home Guard in 1941. The Cotleigh platoon wore 19 DVN on their shoulders of their uniforms with the Home Guard shoulder titles above.'

Shoulder distinctions were worn on both shoulders just below the Home Guard shoulder titles on serge battledress and great coats. In most areas they started putting in an appearance in mid 1941 as the Home Guard armlet or patch on the right arm were being phased out and the new shoulder titles were being sewn to the uniforms.

These first style distinctions arrived on long rolls and were made in two parts so the DVN could be used in conjunction with all the county Battalions.

DVN
4

So, DVN 4 represents the 4 'Barnstaple' Battalion Devon Home Guard. The next Distinction is 10 'Torbay' Battalion Devon Home Guard.

10 'Torbay' Battalion distinctions

Photographs of Exmouth Company 2 'Clyst' Battalion show the early pattern distinctions attached to the uniforms which had the figure 2 at the top thus reading:

2
DVN

This is highly unusual and may only apply to 3 Platoon for some reason. An example of the distinctions being worn like this is the photo of C.S.M. Charlie Havill and his men on exercise on Woodbury Common standing with the heavy machine guns.

Other 'Clyst' Battalion platoons have DVN 2 in the normal fashion displayed on their photographs. For every rule that you will hear about concerning the Home Guard, there is always something new and different to be found!

The following tiles display the distinction DOR 4, which is 4 Battalion Dorset Home Guard. After a while you get used to how to read them if you are looking at old photographs of relatives trying to work out what unit they belong to.

First and Second Type Shoulder Distinctions

The second style distinctions (as above) were printed in one piece and were dedicated to the individual battalion. The DVN representing the county of Devon abbreviation and the 2 representing the 2 'Clyst' Battalion of the Devon Home Guard once again, it was probably austerity measures that introduced these second pattern titles as less cloth was used.

These distinctions were supplied on cloth rolls and had to be sewn on by hand by the Guardsman himself, or more usually his gently-persuaded wife, sister, daughter or girlfriend.

Later in the war the battledress jackets and great coats arrived with the Home Guard shoulder titles already sewn in place. By stand down, Devon had 25 Battalions of Home Guard volunteers all with different distinctions.

Unusually some units adopted the practise of placing the first type distinctions side by side like the 14 'Hapton' Battalion Norfolk Home Guard.

14 NK

There are probably more exceptions to the rule still lurking out there somewhere.

'Z' Rocket Batteries Insignia

A complete set of titles, distinctions and anti-aircraft badge for the Gloucester 101 'Z' rocket battery

The only thing that would change from county to county on the 'Z' Rocket Home Guards uniforms would be the county abbreviation distinctions for instance. BMY 101 would be Bromley and SOM 101 would be Somerset.

Early Rank Badges

Early officer's rank was distinguished by blue strips sewn across the epaulettes of the battledress or denim blouses.

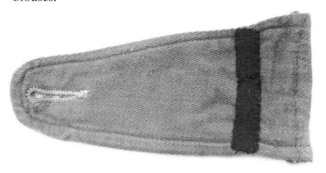

Early Rank system: one thin blue bar indicating Platoon Commander

The Early Ranks were as follows:

- Three thin stripes or one broad stripe:
  Battalion Commander
- Two thin stripes:
  Company Commander
- One thin stripe:
  Platoon Commander
- Nothing:
  Volunteer

From 16 February 1942 the Home Guard adopted the regular army system of rank structure. A public announcement was made in the Exmouth Journal Dated 16 February 1942 declaring from this date that 'Volunteers not holding rank will be designated Private'.

Comparative Rank

Early Home Guard	Army
Zone Commander	Brigadier
Group Commander	Colonel
Battalion Commander	Lieutenant Colonel
Company Commander	Major
Platoon Commander	Captain / Lieutenant
Section Commander	Sergeant
Squad Commander	Corporal / L. Corporal
Volunteer	Private

Officer's rank 'Pip' for Second Lieutenant

Officer's crown

Army Rank System Badges

Three pips one crown	Brigadier
Two pips one crown	Colonel
One pip one crown	Lieutenant Colonel
One crown	Major
Three pips	Captain
Two pips	Lieutenant
One pip	Second Lieutenant
Crown with laurel wreath	C.S.M.
Three stripes	Sergeant
Two stripes	Corporal
One stripe	L. Corporal
Nothing	Private/Volunteer

Company Sergeant Major's sleeve rank badge

Sergeants stripes

Proficiency Badges

These badges were made from red felt and were sewn on to the right forearm after the passing of the exam and presentation of the certificate. The bar worn underneath was for a second advanced test, which incorporated more specialist weaponry and skills.

Home Guard proficiency badges 1st exam and 2nd exam

Both Proficiency Badges on the sleeve of Harry Vincent West Coker Platoon

First Proficiency Badge Topics
1. **General Knowledge.**
2. **Rifle Skills.**
3. **No. 36 Mills Bomb.** (Hand Grenade skills)
4. **Other Weapons.** (e.g., B.A.R., Sten, Lewis, Vickers heavy) Signalling.
5. **Battlecraft.** Coastal Artillery, Heavy Anti-Aircraft, 'Z' Rocket Batteries, Motor Transport, Bomb Disposal.
6, **Map Reading, Field Craft, First Aid.**

When the length of service chevrons were introduced in June 1944, the proficiency badges were moved to the left forearm.

War Service Chevrons

These chevrons denoted the length of service served by the individual. They were issued in 1944 and one was issued for every year of service. They were worn on the right forearm of the battledress blouse and were either printed or machine woven in red on a khaki background.

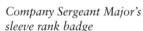

Certificate of Proficiency to Sergeant Clare 1 Northants Battalion

Specialist Armbands

Armbands to draw attention to a specialist trade or skill were worn on the upper arms. Signallers and dispatch riders wore the corps colours of the Royal Signals (white over blue) armbands on both arms. Red

Printed length-of-service chevrons: red on khaki - one year (left) and three years (right)

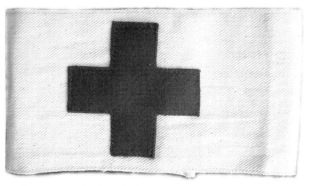

Red Cross Medical Orderly armband

Cross-trained medics and stretcher bearers wore Red Cross armbands on the left arm, when worn in conjunction with the Home Guard armbands, and in later photographs they appear to have been moved to the right arm as shoulder titles appeared.

Traffic Control armband

The traffic control armbands were worn on either arm by Home Guardsmen on point duty directing traffic in London and other blitzed cities. During the preparations for D-Day, they can be seen being worn by Home Guardsmen directing convoys of embarking vehicles to the ports and hards of south coast towns. Once again there will always be exceptions to the rule.

Charlie Atkins of Lower Bockhampton Platoon with four years service chevrons on his right arm

Chapter 15
The Women's Home Guard Auxiliary

The earliest example of Women acting in a supporting role to the Home Guard was probably the Women's Civil Section attached to the 13th County of Durham Battalion. Although not officially allowed to join the Home Guard these women worked tirelessly to support their men in their L.D.V. roles. They were formed in the early summer of 1940 and took on the responsibility for three areas of support.

They formed a first-aid section which ran and equipped a fully operational ward with first-aid trained staff mainly from the Red Cross V.A.D. It was the first dedicated first aid facility for Home Guard use. This facility was in use during the invasion scares of 1940 and treated casualties in the Battle of Britain and also treated minor injuries and wounds caused by the firing of blanks at close quarters during Home Guard training exercises. The fully trained staff also sent medics and stretcher bearers on exercises with the men.

Secondly the women supplied the equivalent of the 'Comfort Services', by collecting wool and knitting warm gloves, balaclavas, pullovers, socks and scarves for the men, who were glad to have them on the freezing nightly patrols during the harsh winters.

The third area in which women took charge was the running, staffing and stocking of a dedicated canteen for the men, so that there was always hot food and drinks available for the men going on and coming off patrol. This section was also able to set up a field canteen during exercises.

Although many women were already serving with Home Guard units on a voluntary basis, since the early days of the L.D.V. they could not enrol officially. In some areas women were already taking on many non-combatant, roles such as medics / stretcher bearers, secretaries, cooks, cleaners and in some cases had been watching for enemy parachutists on Dartmoor and Exmoor with the mounted moorland patrols from early August 1940.

Some women had already been included in a more active role by many Home Guard units who had already trained them to shoot shotguns and .22 ammunition as

larger calibre ammunition was scarce. Although they were not officially recognised by the Government, they gave a considerable amount of help and support to the men. Disgruntled by the lack of support for this recognition, Dr Edith Summerskill, the labour M.P. for Fulham West, with the help of a Women's Champion sharpshooter, organised their own private group of women crack shots called the Women's Home Defence. From the start the appeal of this unit grew and grew to newly emancipated women and they enrolled in their droves to learn how to fire rifles and handguns. It became so popular that by 1943 it had over 20 000 members serving in 250 units all over Great Britain. At this point they had to be taken seriously by the War Office and so it was decided that the Women's Home Guard Auxiliary would be formed in April 1943.

By officially recognising the Women's new role in support of the Home Guard, they had to be afforded the protection of the Geneva Convention and were issued with a certificate, franked by the local Home Guard administration and a plastic cap badge, to ensure they would not be shot as spies.

The Women's Auxiliary Service

The seeds of the Women's Home Guard Auxiliary can be seen to be taking shape as early as 1941 under their name of the Women's Auxiliary Service. Members of the Richmond Surrey W.A.S. were wearing overalls for vehicle maintenance as a uniform and can be seen marching smartly during their training. They later became affiliated to the Home Guard. Early photographs show that some women wore commercially made enamel Home Guard pins on their ties and Khaki/Green W.A.S. armbands.

On the 23 July 1942, Members of the Kensington Women's Auxiliary Home Guard Platoon, one of the first W.A.S. units to be formed were photographed marching in a parade through Whitehall in civilian clothes some with armbands, but were not yet in uniform.

All over Britain women were already helping the Home Guard since its formation in 1940, mostly in small numbers and without being officially recognised as being part of the Home Guard's structure. In many areas these roles carried the title of 'Nominated Women'.

The Formation of the Women's Home Guard Auxiliary

In April 1943, once again at the request of Winston Churchill, the government removed the ban on women joining the ranks. Thus these 'nominated women' women, became part of the official Home Guard structure.

Ninkey Coe was one of the first recruits for the Women's Home Guard Auxiliary in Derby.

Ninkey Coe
'Sometimes, people laughed wondering what a group of women could do but, at the time, there were great fears there may be an invasion and it was important those left back home were able to respond if the worst happened'

Rene Ide
'I Joined the Girls Training Corps in preparation for joining the Women's Services or the Women's Home Guard Auxiliary. The Home Guard taught us to fire rifles on a rifle range, we laid down on mats and sandbags and fired at a target down the range. I loved it and found out I was quite a good shot. We learned how to load and fire a rifle, lie down on your stomach, get it well into the shoulder, and fire! We had the barrel rested on sandbags. We didn't do bayonet training though, it was all great fun.'

The diversity of roles was extended to women, who were now sanctioned to operate field telephones and switch boards, drive vehicles and operate military radio equipment in the field. For this role they received extensive training from the Royal Signal to pass examinations in the transmission and reception of audio messages and morse code, to bring them up to the standard of the regular army signallers. This role was particularly important in the event of an invasion as they would have to communicate with regular army units via the radios and this would have left no room for error.

In 'C' Company 14 'Moorland' Battalion Devon Home Guard, two women excelled in their roles as signallers and went on to become qualified as instructors. In the Moorland Battalion's history the following quote was included in the short piece about the women auxiliaries, which reflects the respect that the men had men for their female counterparts.

'We are proud of our lady signallers, especially so when they proved willing and capable of tackling any communications job which the men were called upon to do, including the taking over of the wireless station on their own.'

In some units, although not permitted to take on a combatant role, the women auxiliaries were trained in rifle shooting. This was mainly limited to instruction on .22 calibre weapons but in some cases .303 Lee Enfield and 30-06 P.17 rifle training was given. Some photographs also show women auxiliaries being trained to throw hand grenades and fire mortars.

Ninkey Coe
'We were a real mixture of women and, of course, some were better than others. I had some crack shots in the group and, on one occasion, we beat the Home Guard in a shooting contest.'

Most sectors eventually ended up with women in their Home Guard units, although some men objected to them being allowed to join. Most however gladly accepted the women and in some cases the women were found to out perform the men. Eventually around 32 000 women were recruited nationally and they were eventually 'Stood Down' with the men in December 1944.

Government Issued Uniform Items
The following items were generally authorised to be issued to women auxiliaries throughout Britain.

• Plastic H.G. Cap Badge.
• Field Service Cap.
• Home Guard Armband.

They also carried their government issued civilian respirators. Some women were later issued with shoulder titles which were sewn on to shirts and coats.

(Left and next page) typical Women's Home Guard Auxiliary uniform of 1943

Home Guard Women's Auxiliary Plastic Cap Badge

A special gold-coloured utility quality plastic-pin-backed Women's Auxiliary Home Guard badge was manufactured by A. Stanley and sons of Walsall in 1943. This badge was intended to worn as a cap badge on the field service cap, but as many women did not have a cap provided, it can be seen on many items of military and civilian head gear. The badge can also be seen being worn as a brooch on a variety of military and civilian clothing. Strangely within the same units it appears positioned on the left or the right side of the blouse or coat.

Photographs of some Devon and Somerset Home Guard Battalions show the badge being worn on the tie and some photos show the badge worn simultaneously on both the headgear and coat or tie positions simultaneously.

It is known that only one badge per auxiliary was issued, so it must be assumed that some HG units had a surplus of badges whilst others had a deficit, or the women could privately purchase additional badges from the company Quartermaster.

The Clevedon, Bristol Signals Squad of six women, wore the badge uniformly on army issued khaki berets. The badge was positioned over the left eye. These auxiliaries, who were also trained to shoot .22 and .303 rifle shooting, also adopted a fine uniform of a khaki shirt with light green A.T.S. issue tie, olive green skirt, tan stockings and brown shoes to compliment the men.

Women's H.G. Auxiliary badge in gold-coloured plastic

Women's Home Guard Auxiliary side cap

In early photographs, most women do not posses any form of uniform clothing at all, except armbands in some cases. In stand down period photographs some women still do not posses any uniform and this could because they have joined recently or couldn't make their clothing coupons stretch to include specialist uniform items.

A full sheet of clothing coupons

Regionally Adopted Uniforms

Because of the problems of finding suitably smart and practical uniforms for the Auxiliaries, not least because of the shortage of raw materials and rationing of clothing, finding a definitive national uniform for them in old photographs is virtually impossible. I have studied carefully as many old photo's as possible of the women auxiliaries from various parts of the U.K. as possible and come up with a great variation in clothing.

When talking with women at Living History events or at museums, women always ask what the women wore; a question raised especially by those who are interested in putting together a costume to attend a Living History event or 1940s dance. I have put together a list of typical uniform items and civilian clothing mixtures that I have seen.

Photographs of Portishead Signal Auxiliaries of the Somerset Home Guard, can be seen wearing smart, light- coloured long mackintosh raincoats although they do not match exactly it provides some uniformity. They also wear olive green skirts, light khaki shirts, light coloured stockings and light coloured ties.

These Auxiliaries can also be seen carrying handbags and civilian respirators. It must have been extremely difficult to have achieved this level of uniformity during the post 1943 period of rationing in Britain, as every piece of clothing for their uniforms would have had to be supplied using their own civilian clothing allowance from their yearly coupon allowance.

Conversely women's auxiliary signallers in 14th 'Moorland' Battalion Devon Home Guard operating a number 19 Radio set in outdoors in cold weather have only civilian clothing and no headgear or badges. They look very smart individually but there is no uniformity in any respect.

In some Somerset units the women are W.V.S. members and can be seen wearing their bottle green W.V.S. uniforms. They wear only the H.G. brooch on their bottle green coats on the left hand side lapel. The W.V.S. badge was worn on their bottle green hats with cherry red ribbon hat band which matches their shirts.

A photograph of a nurse from Woodbury Platoon '2nd' Clyst Battalion Devon Home Guard is wearing her V.A.D. Nurse's uniform with her H.G. badge on her Red Cross apron.

Photographs of Auxiliaries in some Somerset and Hampshire Home Guard units are pictured in wearing V.A.D. nurse's dark blue/black berets with Red Cross cap badges worn over the left eye. The shirts and ties look a light khaki, or possibly light brown or green from the photos and these are worn with light khaki ties. On these ties are worn the women's plastic HG badges. They are carrying regular 37 pattern shell dressing's bags and carrying civilian gas masks in

commercially made covers. Their Red Cross V.A.D. armbands are worn on the right shirt sleeve. Presumably, they may wear their Red Cross great coats in winter.

Stocking colours vary greatly within the same units, from Greenish, thick lisle, possibly obtained from friends in the A.T.S. to fine mesh with every shade through to black in photographs. Basically the women wore whatever was available at the time.

Some women auxiliaries only had their everyday clothes to wear and made no attempt at uniformity with the others. Others went to great lengths to have exact uniformity and looked very smart.

Women in telephonist and secretarial roles, who are usually pictured in H.Q. companies stand down photographs, probably felt that they did not need to wear uniform when carrying out their functions. By stand down in December 1944 there would have been plenty of opportunity to have arranged some kind of uniform.

Women who worked in outside roles such as radio operators, drivers, mechanics and medical orderlies / stretcher bearers, these women were more likely to be quipped with warm practical clothing. Photographs of women in some Suffolk units wear full men's serge battle dress, with coloured field service caps in others W.L.A. issue great coats can be seen and how these were obtained no one will probably ever know!

Other Military Items Issued to Women Auxiliaries

Some women in signals sections can be seen wearing A.T.S. leather jerkins operating radios in cold weather. This may have been because these women also served a dual role as dispatch riders to take messages in the event of radio failures and may have had to been returned to the Quartermaster after use.

Austerity pattern men's denim blouses and trousers were issued to some women when performing particularly messy tasks, such as cleaning or mechanical maintenance of vehicles. Civilian tan brown work overalls 'shopkeepers' coats were also worn by some mechanics.

Duties Performed by Women Auxiliaries

The rules of Geneva Convention forbade the use of women as front line combatant soldiers. So the women auxiliaries performed many support roles. Signallers, Telephonists, Medical Orderlies, Stretcher Bearers, Cooks, Drivers, Mechanics and Dispatch Riders on privately owned machines, were all roles performed by women.

Living Historian Lesley wearing W.H.G.A. Signallers uniform

Living Historian Lesley dressed as a V.A.D.-trained (W.H.G.A.) First Aider

Eva Bishop from Haughley in newly issued 1938 pattern denims 1944

Winscombe and Sandford Home Guard with Women Auxiliaries sitting in the front row, at Stand Down 1944

Lesley from Living History group Blitz and Peaces is wearing a typical outfit for a signaller. On top of her standard uniform she wears an A.T.S. leather jerkin for warmth when sat for long periods in the field. She carries a water-bottle, civilian duty respirator and a 37 pattern signals satchel in which were kept her notepad, headphones and microphone for the radio set. If on exercises she would have also carried or worn a steel helmet.

Dispatch Riders

All Home Guard motorcyclists including women were issued with MK I goggles. Dispatch riders did not wear the army style dispatch rider trousers. They wore standard battledress uniform and were issued with leather jerkins.

Women motorcyclists wore leather jerkins and dispatch riders helmet and men's clothing. Very few appear in photos.

W.H.G.A. First Aiders/Medics/ Stretcher Bearers

The uniform is a period cotton shirt, Red Cross issued Beret and V.A.D. Badge, A.T.S. issue tie, Olive green American made khaki skirt, an A.T.S. issue tie with W.H.G.A. plastic badge worn as a tie pin, flesh colour stockings and brown shoes.

She is holding a shell dressing pouch and a first field dressing pouch and is carrying a Civilian Duty Respirator, 37 pattern medic's haversack (general purpose), and a Mk II steel helmet.

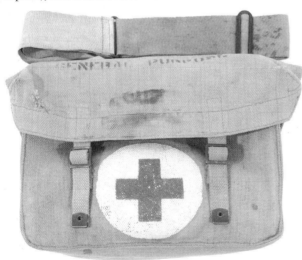

1937 pattern medic's dressings satchel

The 1937 pattern medic's webbing satchel with first-aid kit and shell dressings as carried by HG medics, (These were standard issue and available at all HQs).

Mk II helmet marked with Red Cross

Some medical HG medical units used WWI large packs and army 37 pattern small packs for dressings. These have large red crosses painted on the front.

They were carried and used by Guardsmen or Auxiliaries that had already had Red Cross or St John Ambulance first aid Training.

Young mothers with families joined and also single women. Most of the single women were working for around 40 hours a week in civilian jobs, and a further 12 hours per week in the civil defence organisations, such as the Fire Guard and the A.R.P. Joining a local Women's Home Guard Auxiliary seemed like a natural progression and they were keen to recruit women with medical and radio skills particularly. The women were drawn from all sections of society and all ages, from the landed gentry to working class women. They served Britain with parity to the men.

Williton Home Guard with Women Auxiliaries at Stand Down

Chapter 16
Home Guard Unit Photographs

Officers of Exmouth and Budleigh Companies 2 'Clyst' Battalion Devon Home Guard

Authors Note
Although a copy of this photograph exists it was not of good enough quality to print. I have included the names of the officers in their correct positions, for people who may have a copy in their possession.

Back Row Left to Right.
Lieutenant J.M. Pavey, Lieutenant W.A. Ingham, Second Lieutenant W.A. Britton, Second Lieutenant A.F. Pratt, Second Lieutenant K.H. Coxe. M.C, Lieutenant J.F.R. Richards.

Front Row Left to Right.
Lieutenant H.S. Sutherland, Lieutenant A. Beach, Lieutenant C.R. Rickeard, Captain. A.C.G. Roberts. M.C, Major. J.W. Palmer, Lieutenant R.T. Anderson, Lieutenant S.C. Cassyn. Lieutenant A.R. Smith, Captain. T.C.C. Evans. D.S.O., Lieutenant ?

The Photograph was taken around stand down in 1944.

The picture was taken on the lawn at the end of West Terrace in Budleigh Salterton. Palmer house now stands on the site.

N.C.O.'s of Exmouth 'B' Company 2 'Clyst' Battalion Devon Home Guard at Stand Down

Back Row Left to Right
Sergeant S.G. Seldon, Sergeant T. Mathews, Sergeant W. Croft, ?, Sergeant W. Pascoe, Sergeant H. Lawes, Sergeant Fred Rendle.

Middle Row Left to Right
Sergeant C. Tindall, Sergeant W. Holman, Sergeant J. Brock, Sergeant W. Clarke, Sergeant W. Bryant, Sergeant Reginald Dixon, Sergeant Frank Troulan, Sergeant Roy Fairchild, Sergeant R. Haydon.

Front Row Left to Right
Sergeant L. Hyde, Sergeant W. Pope, Quarter Mater Sergeant A.P. Mc Larin, Company Sergeant Major Charlie Havill, Sergeant F. Havill (Son), Sergeant Albert Edwin Dixon Pollard, Sergeant C. Axon.

The photo was taken in Exmouth Manor Gardens at Stand Down.

Signals Platoon Exmouth 'B' Company 2 'Clyst' Battalion Devon Home Guard at Stand Down

Exmouth Signals Platoon
At present it cannot be established whether this was a section, or, was in fact 1 Platoon.

Back Row Left to Right
?, Dispatch Rider?, George Waldron (Radio Operator)

Middle Row Left to Right
Dispatch Rider?, Bill Homan, Mr. Dowell, Reginald

Dixon, Bill Gorfin, Dispatch Rider.

Front Row Left to Right
?, Sergeant A.P. 'Spud' Mc Larin,?,?,?,?, Company Sergeant Major Charlie Havill, ?,?,?.

The photo was taken in Exmouth Manor Gardens at Stand Down.

2 Platoon Exmouth 'B' Company 2 'Clyst' Battalion Devon Home Guard at Stand Down

Exmouth 2 Platoon

Back Row Left to Right ?,?,?,?,?,?,?,?,?,?.

Middle Row Left to Right Geoff
Wilmott,?,?,?,?,?,?,?,?,?,?

Front Row Left to Right
?,?, S.G. Seldon, Lieutenant (gunners lanyard), Lieutenant (gunners lanyard) , ?,?,?,?,

The photo was taken in Exmouth Manor Gardens at Stand Down.

3 Platoon Exmouth 'B' Company 2 'Clyst' Battalion Devon Home Guard at Stand down

Exmouth 3 Platoon

Back Row Left to Right
?,?,?,?,?, Percy Parsons, ?,?,?,?,?,?

Middle Row Left to Right
?,?,?,?,?,?,?,?,?,?,?,?, Harold Marshall,?,?.

Front Row Left to Right
all unknown

The photo was taken in Exmouth Manor Gardens at Stand Down.

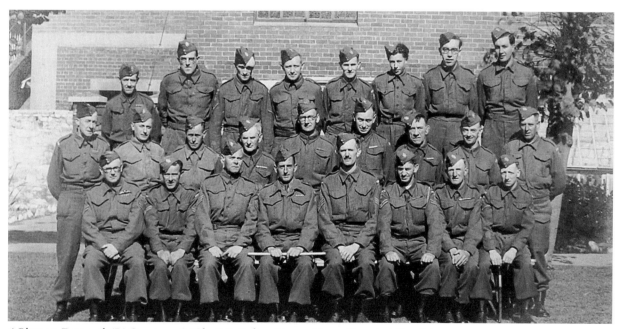

4 Platoon Exmouth 'B' Company 2 'Clyst' Battalion Devon Home Guard at Stand down

Exmouth 4 Platoon

Back Row Left to Right
?,?, Jim Woolacott,?,?, Ray Towill,?,?.

Middle Row Left to Right
?,?,?, Bill Holman, ?,?,?,?,?.
Front Row Left to Right
?, Wilf Capron,?,?,?,?,?,?,?

The photo was taken in Exmouth Manor Gardens at Stand Down.

5 Platoon Exmouth 477 Coastal Artillery Home Guard R.A.

Exmouth 477 Coastal Artillery Battery Royal Artillery Home Guard

Back Row Left to Right
Gunner W.G. Andrews, Gunner A.V. Bolt, Gunner W.J. Doderell, Gunner J.W. Fasey, Gunner H. Long, Gunner A.L. Skinner, Gunner W.J. Richards, Gunner S.W. Martin, Gunner L.H. Farrant, Gunner A. Pemberton, Gunner Raymond A. Steer.

Third Row Left to Right
Gunner Percy W. Gatter, Gunner W.B. Luxon, Gunner C. Thomas, Gunner G. Hitchcock, Gunner J.R.G. Thorn, Gunner W.T. Morrish, Gunner A. Edwards, Gunner Edward J. Derrick, Gunner J. Hyde, Gunner A.J.R. Seager, Gunner C. Dudley, Gunner B. Eley, Gunner Michael A.G. Heard. The only man wearing his Royal Artillery gunners white lanyard.

Second Row Left to Right
Lance Bombardier. R.C. Smith, Gunner E.T. Pannell, Gunner T. Western, Gunner E. Williams, Lance Bombardier J.W.M. Denford, Gunner H. Stowell, Gunner G.H. Slocombe, Gunner A.G. Brailey, Gunner E. McIntosh, Gunner P.L. Harris, Gunner C. Nichol, Gunner P. Sedgemore, Lance Bombardier A.A.G. Searle.

Front Row Left to Right
Bombardier Arthur J. Clode, Sergeant G.M. Walburn Sergeant T.C.V. Burnhill, Second Leftenant G.R.W. Glanville. Captain A.E. Jones, M.C. (seated with stick). Major A.S. Archdale D.S.O. (seated with stick). Second Lieutenant S.J.G. Southon. Company Sergeant Major C.H. Havill. Sergeant H. Swinnerton, Sergeant E.C. Raven, Bombardier Wilf Lowton. Bombardier E. Charlie Bond.

Exmouth's 477 Coastal Artillery Battery Home Guard (R.A.) was photographed on at the Imperial Hotel on the seafront. The Photograph was taken on the morning of September 24 1944, just prior to the national stand down of the Home Guard. The photograph was taken by John Puddicombe.

Exmouth 6 Platoon
No photographs, or list of names of men who served, exist for this platoon at present.

Luppitt Platoon 19 'Seaton' Battalion Devon Home Guard

Luppitt Platoon 19 'Seaton' Battalion Devon Home Guard

The Photograph was taken at Allhallows Playing Fields Honiton Prior to the Stand Down Parade was on 31st December 1944

Back Row Left to Right
Syd Valentine, Charles Crabb, Albie Wright, Charles Coles, Walter Ayres, Captain Rock, Edgar Thorne, Dan Buck, Eli Loveridge, Ralph Rosewell,

Middle Row Left to Right
Geoff Spiller, Len Drew, Ken Pulman, Henry Toomey, Bill Blackmore. Jack Middleton, Gilbert Clapp, Walter Manville, John Wilson, Syd Middleton, Walter Hart.

Front Row Left to Right
Jack Thorne, Carl Churchill, Sam Ewins, Tom Martin, Albie Crabb, John (Jack) Sage, Bill Walden, Wilf Perkins, J. Edwards, Arthur Braddick, Archie Corrick, George Cooper.

Plush Platoon 'Stinsford' Battalion Dorset Home Guard

Plush Platoon 'Stinsford' Battalion Dorset Home Guard

The men are a General Service (Infantry) platoon and have been issued with rubberised haversacks. Taken around Stand Down

Back Row Left to Right
Herb Downton, ?, Fred Bowles, George Bowles, ? Russell, ? Sant, ?, John Parker, George (or possibly Fred Lovell), Reg Atkins, Charles Atkins, Tom Greening, Bert Foot.

Middle Row Left to Right
Fred Parsons, ? Upshaw, Tom Stroud, Charles Symes, ? Tory (or possibly 'Titch' Upshaw, ? Lovell, ? Cosh, Cyril Kingman, Albert Lovell, 'Fido' Harrison, Archie Watts, Fred Thorne, Walt Hyde, ? Tyrell.

Front Row Left to Right
Tommy Cosh, ? Gregory, Bert Crabbie, Phillip Tory, Fred Atkins, John Chapman, ?, Roy Kingman, ?, Jack Wichard,   ? Gregory, Charlie Miller.

In the photo are the Lower Bockhampton section. They met in the old forge workshop situated next to Bridge Cottage. There was no heating in the building so make shift fires were built no chimney either so they got very black with the fumes.

Ivybridge Platoon 16 'Plymouth' Battalion Devon Home Guard

Ivybridge Platoon 16 'Plymouth' Battalion Devon Home Guard

Included in the photograph with positions unknown are;

Edward Moysey, ? Muggeridge, Basil Carey, ? Salter, Jack Hurrell, Fred Andrews, Arthur Bernard, Arthur Johns, Jack House, Clarence Ryder, Edwin Osborne, Bill Hodge, George Yelder, Bill Mortimore, Fred Priddle, Fred Bennett.

Hemyock Company 3 'Cullompton' Battalion Devon Home Guard at Stand Down 1944

Hemyock Company 3 'Cullompton' Battalion Devon Home Guard

The photograph was taken at the milk factory at Stand Down as the men have 4 years service chevrons on their arms.

Back Row Left to Right
Geoff James, Leslie Hart, Stanley Salter, Stanley Lowman, Chris Doble, Frank Lowman, George Salter, Percy Pike, Albert Salter, Stanley Doble, Harry Richards, Leonard Stewart, Jack Wood, Roy Granger, Harold Durman.

Middle Row Left to Right
Arthur Shire, Bill Pike, Jack Trenchard, Frank Simmonds, Dennis Pring, Cedric Jenkins, Eric Cubitt, ? Chichester, Jim Hart, Doctor Muir, George Gammon, Dick Granger, Walter Lee, Jack Lilley.

Front Row Left to Right
Fred Clarke, Fred Lawrence, Jim Lowman, Bill Always, Bill Trickey, Dick Pooley, Harold Cubitt, H. Lowry, R. Thorne, George Franks, Bill Hutchings, Jim Woodgate, Harry Bale , Bill Bradford, Harry Trickey.

'B' Company 2 Battalion Wiltshire Home Guard

'B' Company 2 Battalion Wiltshire Home Guard
This photograph of 'B' Company was taken in June 1943, at the H.Q. hut. No. 5 'Charlton and Hawketon' Platoon. No. 6 'Crudwell' Platoon.No.7 'Minety' Platoon and No. 8 'Oaksey' Platoon are all present.

Back Row Left to Right
L.W. Taylor, C.F. Baker, W.J. Sheppard, A.W.H. Scott, T.S. Clarke, J. Lafford, W.C. Sparrow, A.E. Selby, E.F. Pennell, E.R. Ponting, F.E. Telling, J.W. Westmancott, H.F.L. Parker.

Third Row
Although the following men are in this photograph it has not been possible to match the names to the positions. C.G. Thorne, F.J. Langley, E.G.J. Pugh, J.R.M. Carpenter, L.E. Tucker, S. Juggins, O.F.T. Carpenter, H.S.F. Snuggs, C. Chilverton, C.G. Hannock, H.J. Turner, R. Palmer, J.G. Higgs.

Second Row Left to Right
A.C. Hislop, F.W. Constable, C. Jones, H.C. Starey, C.H. Shores, W.E. Snelling, W.W. Pitter, G.C. Todd, C.E. Timbrell, W. Legg.

Front Row Left to Right
V.S.J. Butcher, P. Webb, G.Webb, P.J. Nurden, R.J. Shaw, W. Harris, S. Collinson, L.P.E. Waldron, W.F. Sherwood.

No. 6 'Crudwell' Platoon, 'B' Company 2nd Battalion Wiltshire Home Guard

6 'Crudwell' Platoon, 'B' Company 2 Battalion Wiltshire Home Guard

The photograph was taken on 5 November 1944 probably taken in the vicinity of the Plough Inn.

Back Row Left to Right
Bert Tidmarsh, ? Smith, Albert Eddolls, Richard Dring, Charlie Tuck, ? Banfield, Bill Teagle, Douglas Kemp, Bob Large, ? Walker.

Middle Row Left to Right
Billy Braid, ? Hayes, Dick Snuggs, Dick Goodfield, William Clutterbuck, Jonnie Casey, Jack Wiggins, Bert Stevens, ? Clack, Frank Ward, Frank Saunders, Richard Waldron.

Front Row Left to Right
Oliver Carpenter, Seymour Clark, R.J. Shaw, Perry Nurden, Bert Selby, H.C. Starey, Charlie Thorne, Reg Carpenter, Bill Sparrow, Jack Lafford, Len Tucker.

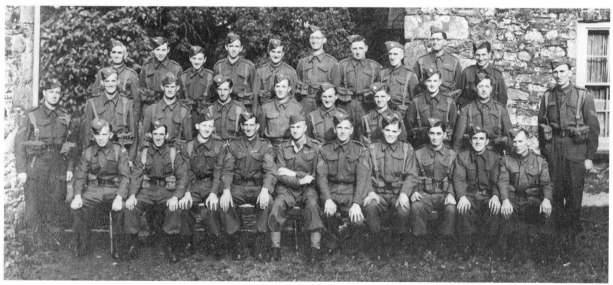

Clearbrook Platoon at Stand Down

Clearbrook Platoon 15 'Plympton' Battalion Devon Home Guard

Members of this platoon are known to have been helping the Royal Engineer with unexploded bombs during the Plymouth Blitz.

William Blackwell Ayers is the only guardsman's names known to be part of this Platoon. Their positions in the photograph are unknown.

Officers and N.C.O's of Woolmers Green Platoon 4 Battalion Hertsfordshire Home Guard at Stand Down

**Woolmers Green Platoon 4 Battalion
Hertsforshire Home Guard**

Back Row Left to Right
Punch Croft, Arthur Warren, Corporal Bill Gates,
Corporal Alf Scott, Corporal Fred Monk, Lance
Corporal Ernie Ayers, Bernie Leggett.

Front Row Left to Right
Sergeant Stan Males, Lieutenant Fish, Lieutenant Eyre,
Sergeant Knowles, Corporal Percy Jeffrey.

'Nestle' Platoon 'Staverton' Company 13 'Totnes' Battalion Devon Home Guard

**'Nestle' Platoon 'Staverton' Company 13 'Totnes'
Battalion Devon Home Guard**

The photograph was probably taken around stand
down in 1944 at the Nestlé factory. No names of the
Guardsman are available.

Officers and Staff of No. 4 'Watchet' Platoon Williton Company, Somerset Home Guard

H.Q. 'Williton' Company 1 Battalion Somerset Home Guard

The photograph is taken at Stand Down in December 1944, hence great coats. It is unusual in that the Sergeant Major is wearing a beret and 1937 pattern webbing and three Women's Home Guard Auxiliaries are present in this small unit. They wear their brooches on their lapels.

Back Row Left to Right

Ernest Stevens, ?, Sergeant Major Bill Venn, Mrs. Beryl Venn, Cyril Thomas, Margaret Branchflower, Maude Trebble, Bill Thompson, ? Stan Baker.

Front Row Left to Right

Sidney Connett, Jack H. Bissell, Victor Danby, Bill Hurley, Major W.T. Greswell, Colonel E.R. Clayton C.M.G., D.S.O., Doctor J. Erskine Collins, (Medical Officer), Edwin Herbert Davis.

4 'Watchet' Platoon 'Williton' Company 1st Battalion Somerset Home Guard

This photo was taken at Stand Down outside the council offices at Williton in December 1944. More than 70 men passed through this unit during the war. As part of their duties they kept nightly watches on the Bristol Channel from an observation point on Cleeve Hill.

Back Row Left to Right

Les Wedlake, Ivor Prole, Frank Warren, Bill Watts, Stan Amies, Hubert Westcott, Arthur Salmon, Len Eveleigh.

Middle Row Left to Right

Cyril Western, Harold Webber, Jack Clavey, Jack Bartlett, Stan Dudderidge, Jimmy Leigh, Ron Prole, Basil Bindon, James Bindon.

Front Row Left to Right

Billy Lee, Tom Bulpin, George Willicombe, Victor Danby, Major W.T. Creswell, Sergeant Major W.J.D. Venn, Bill Thompson, Joe Hunt, Walter Bulpin,

Hempnall Platoon Norfolk Home Guard Photographed at Stand Down

Hempnall Platoon Norfolk Home Guard

James Ladbrooke was the district commander of the Hempnall Platoon. They had initially put an L.D.V. unit together in May 1940 and meetings were held in the cottage near the mill.

Their Quartermasters store was at the Poplars, where ammunition and rifles were also stored.

Back Row Left to Right
Mr. Stopps, Spratt Potter, Will Leatherstich, Phillip Moore, Jimmy Youngman, Nat Davidson.

Middle Row Left to Right
Norman Ellis, Jimmy Leggett, ?,?, Mr. Cunningham, ?, Walter Pigg.

Front Row Left to Right
Ben Hickling, Jimmy Cawthorne, Walter Ladbrooke, Bob Hazell, Jack Waddeldow.

Nynehead and Oake Platoons Somerset Home Guard at Stand Down December 1944

Nynehead Platoon and Oake Platoons
Somerset Home Guard

Back Row Left to Right
?, ?, Jack Hawkins, R. Hartnell, ?, ?, ?, T. Hutchins, F. Pulman, E. Stevens.

Middle Row Left to Right
S. Jones, T. Lock, H. Dunn, R. Marks, Bill Winter, H. Sharland, B. Pavey, ?, L.Stone, E. Derbe.

Front Row Left to Right
Bill Radford, L. Sparks, Reverend Rees Davies, R.B. Hankey, A. Elston, Fred Bickham.

Mere Platoon at Stand Down 1944

Mere Platoon Wiltshire Home Guard

Back Row Left to Right
P. Flower, C.Whitmarsh, ?,

Third Row Left to Right
R. Shave, W. Lawrence, W. Gray, G. Pester, R. Sims, R. Bourton,

Second Row Left to Right
T. Burfitt, A. Warre, F. Bristow, W. Mills, E. Horrell, R. Doddington, H. Abraham.

Front Row Left to Right
R. Warren, A. Coward, R. Stratton, ?, L. Vincent.

No. 3 Platoon 20 'Tiverton' Battalion Devon Home Guard photographed at Stand Down

Tiverton Company 20 'Tiverton' Battalion Devon Home Guard 3 Platoon

The photograph was taken outside the Middle School in December 1944.

Back Row Left to Right
Privates Emmett, Andrews, Bird, Carpenter, Willman, Habgood, Wilkins, Kerr, Allen , Montadon, Lance Corporal, Hookway, Private Payne,

Third Row Left to Right
Privates Leaworthy, Frankpitt, Corporals Searle Gardiner, Mogridge, Gale, Sergeants Day, Cook,

Corporals Greenslade, Davey, Hicks, Lance Corporal Legg, Privates Ashford, Matthews.

Second Row Left to Right
Sergeants Marker, Bicknell, Company Quarter Master Sergeant Ellicott, 2nd Lieutenant P. Bicknell, Lieutenant Heal, Captain Warren, Lieutenant Jenkins, Lieutenant B. Bicknell, Sergeants Cox, Beck, Wills.

Front Row Left to Right
Privates Poole, Paul, Edwards, Jones, Fewings, Forward, Green, White, Mills, Lanchbury, Goff.

No. 4 Platoon 20 'Tiverton' Battalion Devon Home Guard photographed at Stand Down

No. 4 Platoon

This photograph was once again taken outside the Tiverton Middle School, There are no names available for the men in the photograph. It is known that members of the Women's Voluntary Service assisted the Home Guard in Tiverton, as Auxiliaries, but no information or photographs are available.

Tiverton Home Guard was led by the borough Surveyor, Colonel Duncan Arthur and Sir John Amory. A special mounted patrol was formed from members of the local hunt to look for possible paratroop landings on the open spaces. Blundells School had it's own Home Guard platoon and on one occasion, held Sir John Amory under arrest as he had no identification. They refused to release him until his identity could be positively established.

Officers and N.C.O.s of Dartington Platoon 13 'Totnes' Battalion at Stand Down

Dartington Platoon 13 'Totnes' Battalion Devon Home Guard

By September 1940 Dartington Home Guard had 70 members. Their H.Q. had been established at shiner's bridge. They soon built a makeshift rifle range at a nearby disused quarry. One of the main objectives was to defend the vulnerable points at river crossings and the road junction at shinner's bridge and nearby railway line to Malt Bridge.

Unfortunately the names of the Guardsman who appear in this photograph are not known, except for Lance Corporal Reg Newson who stands 5 from the left in the back row.

Dartington Platoon 13 'Totnes' Battalion Devon Home Guard

Back Row Left to Right
Noel Wakeham, Paddy O'Harahan, Eddie Pront, Jack James, Hugh Fowler, Ernest Clarke, ?, Walter Thomas, Jack Last, Clifford Cordy, William Pook, William Ambrose, Walter Harris, Stanley Ivey.

Middle Row Left to Right
Henry Rogers, Tom Dance, Sergeant Bert Helbes, Victor Syms, ? Hines, Tom Blight, Dennis Martin, Jim Head, Harry, Doidge, Reg Denham, Dei MacTaggart, Maurice Clements.

Front Row Left to Right
Harry Walters, Dick Legg, Frank Burrows, Jim Taylor, Jim Martin, Charlie Winston, Clarence Miller, Richard King.

Officers and N.C.O.s of Bampton Company 20 'Tiverton' Battalion Devon Home Guard at Stand Down

Bampton Company 20 'Tiverton' Battalion Devon Home Guard

Back Row Left to Right
H. Weston, Ron Baker, Sam Hill, Tom Cotterell, Les Besley, L. Ekhart.

Middle Row Left to Right
Len Gratton, Evan Collacott, Frank Manley, Colonel Sir Gilbert Acland-Troyte, Len Burnett, Colonel Hockin, Jack Dunn, Albert Chudley.

Front Row Left to Right
Rob Burnett, Ernie Balman, Bill Williams, Donald Jones, Walt Randle.

Bampton Company 20 'Tiverton' Battalion Devon Home Guard 1943

Bampton Company 20 'Tiverton' Battalion Devon Home Guard at Stand Down

Back Row Left to Right
P. Penney, E. Gillard, D. Bowden, R. Smolden, Reverend Jones (Baptist Minister), S. Salisbury, R. Milton, Jack Scott Rundle,

Fourth Row Left to Right
? Tar, R. Graham, A. Woodman, V. Greens lade, G. Hotter, A. Hereford, A. Baker, W. Marley, J. Dunn, H. Tout, R. Baker, R. Ounce.

Third Row Left to Right
H. Hancock, W. Walsh, F. Pook, R. Burnett, T. Peachey,
A. Hotter, H. Counter, F. Baker, H. Bowers, F. Parkman, L. Cleland, C. Cottrell.

Second Row Left to Right
E. Balman, R. Burnett, ? Dunn, G. Hill, W. Williams, L. Elkhart, T. Cottrell, Don Jones,.

Front Row Left to Right
G. Yen, H. Tavernier, F. Dunbar, G. Brewer, J. Hancock, S. Baker, H. Atwater, S. Coles, ?, J. Falter, P. Milton.

Calbourne Platoon Isle of Wight Home Guard

Calbourne Platoon photographed at Westover House 1941

Back Row Left to Right
Dennis Harvey (home on leave from the airborne forces), Les Long, Frank Parnell, Jack Hillier, Les Strickley, George Weeks, (home on leave from the R.A.F.).

Third Row Left to Right
Ted Harvey, Len Pitman, Albert Long, Bill Bradley, Bert Hooker, Jack Simms (possibly Simmonds?), Frank Cassell, Dick Jellis, Ern Pocock,

Second Row Left to Right
Fred Long, Fred Buckett, Bert Hannam, Alf Hayles, Bill Brett, Alf Brett, Dave Angell, Fred Sivier, Joe Critchell.

Front Row Left to Right
Ronnie Weeks, Roy Harvey, Len Brooks, Captain Harry Lee, Lieutenant Michenor, Unknown Army Officer, Unknown Army Officer.

The Calbourne Home Guard Unit of the West Wight Company used an old Austin truck to be taken to defend various vulnerable points on the island. They met regularly at Westover House where they drilled and trained throughout the war.

Blofield Company Norfolk Home Guard at Stand Down December 1944

Blowfield Company Norfolk Home Guard
The Blowfield Home Guard met at the Kings Head, public house.

George Cann Blofield Home Guard
'You joined the Home Guard one week. The next week you got a rifle. Then they taught you how to fire it!'

Back Row Left to Right
Kenny Smith, Ben Frost, Charlie Brady, Tom Dawson, Arthur Browne, ?, Fred Edrich, George Bailey, Billy Brooks, Jimmy Brassy Brown, ?, ?, Leonard Hubbard, Laddy Watson.

Third Row Left to Right
Ted Frost, ?, Mr. Smith, Norman, Marriott, Alfie Allen, ?, Cyrill Trett, Percy Rope, Henry Bowring, ?, ?, Albert Francis, Claude Leeder, Jack Rope, Horace Howard, George Townsend.

Second Row Left to Right
?, ?, Ernest Hanton, Herbert 'Winkle' Layt, Jack Land, Bertie Rope, Hedley Smith, Mr. Golder, Mr. Jack Gowing, ?, Bernard Read, ?, Harry Alden, ?, Fred Fountain, 'Bishy' Baynes, ?.

Front Row Left to Right
Arthur Knights, ?, Ben Richardson, Harry Rose, Walter Parker, George Cann, ?, Jack Marshall, Lenny Hayton, ?, Kenny 'Mucky' Hylton, Baden Hanton, Thomas Houghton, Cecil Parker, ?.

Narborough Company Leicestershire Home Guard at Narborough House, their H.Q. in 1942

Narborough Company Leicestershire Home Guard

Narborough L.D.V were formed on 14 May 1940. Originally two units were formed at Narborough and Pentney, these were later amalgamated into one company. Early members of the L.D.V were: Peter Wright, Sam Goose, Jack Smith, 'Wally' Thacker, 'Pony' Moore, and 'Show' Hunt. Early Commanding Officers were Peter Hayward and David Bun field. A major road block made from concrete blocks Zig Zagging across the road was established on the East Walton Road, which was the main route between R.A.F. Marham to the fuel dump at Harpley.

The area was heavily defended with pill boxes, tank traps, and spigot mortar concrete slab bases, these can still be seen today by the river.

Narborough Leicestershire Home Guard Officers and N.C.O.'s

Back Row left to Right
G. Mobbs, A. Bix, J. Bull, L. Curson, D. Coggles, H. Wilson.

Middle Row left to Right
E. Bray, V. Gotsell, F. Curzon, W. Taylor, G. Gotts, A. Morton.

Front Row left to Right
W. Smith, J. Cooper, P. Heywood, D. Bunfield, J. Gotsell, J. Taylor, R. Taylor.

Sourton Caundle Platoon 'Lydlinch' Company Dorset Home Guard

Sourton Caundle Platoon 'Lydlinch' Company Dorset Home Guard

No names are available for this photograph.

The volunteers from Sourton Caundle were part of the Lydlinch Company. When the L.D.V. was first formed, the lectures and training sessions were held in the village hut, where they gradually became more organised. Patrols were mounted on the high ground at the top of Holt Lane where the L.D.V. members watched for German paratroopers in four hour shifts.

During September 1940, when the code word Cromwell was given, signifying an invasion by German forces, the men of the Lydlinch Platoon were raised from their beds to stand guard on emergency standby. They passed the night trying to keep warm and chatting to each other about what might be coming their way.

After the night of the invasion scare many changes were made to the structure and duties of the Lydlinch unit. More patrols were now mounted one at Cat Lane near Brunsells Knapp, the patrols were also issued with rifles and 5 rounds of ammunition. A rifle range and explosives store was built in an orchard a Barrows Hill Farm. Training with hand grenades and .303 rifles took place here.

An H.Q. was set up at an abandoned cottage at Goldsneys and training and night time exercises were gradually introduced and organised from here.

Willand Company 3 'Cullompton' Battalion Devon Home Guard at Townlands House

Willand Company 3 'Cullompton' Battalion Devon Home Guard

The L.D.V was formed on 15th May 1940 and initially the men drilled with replica rifles.

The prime objective of the Willand Platoon, was to make sure that the railway bridges, including Staunch Hill and the White Ball Railway Tunnel in Somerset were secure. They also mounted road blocks, watches and patrols in the area. When they were eventually issued with rifles, a rifle range was set up at Uffculme Quarries and regular training was given there

Back Row Left to Right
Tom Sanders, Ken Stoyle, Jack Clench, Charlie Dart, Hector Stoyle, Cyril Bryant, Dick Rowland, Douglas Keen, Arthur Vinnicombe.

Third Row Left to Right
Jack Davey, Walt Radford (Junior), Ernie Upham, Ted Austin, Abe Roberts, Les march, R. Chichester, Bill

Head, Frank Chick, Jack Broom, Dick Ousley.

Second Row Left to Right
Stan Villis, Alb Chard, Ron Sanders, Alf Keen, Reg Rowe, Walt Radford (Senior), Bill Knott, Tom Evans, Jack Harnell.

Front Row Left to Right (Seated)
Bill Baker, Henry Eveleigh, Bill Russ, Ted Taylor, Doug Wright.

West Coker Platoon Somerset Home Guard at Stand Down December 1944

West Coker Platoon Somerset Home Guard

The West Coker Home Guard's main responsibilities was protecting a building which was situated at the corner of Pack Hollow and Gooseacre Lane. The building was a recently built 'Repeater Station' for telecommunications, containing the most up to date telephone exchanges and equipment and was crucial to the security and communications of the country. As well as protecting the Repeater Station, half the Platoon was situated at Coker Hill Ridge . Information Supplied by Reg Warr.

Back Row Left to Right
Wilf Baker, Charles Bartlett, Joe Woolmington, Reg Woolmington, George Bonard, ?,

Third Row Left to Right
Bill Lee, Cecil Reed, Charlie Bastin, ?, Gordon Chick, Harry Ricketts.

Second Row Left to Right
Howard Wright, Sid Burt, ?, Eddie Stroud, Maudwyn Adams, Eric Gatcombe, Morgan Chick.

Front Row Left to Right
Henry Trask, Arthur Burroughs, Charles Adams, Victor Booth, Sergeant Richards, Ray Burnett, George Cyril.

Front Kneeling Left to Right
Ted Rendell, Harry Vincent.

Peter Tavy and Cudlipptown Platoons Circa 1943

Peter Tavy and Cudliptown Platoons 7 'Okehampton' Battalion Devon Home Guard

John Vogwill and John Roskilly were men with previous military experience and they formed the initial L.D.V. unit. When it changed to the Home Guard they remained the commanders of the unit.

To get the men fit they practised rout marches between Peter Tavy out to Cuddliptown and back, returning through Horndon and along the main road to Harford Bridge.

Training and exercises with regular troops were also carried out, including mock invasions. The Company Headquarters and First Aid Post were in Peter Tavy. At the school room in Peter Tavy, regular lectures were given on weapons, gas training and field craft, by officers from Okehampton Camp. The quartermasters stores were at Lang Cottage (now Spring House), where Q.M.S. Herbert Stevens looked after the inventory. Uniforms rifles and other heavier weapons

gradually arrived here and were allocated to the men as equipment became available. There was a rifle range and butts at Willworthy where they practised with shotguns, firing W.D. supplied solid ball cartridges and later .303 SMLE rifles.

Nightly Patrols were mounted and guards posted at Harford Bridge over the river Tavy and nightly watches were also mounted at Mary Tavy power station, as this was considered a vulnerable point. A searchlight was stationed at Westlake and on Whit Tor in the joint role of searching for enemy aircraft and lighting the moors in the event of an enemy airborne assault.

A horseback unit was also set up to patrol some of the more remote areas of the region including morning patrols at Cox Tor.

Back Row Left to Right
F.J. Roskilly, W. Smale, J. Perkins, T. Medland, J. Cole, F. Collins,

Middle Row Left to Right
E. Pellowe, J. Osborne, G. Medland, A. Perkins, E. Pengelly, J. Mudge, Mr. Simms, J. Blowey, B. Rickeard.

Front Row Left to Right
J. Bellamy, Mr. Wedd, F. Alford, S.D. Strafford, J. Vogwill, J.M. Roskilly (Senior), Henry H. Stevens, F. Brooks, G. Madge.

Other Known Members of the Platoon
Frederick William Dodd, Frank Littlejohn, John Palmer, Dennis Cannon.

Officers of Looe Home Guard at Stand Down December 1944

East and West Looe Platoons Cornwall Home Guard

In May over 100 men from Looe with an average age of 45, enlisted in the L.D.V. The West Looe Section was commanded by Mr. S. Bowden, whilst East Looe was commanded by Mr. H. Ross from Plaidy.

They had a small hut donated to use for their meetings and two local fishermen also offered the use of their boats in an emergency. Unfortunately, Mr. Bowden

noted with some annoyance that not one young fisherman from Looe had volunteered for service in either unit, but this was mainly due to the fact that the fishermen mainly worked at night. Despite their lack of commitment to the L.D.V. the fishermen did volunteer to cross the channel to Dunkirk to ferry back the Tommies stranded on the beaches. Although preparations were made in Looe for all boats with a draught of less than 2 metres and an engine of more than 12hp to be readied for the crossing, Just before the small boats were due to leave, the order was cancelled as it was deemed that the Looe boats would not be needed.

Back Row Left to Right
Horace Loose, ?, Bob Pengelly, Dick Nason, ?,?,?,

Front Row Left to Right
Harry Whale, ?, Wilfred Neale, Major H.E.Ross, Albert Mutton, Bill Evil, Harry Coad.

Major Ross was awarded the M.B.E. for his services to the Home Guard.

Mulbarton Platoon Norfolk Home Guard at Stand Down

Mulbarton Platoon Norfolk Home Guard

The men in the Mulbarton Platoon are photographed outside the remains of the mill on the common at stand down probably December 1944. The following men are known to be present but there is no indication as to where there positions are.

Otto Arbendroth, Ted Aggas, Leslie Andrews, Bob Bailey, George Barrett, D. Bennington, Louie Bennington, George Bosten, 'Pots' Brighton, Harry Carver, Jack Cooper, Ted Copeman, Tom Cotton, L. Cross, Toby Callum, Russel Dent. Ted Farrow, C. Hooney, Fred Jackson, A. Jenkins, Reggie Ladbrooke, Billy Larter, Horace Lofty, Tony Mc Kelvey, Jimmy Mackerell, Ted nelson, W. Rose, Tony Robottom, Don Skipper, Tom Smith, Fred Wasey, Jimmy Whurr, George Wick, Leslie Woods, Pat Wymer, Plus three other unnamed Guardsmen.

Hindringham Platoon Norfolk Home Guard

There were two sections known to be operating in this area. One in the centre of the village of Hindringham itself, operating out of a hut near the church and the other located at Field House. At field house there was a store for A.R.P. equipment for bombed out families and also the store for the Home Guard ammunition, which included ST grenades and Mills bombs. Rifles and Sten guns were also stored there at a later date and the explosive weapons removed to a safer location.

The area suffered one enemy attack by a German bomber one night which strafed the area including cottages and farm buildings.

A total of around 30 men were in the unit at any time and they were commanded by Lieutenant Bob Sands, and trained by Sergeant Major King who lived in Thursford. No Photograph is available for this platoon.

Members Known to Have Served with Hindringham Home Guard
Anthony Hammond, George Abel Senior, George Kendall, 'Seagull' Bernard Lake, Charles Grieves, Bob Sands, George Edmonds, Russell Jordan, Reggie Jarvis, Sidney 'Shy' Bacon, Don Massingham, Hubert Kinsley, 'Sausage' Alfred Martins, John Wones, Reggie Loades, 'Brit' lake, Gus Howard, Maurice Brewster, Clarence Mace, Jack Lake, Jack Bullen, Charlie Rowe, Arthur Frank Flood, Ernie Money,

Members Known to Have Served at Field House
Bob Scott, Phillip Rounce, Alan Rounce, Ray Rounce, 'Dicky' Bird.

23 Platoon 'Land's End' Company 12 Battalion Cornwall Home Guard

Land's End Company 12 Battalion Cornwall Home Guard

This photograph contains the St. Buryan's Crows-an-Wra section and the Sennen section. The Sennen men's names are marked with an (S).

Back Row Left to Right
Thornley Thomas, John Hosken, Percy Jenkins, Cecil Merrifield (S), James Roberts (S), Walter Hutchings (S), Mathew Nicholas, (S), William Rawlings, (S), Thomas Hill (S), Goerge Wearne (S).

Third Row Left to Right
James George, Frederick Jenking, Gordon Hocking, John Chope (S), William Pender, (S), Donald Williams (S), Garfield Humphrys (S), Donald Warren, Beverley Hitchins (S), Joseph Braunton (S).

Second Row Left to Right
Leonard White, Peter George, Dennis Trembath (S), John Quick, Charlie Berryman, Nicholas Hards, (S), John Hutchings (S), Percy Lugg (S), Cecil Olds, Zacchaeus Nicholas (S), Cliford Jenking.

Front Row Left to Right
William Hutchens (S), Phillip Martin (S), Clifford Withers (S), Herbert Semmens (S), Ashley Cargeeg, Humphry Humphrys (S), William Semmens (S), Samuel Trewhella (S), Charlie Kemp, Percy Waters, Kenneth Cargeeg, Leslie Cargeeg, Sidnay Williams (S).

The following photograph is on page 58 of chapter 8, Additional and Personal Equipment

Carhampton Platoon Somerset Home Guard.
This photograph of Carhampton Platoon was taken in the grounds of Dunster Castle just before stand down,

Back Row Left to Right
George Downer Snr., Frank Passmore, Bert Gunter, Bill Middleton, Sidney Williams, Frank Salter, Arthur Laramy.

Middle Row Left to Right
Arthur Taylor, George Pascoe, Gordon Farmer, Eric Pearce, Mr. Ridley, Henry Pugsley.

Front Row Left to Right
Jim Downer, Harry Simons, Joe Williams, Joe Stephenson.

Chapter 17

Stand Down

By the time compulsory enlistment had finished in September 1944, the Home Guard consisted of 1,727,095 men. The peak figure had actually been 1,793,000 in March 1943 which was effectively the largest regiment in the world. By the time the second front, the liberation of Nazi occupied Europe had been consolidated it was realised by the government that there was effectively very little chance of an Enemy invasion from September 1944.

Because of this, from the 11 September 1944 members of the Home Guard were no longer required to report for duty. Expectations were then relaxed and although many units, such as anti-aircraft and coastal artillery batteries were still on active service, most general service battalion units, continued to meet regularly, but it was more on a social level than being on active duty as the threat of invasion was clearly over by this time.

On 28 October 1944 shocked units all over Great Britain were informed that preparations were being made to stand down the Home Guard from 1 November 1944. To a lot of the men this created a sense of despair as they had enjoyed the training, the spirit and camaraderie of their time in the Home Guard.

On December 3 1944 a Stand Down parade was held in London it was attended by over 7,000 Home Guard members including some of their vehicles and inspected by King George VI. It was at this parade that he spoke to the men saying:

'You have fulfilled your charge; you have earned in full measure your countries gratitude.'

The London Stand Down Parade

The men chosen to represent Exmouth Home Guard in the Stand Down parade in London were.
- Company Sergeant Major Charlie H. Havill,
- Private Harry W. Marshall.
- Private W.A. Westwood.

A joint Devon Company was formed for the London stand down march from the following Battalions:

1 'Loyal' City of Exeter.
2 'Clyst' (Exmouth and East Devon).
3 'Cullompton'.
4 'Barnstaple'.
5 'Bideford'.
6 'Chulmleigh'.
7 'Okehampton'.
8 'Holsworthy'.
9 'Newton Abbot'.
10 'Torbay'.
11 'South Hams'.
12 'Dartmouth'.
13 'Totnes'.
14 'Moorside'. (Tedburn and Dunsford area).
15 'Plympton'.
16 'Plymouth'.
17 'Dockyard'. (Plymouth).
18 'Saltash'.
19 'Seaton'.
20 'Tiverton'.
21 'Devon Post Office'. (33 General Post Office).
22 'Southern Railway'. (H.Q. Exmouth Junction).
23 'Drakes'. (Drakes Island).
24 'Hartland'.
25 'Ilfracombe'.

They left from St David's Station by train for London Paddington. Then travelled by Bus to Chelsea Barracks as part of the joint Devon Company, under the command of Captain H. Grant of the Torquay Battalion. C.S.M. Havill was second in command.

They had a meal at the barracks with brand new cutlery and a mug big enough to take a bath in. They then went for drinks with the regulars in the messes and consumed several pints!

Reveille was at 7.00 a.m. with the soldiers dream, a cup of tea in bed and then a slap up breakfast! This was followed by a slightly rushed hour's sight seeing.

They then assembled for the parade, massed crowds lined the roads and the Home Guard looked very smart, according to on lookers.

They then went back to barracks for another meal and

Britain at War

The Daily Telegraph
and Morning Post

LONDON, MONDAY, DECEMBER 4, 1944

THE KING'S FAREWELL TO THE HOME GUARD

"A SPLENDID AND POWERFUL COMRADESHIP OF ARMS"

DAILY TELEGRAPH REPORTER

In the presence of the King, contingents of Home Guards from all over Britain and Northern Ireland yesterday held their final parade following the recent "stand-down" order. From now they cease to exist as a force in being, but remain ready to answer any emergency.

His Majesty took the salute in Hyde Park from 7,000 Home Guards. They marched through the West End of London on a three-mile-long route lined with cheering crowds.

The King wore the uniform of a field-marshal. He was accompanied by the Queen, in a dark coat and fox fur, and Princess Elizabeth and Princess Margaret, both in grey. Representatives of the United Nations and the Forces were at the blue-canopied saluting base. They included three field-marshals, Sir Claud Jacob, Lord Milne and the Earl of Cavan.

Broadcasting to the nation last night, the King said:

Four years ago, in May, 1940, our country was in mortal danger. The most powerful army the world had ever seen had forced its way to within a few miles of our coast. From day to day we were threatened with invasion.

In those days our Army had been gravely weakened. A call went out for men to enrol themselves in a new citizen army, the Local Defence Volunteers, ready to use whatever weapons could be found and to stand against the invader in every village and every town.

Throughout Britain and Northern Ireland the nation answered that summons, as free men will always answer when freedom is in danger.

From fields and hills, from factories and mills, from shops and offices, men of every age and every calling came forward to train themselves for battle. Almost overnight a new force came into being, a force which had little equipment but was mighty in courage and determination. In July, 1940, the Local Defence Volunteers became the Home Guard.

During those four years of continuing anxiety, that civilian army grew in strength; under the competent administration of the Territorial Army Associations it soon became a well-equipped and capable force, able to take over many duties from regular soldiers preparing to go overseas.

I believe it is the voluntary spirit which has always made the Home Guard so splendid and so powerful a comradeship of arms. The hope that this comradeship will long endure was strong in me this afternoon, while many thousands of you marched past me in one of the most memorable and impressive parades that I have ever seen.

For most of you and, I must add, for your wives too, your service in the Home Guard has not been easy.

I know what it has meant, especially for older men. Some of you have stood for many hours on gun sites in desolate fields or on windswept beaches.

By stand down in December 1944, over 800 men had served in the Home Guard in Exmouth. Those still serving, marched around the town and paraded for the last time. The following report was taken from the *Exmouth Journal.*

With the drums of the Exmouth Army Cadets, and the Queens Westminster Army Cadets, The Salute was taken at the Wessex Territorial Drill Hall at the Sea Front.

Then a parade marched from the sea front, via Alexandra Terrace, High Street, Rolle Street, to the Strand. Later the parade moved on to Victoria Road where they were dismissed after four and a half years of Honourable service.

They later set up an Old Comrades association at the Bastin Hall, home of the St. John Ambulance Brigade with Brigadier Gen .H. Fergus as their Chairman.

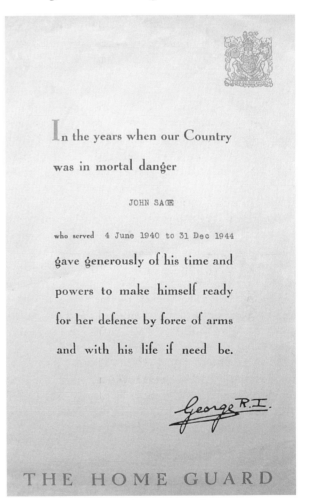

John Sage's Home Guard Service Certificate

The 19 Seaton Battalion had its stand down parade on the 3 December 1944. Religious services were held in Axminster, Honiton and Seaton.

Jack Sage
'The Luppitt Platoon Stand down party was held at Broadhembury Grange. The men's wives did the catering and entertainment was laid on. Although it was very cold everyone had a nice evening.'

Lydford Company march through Tavistock in the Victory Parade

Hazel Rowsell

'Donald was always on time for his patrols and training and really enjoyed it the Home Guard, they had really good times and felt they were doing something to help the country.'

Edwin Hawker

'My time in the Home Guard good fun, but it was also deadly serious. At the time it was generally thought all over Britain, that we were due to be invaded at any time. We had no reason to doubt this because of what had happened in other countries.'

Nationally, the Home Guard was finally completely disbanded on December 31st 1945.

In June 1946 there was a final Victory Parade in London where the some of the Home Guard members met for a last time in their official capacity.

Pictured in this photograph of Lydford Company are Stan Huggins, Louis Screech, Harry Bob Pengelly and Jim Hannaford, Their positions are unknown. But are at the head of the column.

The Resurrection of the Home Guard 1952-56

There was a resurgence of the Home Guard in the 1950s when the threat of nuclear war with the U.S.S.R. reached danger point. Winston Churchill was re elected as prime minister at this time too.

Plans for re-organisation started in 1951 as the build up to the Suez crisis and the Korean War started. Very little changed from the WW II era except that women were admitted from day one, the Home Guard shoulder titles were in red with white writing this time and they wore black berets in line with the regular army.

Chapter 18
Engaging the Enemy

Contrary to popular belief life in the Home Guard was not all beer and skittles

Jack Sage

'We heard German planes flying over all the time, when we were on duty; they were on the route to bomb Bristol.'

'One day, I had my breakfast and went out; I hadn't got very far up the road when I heard planes nearby. I looked up and saw the Swastika on the tail. The plane was headed towards Dunkeswell. It was only one plane and it dropped at least one bomb. Four bombs were also dropped on Luppitt one day and one plane went down through Upottery Valley and crashed.'

'On one occasion a German airman fell out of a plane and hit the ground so hard his heels and backside left an impression in the dry hard soil. He was killed outright and I went to see the mark in the ground.'

I have given just a few examples of the way the Home Guard came into contact with the enemy here, there are too many to list. The main fire fights took place between anti-aircraft artillery and 'Z' rocket batteries and the Luftwaffe.

The Home Guard also came into contact with Luftwaffe personnel who had bailed out of damaged aircraft or had crashed in their patrol areas. In 1941 a German Bomber was shot down at Kenton near Exeter in Devon, the pilot was taken prisoner by two Home Guardsmen. This scenario was repeated all over Britain. They were untested against the German army, but I feel sure that they would have risen to the challenge with a great deal of enthusiasm.

June 1940 Thanet Battalion

Major Witts was a local Lloyds bank manager and Company Commander of the Margate Battalion. Although his 900 men were armed with only 100 rifles and 5 rounds of ammunition for each rifle and they still had no uniforms or steel helmets yet, one Section captured the crew of a German bomber which had crashed offshore.

The Section Leaders report read as follows;
'I have pleasure in reporting that whilst I was on duty with the Kent Local Defence Volunteers a German bomber passed low over my Sub-Section at about twelve feet high, flying from west to east, about 2.15 a.m. at the Bungalow Station, Palm Bay, Cliftonville and crashed roughly one hundred yards from the shore. I immediately had the police phoned, then proceeded to the scene of the crash and found three of the crew in a rubber dinghy. My own men, also the police, spread out fanwise on the shore, keeping the crew covered. I waded out and ordered them to put their hands up. One of the prisoners asked if it was Dover.'

The rest of the report goes on to say how his suit was ruined and that they were badly supplied with uniforms and steel helmets, which considering that they were on the front line was pretty poor The report then concludes with this statement.

'In conclusion I should like to mention that it gives me great pleasure in informing you that a fourth German was found strangled by his parachute hanging from the aft part of the bomber.'

18 August 1940 the Battle of Britain. 1.22 p.m. Kenley Aerodrome.

Oberleutnant Rudolf Lamberty from 9/KG76 was flying his Dornier 17 during a lunchtime raid on Kenley aerodrome. The plane was the lead aircraft flying with a group of 9 flying at around 50 feet above ground level, headed towards the aerodrome. After bombing the hangars and coming under fire from the airfield defences (Lewis guns and Bofors guns) his left wing was hit by an exploding Bofors shell ripping a huge hole in it. The aircraft struggling to keep control was then attacked by Hurricanes of 111 Squadron, first Sergeant W. Dymond and then Sergeant R. Brown. Two of the Aircrew baled out and hit the ground receiving multiple injuries and then a 3rd member let him self and open his parachute just before he let go of the aircraft. Lamberty singled out a large stubble field in front of the aircraft intending to crash land it. On his way he passed a section of the Addington Home Guard who were practising rifle drill with live rounds of ammunition. Their Commander Captain Clarke gave the order for rapid fire at the aircraft as it was flying so low and they noticed that it was on fire.

The 9 Staffel commander Joachim Roth and Lamberty both escaped from the burning wreckage of the crashed aircraft and although were badly burned held up their hands in surrender to the Home Guardsmen who had fired on the aircraft.

In the national newspapers of 22 August 1940 the headlines were 'Home Guard Shoot down a Bomber'. The photograph in the newspaper shows the wreckage of Dornier 17 lying in field, and the Officer congratulating his men on their achievement.

Hyde Park 'Z' Rocket batteries, which were manned mainly by scientists and university lecturers, were extremely effective against the Luftwaffe bombers, having a fearsome reputation with the aircrew. The crews gave them a wide berth after seeing them in action.

During the Luftwaffe's Hit and Run campaign against coastal targets and shipping in the south-west of England in 1942-43, Home Guard anti-aircraft units continually manned the Lewis guns, Bofors guns and 'Z' rocket batteries in the most vulnerable places.

10 'Torquay' Battalion Focke Wulf 190 Kill

The Torbay and Paignton Gas Company platoons claimed one Focke Wulf 190 shot down in an attack by three planes on Holcombe Gas Works. The three raiders attacked from the landward side to put them in the best position to fly out to sea after the attack.

The attack took place at 10.12 a.m. on Wednesday December 30 1942. The following report established the claim for the destruction of one aircraft.

'At approximately 10.12 hours on December 30, 1942, three planes approached Hollacombe Gas Works from landward.'

'Two Planes identified as F.W. 190s approached over Round Hill flying east at approximately 400 feet. The third plane, identified as a F.W. 190, approached via Cockington Valley over No.1 Holder at approximately 150 feet with its machine guns in action, but apparently with no effect.'

'Sergeant W.P. Matthews, in charge as No.1 on U.P. Projector, identified and engaged the two planes flying over Round Hill and approaching the projector position at an angle of 90 degrees to the port side.'

'Ten rounds were immediately discharged at the leading plane. These rounds were extremely well directed and cause the plane to kick violently in the air whilst small sections of material were observed to fall into the sea below. The plane immediately dived towards the sea apparently out of control, but recovered almost on water level and proceeded towards Berry Head at a much reduced speed.'

'It would appear highly improbable that the plane would reach its home base for it was apparently losing speed and unable later to rejoin formation with its flight. I understand from witnesses of the incident that a plane was seen to crash in the sea off Berry Head, but we are unable to say if this is the plane hit by the U.P. discharge by Sergeant Matthews. Our attention was directed at this stage to recharging the projector for further action.'

'The second plane was engaged with the second bank of rocket projectiles, but the shots were not close. This plane continued in an easterly direction, being joined by the third plane mentioned.'

'Lieutenant J.W. Denton, who was present and Private F. Powell, who was No.2 on the gun confirmed the above.'

'In all 18 rockets were discharged, one remaining in the projector and one falling short on the beach and not exploding.'

'The discharged rocket projectile was pulled out of the sand and is now attached by cord to a stake. The matter has been reported to the R.N.O., Torquay and to the Police, Torquay.'

Shortly after the event, Colonel H.G. Hay. Officer Commanding South Devon Group Home Guard sent a signal to the U.P. Rocket Unit after further research to confirm the 'Kill' had been undertaken.

'The Sub District Commander had read with pleasure the report by the Gas Works Company of the Torbay Battalion of their action with enemy aircraft on December 30th 1942.'

'Although no confirmation can be obtained, it is fact that one F.W. 190 did crash into the sea off Berry Head on the Morning of December 30, 1942. I think it can be assumed that this machine was the one hit by Sergeant Matthews.'

'Please convey to Captain Taylor and all ranks under his command, the Sub District Commander's appreciation of the work carried out.'

'It is suggested that a board be placed in the Company H.Q. with record of this and any future machines brought to earth.'

'The Zone Commander and I are very pleased to be able to forward these remarks and wish to add our appreciation to that of the Sub District Commander.'

The following day the men of the U.P. unit painted a swastika on the shield of the rocket projector.

Chapter 19
Courage, Sacrifice and Tragedy

Dennis Davey
'I regret the way that the Home Guard has since become a joke, mainly because of the programme 'Dad's Army', which I agree was funny, but at that time we were deadly serious and worked hard with our training.'

In order to try and create a realistic summary of the duties and responsibilities of the men who served in the Home Guard, I have selected a few examples from a very long list of those who took their commitment to their roles very seriously and which sometimes ended in tragedy.

Home Guard Casualties

A total 1,765 Home Guardsmen were killed or injured whilst on duty during WW II. Most of the casualties caused by enemy action were caused by V1 and V2 rockets in the London and Kent area from September 1944, others were killed as a direct result of bombings and being killed by falling debris in attempts to rescue civilians from burning or bomb damaged buildings.

The Final total of casualties is as follows:

Killed on duty 1208. Seriously injured whilst on duty 557. Admitted to hospital for minor wounds and ailments when on duty 5,663.

These figures include those killed and wounded by other members, misfortune, carelessness, or by accident, they represent less than one casualty per thousand of the men and women who served in the Home Guard. For such a large military formation this represents a very small amount of self-inflicted casualties, considering they were using weapons on a day to day basis in a war zone.

The First Casualty by Enemy Action

In early August 1940 Jack Bosley was on guard duty at a factory during the evening, when it was attacked by 12 German planes. He was shot through the knee and became the first Home Guard casualty caused by enemy action.

7 September 1940
the Start of the London Blitz

The boroughs of Bermondsey, Rotherhithe and Southwark were badly bombed on this night were hit particularly badly in this first raid. The men of the 15 Battalion, County of London Home Guard worked tirelessly to rescue and evacuate patients and staff from Guy's Hospital which was badly bombed. The volunteers from the Bermondsey, Southwark and Deptford areas which were part of the M.1 Battalion and about this time it became known as the General Service Battalion. They worked tirelessly through the first blitz of London, assisting the Police and fire services, rescuing people from wrecked and burning buildings, fire fighting, traffic control and guarding against looters. Sometimes these men worked right the way through the night, to then go on and work a full day at their regular jobs.

10 May 1941 Kennington Company

The Kennington Company of the 15 Battalion County of London Home Guard also received a letter of commendation, signed by the Speaker of the House of Commons and the Lord Chancellor for their services working with the A.R.P. to extinguish fires at the Houses of parliament after a night of bombing. It must be remembered that at this point in the war many Home Guards had no steel helmets during the Blitz and certainly were not issued with any specialist clothes for fighting fires.

Many of the members worked as Fire Guards when not on duty with the Home Guard, they were also called to the

Fire Guard role performed by the Home Guard

Saturday, May 3rd, 1941.

FIRE AT THE POINT
HOME GUARD AND BRIGADE CALLED

Members of the Home Guard on duty on the Point on Saturday night, received an urgent summons to go to help put out a fire at 38a, Shelley-road, The Point, at a quarter to three on Sunday morning. The Fire Brigade was called, and meanwhile attempts were made to put out the fire. It was found that an arm-chair by the fire in the sitting-room had been caught by a spark from the fire, and after smouldering for some time it had eventually burst into flames.

The occupant of the house, Mrs. Sansom, awoke and smelled the smoke fumes. She hurried outside to obtain what help she could, and the Home Guard came to the rescue.

They got the chair outside, and opened the windows to let out the smoke. When the Brigade arrived a few seconds later it was all over.

The owner of the house, Mrs. Quick, of Exeter, was not present. Her tenant, Mrs. Sansom, came down from London about a week ago. Her five children were all in the house with her at the time.

scene of many small domestic fires as well as those caused by enemy action in the general course of their duties, as this account in the Exmouth Journal shows.

Early Home Guard Commendations

Home Guard J.H. Warren.
No.2 Company Thanet Battalion.

For remaining on duty when the building he was guarding had been bombed. He had been badly injured by flying glass remained at his post until relieved and then after his wounds were treated returned to his post to finish his duty.

Home Guard F.J. Pellat.
No.3 Company Thanet Battalion.

For his courage and prompt action in capturing an enemy pilot and preventing him from setting fire to his machine, though he himself was unarmed.

Volunteer K.H. Ritchie. Shoreham Platoon, 'B' Company Sevenoaks Battalion Kent Home Guard.

In September 1940, several delayed action bombs fell on Chevening House and in the grounds.
Volunteer Ritchie immediately went there, investigated the bombs at considerable personal risk and in conjunction with Platoon Commander Duckett and men of the Chevening Platoon, arranged for all the occupants to be evacuated and took measures to localise the explosions of the bombs in the house. His action showed promptitude, coolness and courage.

Volunteer A.E.R. Breenger. 'C' Company, 1st Southern Railway Battalion, Kent Home Guard.

On Sunday 6 October 1940, under the following circumstances; Volunteer Breenger was on duty at an observation post when an alarm had been sounded.

A large enemy bomber dived suddenly out of the clouds in a direct line with his post. Although he was being machine gunned by the crew of the bomber and bombs dropped within 30 metres of him, Volunteer Breenger remained steadfastly at his post and transmitted a warning to the staff on duty at the works, enabling them to get under cover. His courage showed courage and devotion to duty.

Section Commander R.S.G. Worster. Rochester Battalion, Kent Home Guard.

In October 1940, 1940 at 21.35 hours, a high explosive bomb fell. The bomb set fire to a stationary Army lorry, in which were F.A.N.Y. drivers and six members of the A.T.S.

Section Commander Worster, who was about twenty feet away, though partially stunned by the explosion dashed to the lorry and at great personal risk rescued one of the F.A.N.Y. drivers who was badly injured and whose clothing was on fire. He dragged her from the driver's seat, beat out the flames with his bare hands and took her to a place of safety. He then, with the assistance of Mr. R. Hilder of the A.R.P. Service, rescued three of the A.T.S. personnel, who were still alive in the blazing lorry.

Though suffering from his own injuries and shock, Section Commander Worster refused to give up his rescue work until forced to do so. But for his gallantry and presence of mind the death toll of five would have been considerably larger.

Volunteer R. Baker. Tonbridge Battalion, Kent Home Guard.

A stick of heavy bombs fell across his village. As soon as he had picked himself up. Volunteer Baker saw that an oil bomb had been dropped and it was starting a fire. He ran to the spot and single-handedly, put out the flames and then smothered the bomb. By his action he prevented a very serious fire. His conduct is all the more praiseworthy as he is only seventeen years of age.

Volunteer R. Gant. 'E' Company 1st Southern Railway Battalion, Kent Home Guard

One morning in October a hostile dive bombing attack was made on the town. One of the gasometers on the Gas Works was hit and fire broke out. The gasometer had a hole nine inches in diameter made in it and the escaping gas was on fire in the direction of the neighbouring Gasometer.

Volunteer Gant immediately approached the Gasometer to see if any of the railway's property was in danger and to render assistance. He showed considerable courage in climbing the Gasometer and inserting clay in the aperture whilst the fire service played water on the same.

His prompt action probably prevented a serious spread of the fire.

H2 and H3 Platoons Torquay and Paignton Gas Company

On the evening of Friday the 4 September 1942 in Torquay Gas Works was attacked by an attack by a German Hit and Run raider. The One and a Half Million cubic feet gas holder was set on fire by cannon and machine gun fire. Home Guard Platoons H2 and H3 were on duty at the time and worked hard with the A.R.P. and Fire Services to extinguish the blaze before the onset of nightfall.

The blazing Gasometer needed to be extinguished quickly as it would have acted like a beacon in the approaching black out.

At the time, a convoy of ships making their way up the English Channel in the area was in danger of being attacked by further enemy planes operating in the area and fortunately the fire was extinguished. Letters of congratulations and commendation were sent to the following men by Lt.-General. H.C. Lloyd, G.O.C. Southern Command.

Captain R.C. Taylor.
Captain G.H. Fursdon.
Lieutenant J.W. Denton.
Sergeant F. Richardson.
Sergeant J. Vanstone.
Sergeant F.C. Williams.

At later investitures at Buckingham Palace, Captain R.C. Taylor Received the M.B.E. Whilst Lieutenant J.W. Denton and Sergeant F.C. Richardson received the George Medal.

Accident Casualties

The National Totals for Home Guardsmen and Civilians involved in accidents with the Home Guard were as follows.

Killed by the Home Guard or in accidents whilst on service were.

Home Guard Personnel 768. (of the previous overall total)

Civilians. 50.

The figures above include family and friends shot by accident with rifles that were presumed to be unloaded, people shot at checkpoints for failing to stop.

Detailed reports are not available for those who were killed or injured by circumstances not caused as a direct result of enemy action, apart from scattered newspaper reports. The figure of 768 is high in comparison with those Killed by enemy action and this lead to the Home Guard being given the dubious 'Honour' of having killed more of their own side than were killed by the enemy. This of course led to some of criticisms about incompetence which has been directed at them over the years.

In the month of June 1940, every effort was made to arm the L.D.V. with safe and reliable weapons, all the donated early weapons were inspected by the local police and military armourers. Mistakes were made though, which resulted in the death and injury of some volunteers.

Mr. Kenneth Marshall of the Cheltenham L.D.V. was the first casualty when he died from a bullet wound in the back, when newly arrived rifles were, wrongly loaded with live ammunition.

Thomas Lyon a Clydeside dock defence L.D.V. was also killed in the same manner.

Alan Chadwick

In September 1940 a Wolverhampton boy, 15 year old boy Alan Chadwick was cycling home one day, when he was shot and killed at a Home Guard checkpoint. He failed to stop when challenged, because he was deaf. All Home Guard road blocks and check points personnel were under orders to fire on anyone who failed to stop when challenged, as an invasion and fifth column activities were expected at any moment.

Accidents with hand grenades and Molotov cocktails were common. The worst grenade training accident was when a No. 68 Anti-Tank grenade, which had a bad reputation for premature explosion, detonated on leaving an E.Y. cup discharger during a hand grenade lecture in 1944. Six Home Guardsmen were killed.

Killed by an American Truck

Gunner H. Stowell worked at his family business, the Point Iron Works on Exmouth dock. In 1944 he was accidentally killed shortly after his platoon photograph was taken. He was riding his bicycle in Exmouth, down Belle Vue Road near the Highland Garage and was killed outright when he was crushed by an American army truck when turning right at a road junction.

Raymond Kindell an Exmouth Volunteer who was deemed unfit for service, as a result of his post mortem, after he died tragically from over exertion on exercises.

Also included in the statistics is information gathered from recorded attacks on British, Commonwealth, Polish and Czech Pilots who had been shot down and were descending or had landed by parachute. Challenges to downed pilots happened regularly, and although there is no evidence to support that any were killed, some were reported as being injured.

ACCIDENT TO HOME GUARD

Mr. E. V. Gosney, of Holly Tree Cottage, Lympstone, signalman at the Lympstone railway station, was admitted to Exmouth Hospital on Wednesday night suffering from injuries sustained in an explosion while on Home Guard duty. On inquiry at the Hospital later it was reported that he was going on very well.

Injury Sustained in a Hand Grenade Accident

Occasionally equipment malfunctions were responsible for death and injury.

Newspaper Headlines the Torbay Herald

'Six Lives Claimed in Gun Site Tragedy'
Gun Tragedy at Corbyn Head

Tragedy struck the men of the Devon Home Guard when, during a practice shoot at Corbyn Head Battery (sister to Brixham Battery) on Sunday August 11 1944, during the shoot, a shell in the breach exploded on one of the 4.7 inch guns due to the failure of the retracting pin.

Gunnery Sergeant Ron Coleman of the 10 (Torbay) Battalion Devon Home Guard was on duty during the practice shoot.

Ron Coleman

'Five members of the 10 Battalion "Torbay" Home Guard are buried in the "Heroes Corner" of a Torquay cemetery. Killed when a 4.7" Coastal Artillery gun exploded when training in 1944'

Account by
Captain C.H. Fursdon

The evening of August 11, 1944 was clear. A cool breeze whispered through the trees around Corbyn Head Battery of coastal artillery. We were there to witness another practice shoot, as was the Brigadier Royal Artillery, Southern Command and the Commander Coast Artillery, South West District.

The spectators gazed seaward. We were proud of this detachment attached to a Regular Coastal Artillery unit. They had earned praise for consistently good work and fine shooting and we raised our binoculars in expectation.

Fire! There was a muffled explosion.

The guns were firing at over three thousand yards, but the round had plunged into the sea one thousand yards away. And looking towards the offending

The Death of Guardsman Raymond Kindell Reported in the Exmouth Chronicle and Exmouth Journal in June 1943

Home Guard's Death

The death of Mr. Raymond Kindell, reported on our front page this week, reveals the danger of strenuous drill and fatigue run by men of middle age and not too strong.

After hurrying from his home at Courtlands Cross in uniform, with rifle, last Sunday morning, and going through the routine, he collapsed soon after returning, and died.

Judging by the post mortem upon the deceased, he would never have been passed fit for

Tragic Death of Home Guard

After doing strenuous Home Guard exercises at Exmouth, on Sunday, Mr. Raymond Herbert Kindell, age 47 years, of "The Tors," Round House-lane, Exmouth, returned home in a state of exhaustion. Within half an hour he collapsed and died. A post mortem examination was subsequently made and the doctor was able to give a certificate as to the cause of death without holding an inquest. His brother, Mr. H. E. Kindell, stated that deceased rushed off on Sunday morning to his Home Guard duty, a distance of over two miles, and came back worn out. He was keen on the work and during the last war received four medals for his services, he having been attached to the Civil Service Rifles (15th London Division). He had gained the Military Medal for bravery in

gun we observed a sheet of flame creeping outside the gun emplacement, devouring grass and camouflage and though the situation had not dawned upon the majority, tragedy was enacted before our very eyes.

And then realisation came. The breech of the gun had blown and men had died. Others were seriously injured or badly burned. Only the very lucky ones escaped.

And with this knowledge things began to move. Our medical officer took charge of the lecture hut, which was turned into a dressing station and in his quiet, efficient manner, proceeded to do his best for the injured. An ambulance was soon on the scene and other doctors came to his aid. The flames too were soon under control.

The casualties were hurried to the Torbay Hospital and a hush of horror descended on those left behind. Four Home Guards had been killed instantaneously and one regular artilleryman and another Home Guard later died of their injuries.

Then came the role call and a few words of encouragement from the B.R.A. Men manned and fired another gun to break the spell, the assembly dismissed and we went on our ways.

To Captain Grant, the officer in command of the Home Guard detachment, accompanied by the Adjutant, fell the duty of breaking the sad news to the relatives of the casualties.

One cannot pass on without recording the deep sympathy and keen interest shown by the B.R.A. and personally interesting himself in all their needs.

In recognition of the great sacrifice the dead had mad, a full military funeral was ordered and this took place on Tuesday 15 August, 1944, the bodies being interned in the 'Heroes' Corner' of Torquay Cemetery.

The parade assembled at 2.15 p.m. outside the cemetery's main gates and from their, led by a detachment of Royal Artillery, the procession slow marched along the road to the new part

COURAGE AND SACRIFICE AND TRAGEDY

of the cemetery. A Royal Artillery band from southern Command playing the 'Dead March' followed the leading detachment.

Then came the gun carriages bearing their coffins draped with Union Jacks. Two lorry loads of wreaths bore silent witness to the tribute being paid.

Following the gun carriages, came the cars carrying the relatives and chief mourners and then came a long khaki procession of military mourners. Among those present were the Sector Commander, Colonel H.G. Hay, C.B.E., D.L, representing the Lord Lieutenant of Devon; the Mayor of Torquay, Mr. E.H. Sermon; Brigadier J. Wedderburn-Maxwell, D.S.O., M.C., representing Lieutenant General W.D. Morgan, C.B., D.S.O., M.C., G.O.C-in-C. Southern Command; Brigadier E.T. Weigall, C.C.A., South Western District; Captain R.H. Wilson, R.A. representing Brigadier R.J. Wyatt, M.C., T.D. Commander, Devon Sub District; Major Sir Francis Layland-Barratt, representing South Devon Sector Home Guard; Lieutenant Colonel A.J.H. Sloggett, D.S.O., Commanding 10 'Torbay' Battalion Devon Home Guard; and officers representing the 9 'Newton Abbot', 11 'South Hams' and 13 'Totnes' Battalions Devon Home Guard and many others; a special detachment of Home Guard gunners and a unit of nearly two hundred Home Guard officers and other ranks.

We buried our dead and saluted them to the sound of the 'Last Post,' and moved off to fall in once again on the road and marched away, past the B.R.A., to dismiss.

We lived the next four days with the hope in our hearts that other seriously injured would survive, but this was not to be.

On August 19 Gunner Houghton also succumbed to his injuries in the Gloucester City Hospital. We laid him to rest with similar full military honours beside his comrades whom we had buried only nine days before.

A court of enquiry sat at once and investigated the whole sad affair, but the exact cause will never be determined. No blame however attaches to anyone.

To the relatives of those who gave their lives our deepest sympathy; the dead will be remembered with reverence.

The damaged gun was quickly replaced for the purposes of morale! A Home Guard Memorial Stone now exists on Corbyn Head and nothing else is left of the 'Emergency Battery'.

Corbyn Head Casualty List

Home Guard Personnel Killed
Gunner G.I. Buckingham – Killed.
Lance Bombadier J.H. Fishwick – Killed.
Lance Bombadier FG Wellington – Killed.
Gunner W.G. Houghton – Died later from injuries.
Gunner W.S. Kinch – Died later from injuries.

Home Guard Personnel Injured
Lieutenant S.C. Gorrell H.G. – Seriously injured.
Gunner F.M. Bailey – Seriously injured.
Bombadier H.V. Grills – Shock.
Lance Bombadier D.M. Fraser – Shock.

Royal Artillery Personnel Killed
1059461 W.O. I (R.S.M.) F.W.J. Blackett - Died later from injuries.

Royal Artillery Personnel Injured
1708352 Gunner W. Gammon - Seriously injured.

R.E.M.E. Personnel Injured
7601860 W.O. II (A/Q.M.S.) G.F. Cole – Seriously injured.

Chapter 20
Medal and Decoration Recipients

Listed here, are details of a few of the many awards to Home Guard personnel during WWII.

The George Cross

Two Crosses were awarded posthumously to Home Guard personnel during WW II.

Sector Commander George Walter Inwood 30 Battalion, Warwickshire Home Guard. Bomb damage rescue. 27-May-41.

George Inwood died rescuing people from the wreckage of an air raid.

Lieutenant William Foster. 7th Wiltshire (Sby) Battalion, Wiltshire Home Guard. Grenade self sacrifice. 27-Nov-42

William Foster was a 61 year old Lieutenant, who had previously served as far back two South African He threw himself on a live grenade which had rolled back in to a trench during hand grenade training.

The George Medal

Thirteen medals were awarded to Home Guard personnel during WWII.

Section Leader A.H.G. BRUNGES
Patrol Leader C.W.L. TOZER
2nd Birmingham Battalion
(Later 22nd (Birmingham) Battalion Warwickshire Home Guard).
'On the 26th October 1940 a bomb explosion caused the destruction of a public shelter. Section Leader Brunges and Patrol Leader Tozer showed the utmost bravery and devotion to duty in going to the assistance of a considerable number of persons who were trapped in the debris. The work of rescue seemed hopeless as the basement was filling rapidly with water. Loose beams had to be removed where possible but this was highly dangerous owing to the possibility of huge blocks of concrete from the floor above becoming dislodged. Section Leader Brunges and Patrol Leader Tozer took the risk of moving these beams without a moment's thought for their own safety. The debris they removed with their hands, mostly under water and in kneeling or half laying positions.'

'Heavy bombs were falling in the vicinity, but work was carried on until between fifteen and twenty persons had been extricated, about half of them still being alive. It was not until it was impossible to discover any further victims that Section Leader Brunges and Patrol Leader Tozer gave up their work of rescue.'

L.G. 30.9.1941
Source: The Times 1.10.1941
Investiture: 29.9.1942

Volunteer A.W. BAILEY
6th Birmingham (Factories) Battalion
(Later 26th (Birmingham) Battalion Warwickshire Home Guard).
'On the night of 19th November 1940 Volunteer Bailey was due to report for duty with B.S.A. Guns Ltd. Home Guard at 9.30 p.m. Hearing bombs; however, he arrived at about 7.00 p.m. and remained on duty helping to deal with incendiary bombs. At about 9.00 p.m. he reached the unit headquarters where he met an officer who called for volunteers to rescue people trapped under the debris of a building that had suffered direct hits by bombs. He first helped to rescue a Home Guard and later, with another Home Guard, got out two workmen from the same place. He then went to the other side of the debris and helped out a man and then a girl.

He then tried to crawl into the building through a hole but was obstructed by some concrete. On attempting to knock a hole through the concrete he found that a girder prevented further progress. An oxy-acetylene cutter was used to cut through the girder and a girl and four men were released one at a time. A fierce fire was burning inside and was being fought from outside but Bailey held up a piece of concrete with his raised arms for some time and was saturated with oil and water. He finally collapsed near the entrance to the hole and was taken home in an ambulance.'

L.G. 11.2.1941
Source: Birmingham Gazette 12.2.1941; the Times
12.2.1941
Investiture: 18.7.1941

Platoon Commander T. Simpson.
6th Birmingham (Factories) Battalion
(Later 26th (Birmingham) Battalion Warwickshire
Home Guard).
'On the night of 11th December 1940 Platoon
Commander Simpson actively assisted in rescuing
several persons who were trapped beneath debris when
an A.R.P. depot was hit. He had to crawl through
debris with men supporting props and there was great
danger of other parts of the building collapsing on
him. He managed to saw through steel pipes and
removed debris which was lying across trapped
persons. He showed conspicuous gallantry and
devotion to duty.'

L.G. 27.5.1941
Source: The Times 28.5.1941
Investiture: 10.3.1942

Platoon Commander R. Haigh.
9th Birmingham (Public Utilities) Battalion
(later 29th (Birmingham) Battalion Warwickshire
Home Guard).
'At about eight p.m. on 22nd November 1940 a
number of incendiary bombs fell on the Wagon Repair
Shops and on Washwood Heath Gas Works. Haigh
was P 19 Company Duty Officer and after one or two
small fires in P 19 area had received attention, he
proceeded, with Volunteer S. A. Tyler, to the Gas
Works. They found two fires in the coal stack and
extinguished them. Two smoke screen containers had
been ignited and were burning with considerable
flame. These, in the absence of equipment for dealing
with oil fires, were extinguished with some difficulty.
There was a plume of flame in the crown of one
gasholder; at the time the crown on the gasholder was
some 200 feet high. Haigh, taking the initiative and
with three other men, ascended to the crown of the
holder carrying sacks, and after considerable effort
extinguished the fire and partially stopped the escape
of gas with bags and clay. Another aperture in the
crown of the holder, through which gas was escaping
but not burning, was dealt with in the same way. No
protective equipment was carried. The raid was still in
progress, with bombs dropping in the vicinity, and the
flame from the holder must have provided a
continuous beacon. The action taken by Haigh and the
other three men not only promptly removed the
beacon, but also saved a considerable quantity of gas
from escaping.'

L.G. 11.2.1941
Source: The Times 12.2.1941
Investiture: 18.7.1941

Platoon Commander R. E. Cooke.
F7 Company (Austin Aero Engine Co. Ltd.),
Birmingham Zone [later part of 43rd (Birmingham)
Battalion Warwickshire Home Guard].
'On 28th October 1940 a 550-lb bomb with delayed
action fuse was located at the factory of Messrs.
Burman Ltd., Hyland Road, Birmingham and the clock
was found to be still ticking. The bomb had been down
for approximately 45 hours and from experience an
explosion was considered so imminent as to justify
withdrawal of the working party. An attempt to
remove the fuse failed and the officers concerned,
together with Cooke, who was present the whole time,
withdrew to consider the matter. 'In view of the
importance of the factory it was decided to attack the
fuse a second time using a heavy crowbar. Three people
were necessary and Cooke volunteered to make up the
party. This time the fuse was partially removed but the
ticking clock and the detonators still remained intact.
It was then decided to flood the pit in an endeavour to
stop the clock and Cooke's assistance again proved
invaluable in what turned out to be a successful
operation. The bomb was safely removed.'

L.G. 11.3.1941
Source: P.R.O. (Public Records Office) Air 2/9504
Investiture: 29.7.1941.

Lieutenant H. W. Roxborough.
7th (Okehampton) Battalion Devon Home Guard.
'On 6th June 1943 at Hele Bridge Rifle Range,
Hatherleigh, this officer made a faulty throw with a
No.36 grenade, which fell close to the pit. Thinking
that the lives of others might be endangered, he
immediately picked up the grenade, which exploded
in his hand. As a result he lost his right hand and left
arm.'

L.G. 10.3.1944
Source: H.G.I.C. No.48-24.5.1944/P.R.O. (Public
Records Office) Air 2/9001
Investiture: 24.10.1944

Platoon Commander A. R. Ballantine.
2nd Battalion Dumbartonshire Home Guard.
'On the night of 13th/14th March 1941, while on
Home Guard duty in Singer's factory, Clydebank,
during an intense air raid, Platoon Commander
Ballantyne took command of all available Home
Guards.

Large quantities of incendiary and high explosive
bombs were failing and he organised the fire-fighting
with an utter disregard for his own safety. He then
found a timber yard ablaze and personally assisted the
Works Fire-master to carry hoses into the heart of the
fire. Later, the Shipping Department took fire and he
entered the building at great risk to himself and fought
the fire. At 5.00 a.m. on 14th March, when the

building containing the rifles, automatic weapons and ammunition of the Home Guard caught fire, he succeeded in saving all the weapons and practically all the ammunition. The factory was the focal point of this exceptionally heavy raid which was repeated on the following night'.

'During both periods, in spite of extreme fatigue, he displayed conspicuous courage, energy and determination in the face of great danger and was an inspiring example to his men.'

L.G. 8.7.1941
Source: The Times 9.7.1941
Investiture: 8.12.1942.

Volunteer S. J. Ferguson.
1st Battalion 'K' Zone, London
(later 12th (Barking and Ilford) Battalion, City of London Home Guard).
'On the night of 17th/18th October 1940 during a heavy enemy attack from the air, in the Barking area, Volunteer Ferguson, who was on duty at his company headquarters, proceeded to a group of houses which had received direct hits.'

'It was reported to him that a woman - a resident of one of the houses - was imprisoned under the wreckage. Despite the fact that the walls of the dwelling were collapsing, he made his way without hesitation into the ruins and found a woman bleeding from a severed artery. Ferguson at once applied first aid amid the flames of incendiary bombs and gave every help to her, at risk of his own life. He remained beside her until it was possible to remove her for conveyance to hospital.'

L.G. 11.2.1941
Source: The Times 12.2.1941
Investiture: 25.7.1941.

Volunteer D. Lazarus.
2nd Battalion 'H' Zone, City of London Home Guard.
'During an enemy air raid in the Aldgate district Volunteer Lazarus, a Home Guard aged 17, was on his way to report for duty when a bomb fell on a block of tenement flats. The explosion caused great havoc and the building was reduced to ruins. Masonry and other debris was falling continuously but Volunteer Lazarus, with complete disregard for his own safety, entered the ruins and began to remove quantities of wreckage with his hands in order to get to four people who were imprisoned. He managed to bring them all out, despite the fact that he had already sustained injuries. Instead of seeking first aid for himself, however, he made an attempt to rescue a fifth occupant of the flats, but a wall collapsed and buried him. He was taken to hospital suffering from multiple injuries to the head, arms and body.'

L.G. 11.2.1941
Source: The Times 12.2.1941
Investiture: 18.7.1941.

Volunteer W. T. Whitlock.
L.M.S. Railway Unit, Euston Station.
(Later 37th (L.M.S. Euston) Battalion. County of London Home Guard.
'On 19th October 1940 a building (Hampstead Heath Station) received two direct hits from high explosive bombs. Volunteer Whitlock, who was on Home Guard duty, received severe injuries to an arm, leg and side; his eyes were also injured by the blast. He was thrown more than twenty feet and over a wall but, ignoring his injuries, he made his way back to the offices which had been wrecked. At great personal risk he pulled his section leader from the wreckage, thus saving his life.'

L.G. 29.4.1941
Source: The Times 30.4.1941
Investiture: 15.7.1941.

Company Sergeant-Major J. A. Leslie.
6th (Bath-Admiralty) Battalion, Somerset Home Guard.
'Company Sergeant-Major Leslie showed outstanding courage and personal bravery in rescue work during the night of 26th/27th April 1942, and in the following days at Bath. The Regina Hotel had been hit and although the raid was still in progress he made his way into the basement through a small hole which allowed only one man to enter at a time, and himself rescued a number of people. A woman was trapped by falling masonry and hanging by her knees. Company Sergeant-Major Leslie supported her for a considerable time while other men worked at the masonry to release her. During this time there was such danger that both might be killed by failing masonry that they were covered with a sheet so that they could not see the blocks if they fell. There was imminent danger of fire and at one period Company Sergeant-Major Leslie had to be doused with water to prevent his clothes catching fire, but throughout it all he never wavered. During the same night Company Sergeant-Major Leslie swarmed up the side of a shop and tore down the blazing shop blind and fixture in an attempt to prevent the spread of fire after the firemen had given up the task as hopeless.'

L.G. 3.12.1942
Source: Bath and Wilts Chronicle and Herald 4.12.1942
Investiture: 16.3. 1943.

Section Leader A. H. Tilyard- Burrows.
Vickers-Armstrong Aircraft Factory Ubit, Weybridge Home Guard (later part of 10th (Vickers-Armstrong) Battalion, Surrey Home Guard. Later become part of 3rd (Weybridge) Battalion, Surrey Home Guard).

'On the morning of 21st September 1940 at about 08.30 hours the Vickers Aircraft Factory at Weybridge was attacked by an enemy aircraft. Three bombs were dropped, two of which exploded, doing slight damage. The other, a 500-lb. bomb, penetrated the factory roof, passed through a wall at the end and came to rest on the concrete driveway outside the erecting shed, having failed to explode. As the explosion of the bomb at the position where it rested would have caused considerable damage, its immediate removal was a matter of national importance.

Lieutenant J. M. S. Patton, Royal Canadian Engineers, undertook to remove the bomb to a place of comparative safety and Section Leader Tilyard-Burrows together with Volunteers W. J. Avery, E. A. Maslyn and C. E. Chaplin, with complete disregard of personal safety and having no previous experience of handling unexploded bombs, immediately volunteered to assist.'

'The bomb was lashed to a sheet of corrugated iron, attached to a truck by wire cable and towed to a crater about 200 yards away where it could do no harm. The task was accomplished in little more than half-an-hour from the time the bomb had fallen. The bomb exploded the following morning.'

'Throughout the operation these men displayed cool courage of the highest order and contributed largely to the removal of a serious threat to the production of this factory.'

L.G. 22.1.1941
Source: P.R.O. (Public Records Office) Air 2/9537
Investiture: 18.7.1941.

Many C.B.E.s, O.B.E.s, M.B.E.s and B.E.M.s were awarded to members of the Home Guard that had served with distinction. Far too many to list here unfortunately.

The Defence Medal
Guardsmen who had served for three years or more were eligible for the Defence Medal only. Some Home Guardsmen who were killed or injured whilst on duty, were not even eligible for this medal as they had not served in the Home Guard for long enough. A Home Guard medal was never instituted.

The Defence Medal

Chapter 21
Living History

Living History groups have cropped up all over Britain in the past 20 years. They collect equipment and information about significant periods in Britain's history and share it with communities, schools, museums and at specialist events. In these days of an alarmingly health and safety conscious Britain, living historians, help people to understand what life was really like in days gone by, rather than keeping everything behind sheets of glass.

Without their help I could not have made this book. If you are at an event where there are living historians take your time to talk to them as they will be only too pleased to chat about their specialist subject. Thanks!

Living Historians Andy Youngs and Lee Marshall man the Vickers machine gun

Brixham Battery

If you would like to see a WW II 4.7" Gun Battery I can recommend a trip to Brixham Battery in South Devon (about an hour's drive from Exeter). Brixham Battery was opened in 2002 by the National Trust who has preserved the remaining battery buildings. This is overseen by a group of WW II living historians with a lot of excellent knowledge of national and local defences and the Home Guard in WW II. The original gun casemates, battery observation post, magazines, searchlight and weapons pits and other features can still be seen. Brixham Battery has an ongoing commitment to research and restoration of the site and has recently restored the tunnels underneath the site.

The Battery is open to visitors every Sunday, Monday, and Friday from 2pm–4pm throughout the year. There is no admission fee to the Museum and Battery Gardens.

The Brixham Battery living history 'Meet the Home Guard' event is yearly on the first Sunday in June.

Decay! The living enemy of the Living History group

Brixham Battery volunteers and Living Historians

Dale Johnson in his restored Austin 7 Van

Appendix I
Threat of Invasion Timeline

1939

1 September	Mass evacuation of Children from London Begins. Germany invades Poland.
3 September	Britain and France declare war on Germany.
12 October	British Expeditionary Force fully deployed along the France – Belgium border.

1940

10 May	Germany invades France, Holland, Belgium and Luxembourg.
14 May	German 1st Panzer Division crosses the Meuse river at Sedan. Anthony Eden broadcasts an appeal on the radio for able-bodied men, between the ages of 17 and 65 to join the Local defence Volunteers.
15 May	Thousands of British men of all ages sign on for the L.D.V. at local police stations all over Britain. The L.D.V. are formed.
18 May	Tyler Kent and Anna Wolkoff arrested for spying and passing information via Italy to the German Abwher.
21 May	German 1st Panzer Division reaches the French coast. Admiral Raeder meets with Adolf Hitler to discuss the principles of an invasion of Britain.
26 May	Operation 'Dynamo' the evacuation of British and French and Canadian troops of the B.E.F. begins,
30 May	Transfer of L.D.V. Command from G.H.Q. Home Forces (Regular Army), to the War Office
4 June	The evacuation of Dunkirk is completed.
22 June	Armistice between Germany and France signed by General Keitel (Germany) and General Huntziger (France) in Compiegne.
30 June	Germans invade the Channel Islands.
10 July	Battle of Britain. The first day. Widespread raids of mainland Britain. Dover, Falmouth, Swansea, Pembrey.
16 July	Adolf Hitler issues the directive to initiate full plans for Operation Sea Lion.
19 July	Hitler's 'Last Appeal to Reason' speech in the Reichstag.
23 July	The L.D.V. are renamed the Home Guard at the behest of the Prime Minister Winston Churchill.
1 August	The Luftwaffe drop leaflets with Hitler's 'Last Appeal to Reason' speech all over southern and south-east England.
3 August	The Home Guard affiliated to the regular army County Regiments.
13 August	Adler Tag (Eagle Day). The Luftwaffe's offensive to destroy R.A.F. Bases starts.
27 August	Operation 'Sea Lion', is modified by Hitler to be made on a much narrower front between Eastbourne and Folkestone. Germany's Planned invasion date is 15 September 1940.
3 September	Hitler postpones the invasion of Britain from the 15 September to 21 September. Two German spies landed by boat at Hythe, both apprehended within a few hours. Two more German spies landed at Dungeness, both apprehended within two days. Three were later hanged at Pentonville Prison.
4 September	Hitler's 'Invasion of Britain' speech in Berlin.
5 September	Kriegmarine lay mines in the Dover straights.
6 September	German spy, Caroli landed in Oxfordshire by parachute.
7-8 September	The Blitz of London Begins. The 'invasion imminent' code word 'Cromwell' is sent by G.H.Q. Home Forces to Southern Command and Eastern Command. Elements of the regular army and the Home Guard are put on action stations. German S-Boats lay mines in the straights of Dover. Bodies of German troops in British and German Uniforms washed ashore at Dimchurch, Portsmouth, Southhampton, Exmouth. Church bells are rung all over the south and south-east of England to sound the invasion warning.
10 September	German spy Schmitt, landed by parachute in Oxfordshire.
11 September	Dover suffers its heaviest attack of the war.
14 September	Hitler postpones the final decision to invade Britain until the 17 September.
15 September	Battle of Britain Sunday. The R.A.F. ward off two huge attacks by the Luftwaffe.
17 September	Hitler orders the indefinite postponement of the invasion of Britain.
19 September	Hitler orders the dispersal of the entire German invasion fleet, which is anchored in the French and Belgian channel ports, for fear of it being destroyed by R.A.F. bombers. Britain still does not know that Operation Sea Lion has been postponed. There are 1,277 landing barges, 1,161 motor launches 471 tug boats, 155 troop carrying steam ships,
30 September	Three German spies, two men and one woman, landed by rubber dinghy from a seaplane at Banffshire. All were apprehended within a few hours, the men were later hanged. The woman became a double agent Vera Von Shalburg and disappeared.
21 October	Winston Churchill broadcasts his mocking speech about the threatened invasion of Britain. 'We are waiting.......So are the fishes,' he taunts.

Many periods existed after this date where the War Office considered that the risk of invasion, or invasion was imminent and the Home Defence Forces were put on alert. Most are mentioned in the main text.

Exmouth Men Known to have Served in the Home Guard

Southern Command

The Exmouth men served under Southern Command. Listed below are the combined members of Exmouth Company 2 'Clyst' Battalion and the 477 Royal Artillery Coastal Battery.

There are no official records held to give all of the names of these men. This list had been put together with the aid of photographs and the last surviving members of the Exmouth Home Guard.

There are approximately 650 Guardsman's names who served missing from this list. I am keen to complete this information if possible. Please forward any names to my e-mail address: www.blitzandpeaces.co.uk

Exmouth Home Guardsman's names listed by rank, then alphabetical order.

Officers

Majors
Major A.S. Archdale D.S.O. Major. J.W. Palmer. Major John Gerald MacCovaghy CB DSO MVO.

Captains
Captain. T.C.C. Evans. D.S.O. Captain A.E. Jones, M.C. Captain. A.C.G. Roberts. M.C.

Lieutenants
Lieutenant. A. Beach. Lieutenant. R.T. Anderson. Lieutenant. S.C. Cassyn. Lieutenant. W.A. Ingham. Lieutenant. J.M. Pavey. Lieutenant. J.F.R. Richards. Lieutenant. C.R. Rickeard. Lieutenant H.W. Sharp. Lieutenant. A.R. Smith. Lieutenant. H.S. Sutherland. (Quartermaster).

Second Lieutenants
Second Lieutenant. W.A. Britton. Second Lieutenant. K.H. Coxe. M.C. Second Lieutenant G.R.W. Glanville. Second Lieutenant. A.F. Pratt. Second Lieutenant S.J.G. Southon. Second Lieutenant. A.G. Yates. Second Lieutenant. Edward George Arthur Simms. Second Lieutenant. Albert Richard Smith. Second Lieutenant. George Craggs. Second Lieutenant. Gerald Roy Tucker. Second Lieutenant. Arthur William Glenton Lennard. Second Lieutenant. Thomas Harold Nash-Peake.

Non Commisioned Officers

Company Sergeant Major
Company Sergeant Major Charlie H. Havill.

Quartermaster Sergeant
Quarter Master Sergeant. P. Mc Larin.

Sergeants
Sergeant. C. Axon. Sergeant. John Brock. Sergeant. W. Bryant. Sergeant T.C.V. Burnhill. Sergeant ? Challis. Sergeant. W. Clarke. Sergeant. W. Croft. Sergeant. Reginald Dixon. Sergeant. Roy. Fairchild. Sergeant ? Goldsmith. Sergeant F. Havill. Sergeant. R. Haydon. Sergeant. W. Holman. Sergeant. L. Hyde. Sergeant. Harry Lawes. Sergeant. T. Mathews. Sergeant. W. Pascoe. Sergeant. Albert Edwin Dixon Pollard. Sergeant. W. Pope. Sergeant. J. Pover. Sergeant E.C. Raven. Sergeant. Fred J. Rendle. Sergeant. S.G. Seldon. Sergeant H. Swinnerton. Sergeant. C. Tindall. Sergeant. Frank Troulan. Sergeant G.M. Walburn

Bombardiers and Corporals
Bombardier E. Charlie Bond. Corporal Babbage. Bombardier Arthur J. Clode. Corporal. K. Ford. Corporal. F.R. Grimes. Corporal. D.E. Hamson. Corporal. C. Harding. Corporal. H. Lavis. Bombardier Wilf Lowton. Corporal. D.C.A. Miller. Corporal. Archie E. Sandcraft. Corporal E. Sprague. Corporal. C. Young.

Lance Corporals and Lance Bombadiers
Lance Corporal. A. Axon. Lance Corporal. E.T. Bradford. Lance Corporal. R.D. Bradford. Lance Corporal Laurie Butler. Lance Corporal. H.G. Carder. Lance Bombardier J.W.M. Denford Lance Corporal. D.B. Mear. Lance Bombardier A.A.G. Searle. Lance Corporal Bill Sleeman. Lance Corporal. D.H. Smalldon. Lance Bombardier. R.C. Smith. Lance Corporal. C.J. Tolman.

Privates and Bombardiers
Private J. Abbott. Private. C.W. Andrews. Gunner. W.G. Andrews. Private. F. Arthur. Private. J. Bain. Private. F. Basgleoppo. Private. S.G. Bastin. Private. S.G. Bastone. Private. F.E. Beach. Private. A.H. Beer. Private. A. Blackler. Gunner A.V. Bolt. Private. M.T. Bowden. Private. Bernard J. Bradford. Private. W.L. Bradford. Private J.G. Bennett. Private. T. Bennett. Gunner. A.G.

Brailey. Private. L.G. Bromley. Private. S.C. Bronsdon. Private. C. Brown. Private. J.P. Burford. Private. Wilf Capron. Private. H.W. Clarke. Private P. Clode. Private Tony Cockington. Private. A.G. Coles. Private. T. Coles. Private. A.W. Crispin. Private Dennis Davey. Gunner Edward J. Derrick. 22. Gunner W.J. Doderell. Private. Henry George Down. Private. ? Dowell. Gunner C. Dudley. Private. E.C. Edwards. Gunner A. Edwards. Private. W.G. Edwards. Gunner B. Eley. Private. W.A. Elliott. Gunner L.H. Farrant. Gunner J.W. Fasey. Private W. Fletcher. Private. L.J. Franks. Private. W.H. Gardner. Gunner Percy W. Gatter. Private. A.E. Grant. Private. W.E. German. Private. S. Hall. Gunner P.L. Harris. Private. C. Harrison. Gunner Michael A.G. Heard. Private. P. Hellier. Private. S.P. Helson. Private. A.G. Hillman. Gunner G. Hitchcock. Private. H. Hitchcock. Private Hodge. Private C.H. Howden. Private. R. Horn. Gunner J. Hyde. Private. G.A. Islip. Gunner Harry Long. Gunner W.B. Private. T. Maden. Private. H.D.M. Edwards. Private. L.K. Yardley. Private. W.E.C. Slocombe. Private. H.W. Marshall. Private. A.L. Martin. Private. L.P. Martin. Gunner S.W. Martin. Gunner E. McIntosh. Private. S.E. Morris. Gunner W.T. Morrish. Private. P.L.S. Mortimer. Gunner C. Nichol. Private. W. Osborne. Private. R.A. Palmer. Gunner E.T. Pannell. Private R. Pannell. Private Ken Parker. Private. A. Parkhouse. Private. Percy J.R. Parsons. Private. G.R. Parsons. Private. G.W. Parsons. Private. W.J. Payne. Gunner A. Pemberton. Private B.G. Pemberton. Private. E. Perry. Private. R.S. Peters. Private G. Phillips. Private. R.E. Piners. Private. A.G. Pike. Private. G.A. Pike. Private. L.S. Pike. Private. J. Powell. Private. J.M. Priddis. Private. P.G. Richards. Gunner W.J. Richards. Private. W.F. Rockey. Private. W.G. Salter. Gunner A.J.R. Seager. Gunner Percy Sedgemore. Gunner A.L. Skinner. Private. P.C. Skinner. Private S. Skinner. Private G. Skinner. Gunner G.H. Slocombe. Private. G. Smale. Private. L.V. Soper. Gunner Raymond A. Steer. Private. F.G. Stone. Gunner H. Stowell. Private. John Street. Private. A.R. Stuart. Gunner C. Thomas. Private C. Tate. Gunner J.R.G. Thorn.Private. W.G. Tolman. Private Ray Towill. Private. C.C. Turl. Private George Waldron. Private ? Webb. Private. A.H. Weekes. Private. R.T. Weller. Gunner. T. Western. Private. W.A. Westwood. Private. Geoff Wilmott. Private. R.E. Whiddon. Gunner E. Williams. Private. L.M.O. Wills. Private. ? Wonnacott. Private C.J. 'Jim' Woolacott.

Women's Home Guard Auxiliaries

No names have come forward for the Women Auxiliaries, except possibly. Miss Whiteway. The Home Guard's Secretary, who worked at the Sailors Rest.

Exeter Home Guard dispatch riders

The Home Guard Select Bibliography

Britain's Air Defences 1939-45
By Dr. Alfred Price.
Illustrations by Darko Pavlovic.
Published by Osprey Publishing.

Britain at War
By Roger A. Freeman
Published by the *Daily Express*.

British Homefront 1939-45
By Martin J. Bradley
Illustrated by Malcomb McGregor
Published by Osprey Publishing.

British Home Defences 1940-45
By Bernard Lowry.
Illustrated by C. Taylor and V. Boulanger.
Published by Osprey Publishing.

Churchill's Secret Army
A History of the Auxiliary Units in WW II.
By John Warwicker.
Published by Frontline books.

East Devon at War
By Ted Gosling and Ray Chapple.
Published by Alan Sutton Publishing.

Exeter a Shattered City
The Exeter Blitz Illustrated.
By Peter Thomas.
Published by Halsgrove.

Exmouth at War
By Arthur Cook
Published by Halsgrove.

Keep Smiling Through
The Home Front 1939-45
By Susan Briggs.
Published by Book Club Associates.

Modern Small Arms
An Illustrated Encyclopaedia of Famous Military
Firearms.
By Major Frederick Myatt M.C.
Published By Salamander Books.

Operation Sea Lion
By Ian Fleming
Published by Pan Books 1975

Somerset Verses Hitler
Secret Operations in the Mendips 1939-1945.
By Donald Brown.
Published by Countryside Books.

The Home Front
British Wartime Memorabilia 1939-45
By Peter Doyle and Paul Evans.
Published by. The Crowood Press.

The Home Guard
By Neil R. Storey
Published by Shire Books

The Home Guard
By S.P. Mackenzie
Published by Oxford Press.

The Way 'Twas
A Devon Country Boy's Memories
by Preston Walter Isaac.
Published by P.W. Isaac.

Winston Churchill's Toyshop
By Colonel Stuart Mc Crae.
Published by Kineton: The Roundwood Press. 1971.

Wartime Publications

14 (Moorside) Devon Home Guard
No Author Named. No Publisher Named.
Book number W356-1.

'Forever Faithful'
The Story of the 1 'Loyal' Battalion of the Exeter
Home Guard.
By Lt. Col. H.J. Wiltsher O.B.E.

**On Guard! 10 Battalion of the Devonshire Home
Guard.**
Edited By G.H. Lidstone.
Published By The Battalion Publication Commitee.

The 5 'Bideford' Battalion of the Devon Home Guard
By Colonel D.C. Crombie C.B.E.

The Home Guard of Britain
By Charles Graves
Published by Hutchinson and Co. London/New York
/Melbourne. 1943.

The Home Guard Manual 1941
Published by H.M.S.O.
A reprint of this book is now available.
Published by Tempus Books

The Home Guard Pocket-Book 1942 (Second Edition)
By Brigadier General. A.F.U. Green, C.M.G, D.S.O.,
P.S.C.
A reprint of this book is now available.
Published by Conway Books.

The 'New' Rapid Pocket Ready Reckoner.
By J. Gall-Inglis, F.R.S.E.
Published (1941) by Gall and Inglis.

The Picture Post
Volume 8 Number 12. September 21st 1940.
'The Home Guard Can Fight'
By Tom Wintringham.